LOVE
DOES NOT
CONTROL

Therapists, Psychologists, and Counselors
Explore Uncontrolling Love

ANNIE DEROLF, CHRISTY GUNTER,
JOHN LOPPNOW, LON MARSHALL,
and THOMAS JAY OORD, eds.

 **Sacra**Sage

SacraSage Press (SacraSagePress.com)

© 2023 SacraSage Press

SacraSage Press provides resources that promote wisdom aligned with sacred perspectives.

Interior Design: Nicole Sturk
Cover Photo: Thomas Jay Oord

Print (Paperback): 978-1-948609-85-2
Electronic: 978-1-948609-87-6

Printed in the United States of America

Library of Congress Cataloguing-in-Publication Data

Love Does Not Control: Therapists, Psychologists, and Counselors Explore Uncontrolling Love
Annie DeRolf, Christy Gunter, John Loppnow, Lon Marshall, and Thomas Jay Oord, eds.

TABLE OF CONTENTS

INTRODUCTION

*T*he Apostle Paul prefaces his famous poem to the Church in Corinth with these words: "I will show you a still more excellent way" (1 Cor. 12:31). The more excellent way he has in mind is love.

Although Paul never defines love in what is now known as the thirteenth chapter of 1 Corinthians, he describes many of love's facets. He concludes by saying, "faith, hope and love remain, these three, and the greatest of these is love" (13:13).

Midway through his proclamation of love's superiority, Paul writes what in Greek are these words:

οὐ ζητεῖ τὰ ἑαυτῆς

The phrase has been translated in various ways, which is understandable given its poetic nature. Depending on the translation, it says love "does not demand its own," "does not force its own way," "does not insist on itself," or "does not control others."

That love is uncontrolling seems obvious to many people. And yet the temptation to control—often with good motives—is strong. The long-term results of trying to control others damage everyone.

Open and relational theology fits nicely with the belief that love is uncontrolling.[1] It rethinks divine power in light of love. Traditional theologies, by contrast, portray God as "in control." God so depicted causes or at least allows all evils we experience personally or witness in the world.

---

1. For an academic explanation of uncontrolling love, see Thomas Jay Oord, *The Uncontrolling Love of God: An Open and Relational Account of Providence* (Downers Grove, Ill.: IVP Academic, 2015). A book of essays exploring the topic from various angles is published as *Uncontrolling Love: Essays Exploring the Love of God* Chris Baker, Gloria Coffin, Craig Drurey, Graden Kirksey, Lisa Michaels, and Donna Ward, eds. (Grasmere, Id.: SacraSage, 2017). A popular explanation is found in Thomas Jay Oord, *God Can't: How to Believe in God and Love after Tragedy, Abuse, and Other Evils* (Grasmere, Id.: SacraSage, 2019).

It's hard to imagine the traditional God *actually* loving everyone all the time. As the omnipotent ruler of all, that God *does* demand, insist, and force His own way!

The present book explores the uncontrolling love vision of God. And it does so from the perspective of therapists, psychologists, and counselors. This group came together to ponder what uncontrolling love might mean for human healing in varying dimensions.

Open and relational theology is diverse, and a wide range of beliefs fall under its umbrella. This diversity shares in common three ideas:

1. God is relational. God not only influences us and creation, we and creation influence God. God gives and receives because God is passible, to use ancient language. Most who affirm this view also think we live in a relational universe, so that what we do has wide-ranging effects on ourselves, others, and the planet.

2. The future is open. God neither predestines everything that occurs nor foreknows all that will happen. Rather, God and creation move through time into an open and undetermined future. The past is settled; the present is happening; the future is a realm of possibilities yet to be actualized.

3. Love is central. Most theologies will *say* God is loving. But the way they describe God makes one wonder! The God described in them is controlling, unaffected, sends some to hell, and more. Open and relational thinkers follow the logic of love as they consider who God is and how God acts. And they say we should imitate this loving God.

The essays in this book are diverse. You may even discover some differences of opinion. Essayists share in common the quest to explore what uncontrolling love means for issues in counseling, psychology, and/or therapy.

These essays are more than mere theoretical musings, however. Their ideas have the capacity to transform our lives in a myriad of ways. Consequently, reading this book has the potential to be an exercise in love itself!

We hope these writings woo you into an adventure of love that does not control.

Annie DeRolf, Christy Gunter, John Loppnow,
Lon Marshall, and Thomas Jay Oord, Editors

Five Core Themes from an Open and Relational Informed Psychotherapy

Mark Gregory Karris

Five core themes emerge from an open and relationally informed psychotherapy.

*G*od, who is thoroughly *relational*, whose love is *uncontrolling*, and whose *compassions* are endless, has co-created life to be *open* and full of vast potentials. God's faithful relationality, uncontrolling love, unceasing compassion, and unscripted dance with humanity has profound implications for me as a licensed marriage and family therapist. In this short essay, I briefly explore five themes as to how an open and relational theological lens shapes me as a clinician and powerfully informs my work with my clients.

Compassionate Wit(h)nessing

The prophet Jeremiah was a mystic and a prophet—one who cherished a deep experience with the Divine and gave voice to God's inner nudges to his community. Jeremiah wrote from his experience that God's compassion never fails and that God's compassion is new every morning. I go a step further. I believe God's compassion is new every moment. God values relationality so much that in each moment God cannot help but be compassionate. Holding to a compassionate and relational view of God inspires me as a therapist to embody the same qualities with my clients.

Compassion is comprised of two fundamental aspects. Compassion involves: (1) a profound sensitivity and awareness of suffering and (2) the motivation to alleviate that suffering. Jesus beautifully modeled a compassionate way of life. In his first sermon ever preached in the synagogue, Jesus stated that his primary mission and the very reason that the Spirit was upon him was to preach good news to the poor, proclaim freedom for the prisoners, open the eyes of those who are blind, release the oppressed, and proclaim the year of God's favor for all (Luke 4:18-19). Jesus was wide-eyed to the suffering all around him, and he felt that his primary calling—the very reason the Spirit anointed him—was to alleviate that suffering.

As a therapist, I am inspired by the "Father of compassion and the God of all comfort" (2 Cor. 1:3). I see myself as an ambassador of compassion. I intend to be a wit(h)ness— a person who seeks to be compassionately and wholeheartedly present with those who feel emotionally poor, inwardly oppressed, and imprisoned by maladaptive habits that cause them to feel blind to the reality of their worth and lovableness. It is the compassionate Spirit who has comforted me in all my troubles, which moves me to comfort those who venture into my office, and collaboratively seeks to alleviate my clients' suffering.

Invitational vs Control or Coercion

I am amazed how God can be so powerful, but God chooses to use that power *with* me, instead of *over* me. Contrary to believing in a more deterministic worldview and God who is in control of everything type of theology, I believe that God does not dictate every action, reaction, or happening in this world. The Apostle Paul says that the "weakness of God is stronger than human strength" (1 Corinthians 1:25). God's empowering and healing presence, which always invites us toward greater measures of wholeness, is stronger than the forceful, controlling, manipulating, and narcissistic love that human beings can demonstrate.

God's uncontrolling love has impacted how I use my power in sessions with my clients. I am sensitive to issues of race, heteronormativity, class, and cultural dynamics. Working with many clients who are healing from religious trauma, I am sensitive to not becoming another coercive guru or authoritarian pastor in people's lives. I intend to be like God in God's uncontrolling love, and not impose my will on my clients. I do not engage in coercion, try to force clients to see from my perspective, or give them moral demands that I expect them to follow.

I consider their will and freedom to choose to be sacred. I dare not usurp what they want and disregard how they want to get there. I want to know what *their* goals are and what approach *they* are looking for. When a client is experiencing emotion and I can see it non-verbally, it is common for me to say, "Is it okay to make room for what is coming up for you?" If I feel like a particular intervention may be helpful for a client, I might ask, "There is an intervention that may be helpful to work through your ambivalence, are you up for a brief exercise?" Invariably, when working with couples, some partners ask me, "Should we stay together? Or should we just get divorced?" I never tell clients what they should do. I invite them to look at different perspectives and options, which is what I believe God does for us. I seek to lead with uncontrolling love that is collaborative and honors their freedom. Following the creed of the wise Mandalorians: *This is the way.*

Trauma is Not Predetermined

Lurking within the psyche of many of the clients who come into my office are conflictual beliefs about God. Some have lingering cognitive dissonance and spiritual disorientation due to tragically losing a loved one, being abused, living through war, or witnessing and/or experiencing other evils and traumas. They may wonder how God can allow such pain in one's life. Our beliefs not only draw us closer or farther away from God, but they also have powerful effects on our psychological health and relationship with ourselves and others.

Secular researchers have found a correlation between a person's mental health and inner struggles about God—what they call *divine struggle*. Researchers have shown that "divine struggle" can be linked to many forms of psychopathology including anxiety, depression, and obsessive-compulsiveness. Divine struggle is also related to lower levels of self-esteem, life purpose, problem-solving skills, and life satisfaction and may also impact physical health.

I have found it beneficial to introduce clients to a new perspective on *theodicy*. Theodicy refers to the attempt by humans to make sense of how a good, loving, and omnipotent God promotes harsh evils and suffering in the world. Of course, this introduction is by invitation only. I always approach these conversations cautiously so as not to place my biases upon them. However, after a client has talked about how they are angry at a God, who they believe is sovereignly in control of all things, for scripting some kind of traumatic suffering or evil in their lives, I might share "Would you be open to hearing another perspective on God's love and God's manner of interacting in the world?" Some say, "No," and with the utmost care and respect I follow their lead. Some say, "Yes." Then, I present them with an open and relational view of God's uncontrolling love; we often have the richest of conversations. It is always a joy to witness a client's decrease in divine struggle and cognitive dissonance as they begin to embrace a fresh, liberating, and more coherent view of God for themselves.

God Relates to Our Whole Family

The greatest commandment is to love God with all our heart, mind, soul, and strength. In many Christian traditions, there has been more of a focus on the mind, above anything else. It seems like as long as you have the right propositions about God, then what awaits is the pearly, golden gates in the eternal heavenly future. The problem is that we are more than just our thoughts. We have emotions, we have bodies, we have a spirit, and we have many sub-personalities or an *internal family* as it is commonly known in psychotherapy circles. God also wants to relate to these aspects of ourselves.

We have many sub-personalities within us, commonly experienced as different *parts* of us. They all make an inner family. It is understood that our parts have their own thoughts, emotional experiences, motivations, and personality. You may remember a time when you may have had to make a complex decision and heard one part of yourself saying, "This would be great!" and another part saying, "I am not sure it is a good idea."

We have secure parts of ourselves and insecure parts. We have adventurous parts and parts that enjoy familiar comforts. We have very young parts and older parts. We have apathetic parts and parts that are deeply sympathetic. Some parts are healed, and others are wounded. We have parts that want to be close to and connected with people, and we have parts that just want to be alone. An *Open and Relationally Informed Therapy* inspires me to value relating to my clients' different parts, especially the exiles and marginalized within them. God's interrelatedness extends not just to my clients' minds, as if just relaying information alone will bring transformation. God's uncontrolling loving relationality and an open future extends to all my clients' internal family. God desires for me to extend compassion to my clients' precious parts so that they can become integrated and experience themselves as more whole human beings, not just for their sake but for those they encounter.

Each Moment is a New Moment

The idea that moment-to-moment, in every creature's life, God is seeking to maximize goodness, beauty, truth, love, and healing, while minimizing evil has been a profound truth for me and my work with clients. Addiction, hopelessness, debilitating anxiety, entrenched negative cycles of couple distress, constricting emotions, and fortified defense mechanisms that do more harm than good, do not have to have the last word. Each moment is ripe with healing potential.

The power of choice and moment-to-moment experiencing is paramount in my work. My clients know me well. Just as I am about to say my pithy pearl of wisdom, they say, "I know Mark. Each moment is a new moment to experience something novel and do something different." I love to continually inspire them with such a statement. Why? Because it infuses them with hope. While one minute they may feel hopeless, they know they can accept the painful thoughts and emotions rising to the surface, tune into their bodies, realign their hearts to their truest intentions, and move forward and live according to their values.

In couples therapy, I used to become startled like a deer in the headlights when a client escalated and yelled at their partner. Now, keeping in mind the principle that *each moment is a new moment to experience something novel and do something different,* I do not fear reactivity will have the last word. I have a firm belief that love, and healing can pulsate forth from each new moment. I can now center myself and help the partner who just snapped at their wife to slow down, feel the anger pulsating in their bodies, help them remember the value of respectful communication, and assist them to move toward repairing the relational injury with their partner. Each moment is a new moment to trust that love wins!

Conclusion

Death in all its forms never has the last word. As a therapist I can drop the ball and misattune to the Spirit of love and to my clients. There are times when my clients can choose pain, reactivity, and maladaptive patterns. However, each moment is infused with hope. God, who is thoroughly *relational,* whose love is *uncontrolling,* and whose *compassions* are endless, has co-created life to be *open* and full of new opportunities. Each moment with my clients is a new moment for us to be invited into the Divine's healing love in all its kaleidoscopic forms.

Dr. Mark Gregory Karris is a licensed marriage and family therapist in full-time private practice in San Diego, California. He is a husband, father, and recording artist. He's a voracious reader, researcher, and all around biophilic. Mark is the author of the best-selling books Religious Refugees: (De)Constructing Toward Spiritual and Emotional Healing *(Quoir, 2020). MarkGregoryKarris.com*

– 2 –

Transforming, Healing **LOVE**

PAULINE E. DOTY

*With mental illness and #MeToo, I have miracles of healing in
ongoing recovery process, forgiving myself and others.*

The path of recovery, healing, forgiving, and finding hope has been my journey.
Thank you, God, for all of your love and mercy that have kept me these 74
years!! It has been a whole lot to go through, to live through. When I review my
hardest years and hardest losses, I see again and again the loving work of the Holy
Spirit, Redeeming Love, and Amazing Grace.

A sophomore in college, at 20 years old, I caved into psychosis. After several
weeks in a state mental hospital, finally I knew I had experienced serious mental
illness. There were so many unanswered questions. Some months later, with extraordinary gifts of courage and support, I was back in classes and struggling to
find my way. I took Philosophy of Religion and learned about Process Philosophy.
I began to understand and believe more in the God of *persuasive love*, not the God
who many believe judges and condemns people to hell.

Why is there so much suffering and evil in the world? Why is there acute
mental illness, even for people like me who were trying hard to follow Jesus?

As I struggled with my questions, I concluded it is not "God's will" or the
"devil's fault" so many persons suffer with mental health issues, reckon with
trauma from childhood, and war continues to destroy whole nations so needlessly.
I affirmed in faith that this is the present state of the world, with the gift and
dilemma of freedom. And God is suffering with the pain, the evil, and the tragic
death of persons and the environment as we are.

In therapy I began to look at all my relationships. I needed answers, and I wanted to find and be a part of the "answer:" How to provide hope for the world, and hope for persons like me who suffered with acute mental illness and ongoing challenges with depression. There was so much pain and tragedy.

In therapy sessions I had the courage to talk about all the feelings and history of my childhood and adolescence. Many times I had not felt loved by my father. In fact, his many harsh attacks with physical punishment had left me with loads of anger buried inside. Could I forgive?

As I shared with counselors, went to church often, and kept a daily practice of prayer, journaling, and meditation, the transforming work of healing and forgiving grew year by year. I was growing into the faith that I was a beloved daughter of God. I was beautiful, deserving, and gifted.

In a revival meeting, I "heard" the Holy Spirit confirming my "call." I changed my major to religious studies and decided to go to seminary. I took theology and philosophy seminars and practicums in pastoral care. I was learning from and through my story of brokenness, healing, and recovery.

Yes, there have been many times in my life when I did not feel confident. My healing and forgiving journey from physical, emotional, and sexual abuse has been a long process. When the painful and abusive experiences have been too many as a child and teenager, and new wounding messages and relationships follow later, the extreme need for *grace* and healing, mediated through loving relationships, therapy, meditation, and prayer are key.

Like Hagar, the mistress servant of Abraham, I have lived through harsh realities of "wilderness." Yet the many, many encounters with God's loving presence protected me and healed me in the midst of suffering. I stayed in therapy, and worked with all the pieces of my forgiving journey.

Grace brings me the strong message that God loves me, forgives me, and will enable me to continue growing into mature spiritual adulthood. I stay with the forgiving journey. It is a process. Grace enables me to forgive those who have hurt me. Grace enables me to forgive myself. I am freed to love and accept myself and to love others. I don't have to go on in despair, wishing to die, to give up. The "demons" and despair of my past and present are overcome.

My journey of healing continues in all the tensions and times when I suddenly drop into more suffering, depression, and uncertainty. The questions of evil and suffering are never easy to reckon with or to reconcile. I am still growing into the beautiful, creative, loving, engaging, and forgiving woman that God meant for me to be.

We will spend our whole lives affirming, and teaching about the *faith answers*, and still know our moments of personal inadequacy when we are face to face with great injustice, severe mental or physical pain, unending suffering, and mass shootings. I return again to read Apostle Paul's Love Chapter (I Cor. 13). It helps to sustain me in my most troubled hours.

"For now we see in a mirror, dimly, but then we will see face to face. Now I know only in part; then I will know fully, even as I have been fully known. And now faith, hope, and love abide, these three; and the greatest of these is love (I Cor. 13:12-13)."

Here I AM! GRATEFUL for how God continues the healing and growing, strengthening and forgiving work in me today and in all these years. I can share my love and support with others. Often there is a strong sense of *gift* and *miracle* as I listen, respond, and pray with others. This sense of gift and miracle is not unique with me. It happens in many ways every day as pastors, chaplains, counselors, rabbis, priests, imams, gurus, and individuals listen, pray together, and share compassion.

I am grateful for each time I share conversation, careful listening, and encounter a great sense of loving *Presence* as our prayers together enable peace, healing, and acceptance.

My grounding position for faith, hope, forgiving, and healing includes a great appreciation for my Christian faith heritage. And I've come to believe that God is working in and through all religions to teach people to grow in compassion, as we learn to love ourselves, love others, and work for peace in our world.

We live with fear for our future with all the issues of climate change and the threat of nuclear war. The number of people with mental health challenges has risen during these COVID pandemic years along with gun violence, mass shootings, and deaths by suicide.

There is waste and loss in this creative process, but it seems to be the only way that God's higher values of freedom and creativity can be accomplished in this world with imperfection at all levels. It seems to be the only way to build the kingdom of God, the divine commonwealth, on earth, as it is in heaven.

On this healing journey, I will continue to learn, practice, and teach redeeming love and non-violence. It is not an easy path. But I believe this is how we find and keep hope, and receive healing, as we face all the challenges of our personal lives and our divided and suffering world.

As I prayed in 2017 and wrote in my journal, I pray again today:

Lord, release me! Forgive me for not being able to forgive completely. And grant me a new experience of releasing my pain, my shame, my anger, my outrage. For how I've been put down. So my forgiving many persons will take me to another level of freedom and loving experience for myself and others. Lord, let your will be done in my life! For whatever you have for me to do. With however many days you have left for me to serve, to share, to teach, to love.

I know in my best assessment that You, Loving Creator, Holy Spirit, Jesus the Christ, enabled or allowed this very exact journey for me, so I would be most able to see and experience the world of tragedy and loss, and to see, experience, believe, and participate in the transforming "power of the resurrection" working in me and in others! To enable the bringing together of all God's people. For One Family. No more Jacobs and Esaus! Betraying, competing, and then wanting to kill and destroy in jealousy and fear. No more believing that God wants to favor one race over another, one tribe over another! Jew is not more than Greek, or more than Palestinian.

So heal me today, even more, as I present myself to you for loving service. I review this past history, and I'm grateful for every year, every step that I have been following, seeking healing, forgiving, and *Peace*. Your *transforming grace* has been so present for me. In every counseling session. In many friendships. In many spoken and shared prayers. How your mercy has continued.

I thank you, Mother Father God! For your mercy and love today. May your echoes of Mercy and whispers of Love grow even stronger in my ears, in my life, so I can be bold to share more of the truth, and your healing work in my life.

In Christ's name, Amen.

Pauline is a retired chaplain, and provides leadership for NAMI Connection Support groups. She earned her M.Div. from Chicago Theological Seminary, Th.M. from Columbia Theological Seminary. She is the author of Echoes of Mercy, Whispers of Love: My Journey and A Theology of Hope *(AuthorHouse, 2010) and* From Despair Into Healing: Workbook for Spiritual Change *(AuthorHouse, 2022).*

– 3 –

Spiritual Direction as an Uncontrolling Practice that Reveals an Uncontrolling God

Douglas S. Hardy

Spiritual direction provides a relational space in which a person can experience an uncontrolling process that introduces them to an uncontrolling God.

One of the ways that I participate in the uncontrolling love of God is through my work in spiritual direction. Spiritual direction is a practice that has a lot of similarities to and resonances with the practices of counseling and psychotherapy. They all draw from psychological insight into the human condition and involve a one-to-one (or in some cases, group) relationship with the goal of providing help through careful listening. A key difference, however, is in the orienting purpose of each practice; for spiritual direction, the purpose is to help people become more aware of and responsive to God (the Divine) in their lives and world. A spiritual director (or guide) does this by meeting with a directee (or seeker) for listening and conversation that focuses on the directee's experience and reflection on that experience.

Both directees and directors engage this work out of their own relationship with God, that is, from their growing awareness of and responsiveness to God's presence and influence in their lives and world. As a Christian spiritual director in particular, I do my best to not only make God the *focus* of spiritual direction conversations, but also to reflect God in the *process* of relating to the directee. So, for example, because God is compassionate, I want to be compassionate; because God welcomes all as they are, I want to welcome all as they are; and because God is uncontrolling, I want to be uncontrolling.

Given the growing popularity of spiritual direction in recent decades and the reality that increasing numbers of people are looking for spiritual directors, it is important to clarify that this *is* an uncontrolling practice. The word "direction" could imply that a spiritual director tells a person what to do in a very pointed way, just another expression of what often happens in religious settings, viz., an authority carefully controls the content and outcomes of programming. Although this has occurred and can occur in some settings and historical periods under the auspices of spiritual direction, it is not the norm, nor the best practice. To the contrary, it robs directees of their freedom and agency. Further, it can be a setup for abuse and trauma. All of this violates the nature of a healthy relational engagement with God based on invitation and response.

People seek out spiritual directors for a variety of reasons. Some need to make a major life choice and want someone to help them discern a good decision. Some feel a deep longing for God, a stirring of desire within that they are not sure how to respond to. Some have difficulty connecting with God, perhaps experiencing God as distant or absent, and this provides a crisis of faith. Some spiritual seekers grew up in or had significant exposure to very controlling religious communities, but eventually rejected them. A damaging consequence for these seekers can be a fear of God as One who only wants to tell them what to do i.e., control their lives, often in ways that go directly against what they are learning is good for their well-being. They know deep inside that this is wrong, and wonder if there might be another way forward for them that honors their spiritual desire. Spiritual direction can be an incredibly important ministry to these spiritual seekers (sometimes referred to as "spiritual-but-not-religious" or "recovering fundamentalists" or "survivors of toxic religiosity") because it provides a relational space in which a person can experience an uncontrolling process that introduces them to (or, in some cases re-acquaints them with) an uncontrolling God. It can open up a vision for and willingness to engage God in a whole new way—not in fear or for conformity but as a loving companion who grants freedom, honors desire, and seeks to co-create.

Regardless of what initially brings a person to spiritual direction, at their core they need to discover, know, and live into God's love for them, a love that is unconditional, uncontrolling, and which invites them into a partnering relationship. Spiritual directors can model this, help a directee to experience it in a session, and guide directees into practices that help the directee more habitually keep that relational space open.

Because of the vulnerability required for spiritual direction work, many spiritual directors who write about their work emphasize how important it is to not take advantage of their position of authority or power, but rather to be uncontrolling in how they relate to their directees. Here are some of the disciplines (practices) a director can employ to embody this:

Looking to the directee to set the agenda and priorities. Within the broad frame of listening for God with the directee, a spiritual director does not determine the focus of the relationship or a particular session. Controlling the agenda of a session can lead to the director's agenda interfering with what God and the directee need to work on.

Asking open-ended questions. These questions give maximum freedom for the directee to choose how to respond, and what and when to articulate. Over time, these questions encourage the imagination of the directee, modeling the evocative imagination and creativity of God.

Allowing for as much silence (not-talking) as the directee needs. This both keeps the director from dominating and provides space and time for the directee to govern the pace of the session.

Regularly checking in with the directee for consent. The temptation to control can re-emerge unexpectedly and a director may not know in the moment to what degree they might be imposing on a directee in a controlling way. Checking in and asking for consent reminds both participants in this practice that the healthy way forward is uncontrolling.

Letting go of a need for a particular outcome in any given session and stretch of sessions. Because God is uncontrolling of the directee, exhibiting patience and gentleness, directors can be patient with the "progress" of their directees and choose to be gentle when feeling frustration with the pace. Forcing an issue when it has not yet been discerned as something the seeker in their relationship with God owns as important or timely shifts the dynamics of the spiritual direction work toward the power of the director and "seeking to please" on the part of the directee.

An uncontrolling posture is not the same thing as being passive or laissez-faire. The disciplines of a director require constant attentiveness to God, the directee, and the director's own interior life. Further, directors know they influence their directees through the creation and cultivation of hospitable space, and through positing questions or sharing observations with intentionality. Spiritual direction is a ministry of guidance and, as such, directors function as guides. In this way they reflect the nature of God as a Guide who influences us, offers direction, and invites us into life-giving paths, sometimes by pointing out things in ourselves or in our world that we were not seeing clearly or willing to engage.

Similarly, a directee cannot benefit from spiritual direction if they bring to it an overcontrolling posture. While honoring their own freedom and agency, directees need to help create and discover that uncontrolling space along with their directors (and God) such that they are open to being influenced, guided, directed. Surrounding this relational matrix is the Spirit of God who enables both director and directee to live into the love that makes uncontrolling responsiveness possible.

My favorite Scripture example of a spiritual direction relationship is found in the first chapter of the Gospel of Luke (verse 39 and following) which tells the story of a pregnant Mary visiting her also-pregnant cousin Elizabeth. It presents a beautiful picture of companionship in which an older, more experienced person of faith (Elizabeth) provides hospitable space and spiritual direction to a younger, less experienced person of faith (Mary). Mary no doubt had many questions about her pregnancy, the child within her womb, and her identity going forward, but Elizabeth did not respond in a controlling way. Rather, she welcomed Mary into her home, greeted her (acknowledging her as a unique person), and tuned into the Spirit of God. Inspired by that Spirit, Elizabeth affirmed all that God was already doing in Mary—forming and birthing God through Christ in her—in a spirit of amazement and curiosity. The outcome was wonderfully responsive and relational—fetuses and the mothers carrying them were moved to joy, and Mary, the seeker, turned her whole being toward God in love.

God is already with us, within us. But this presence is almost always hidden, unrecognized, not forceful; rather, it is lovingly invitational. God's uncontrolling love is expressed as an invitation *to* us but also as a response of invitation *from* us—we ask of God in return, out of our agency, our spirit resonating with God's Spirit. Spiritual direction reveals and helps give expression to this amazing, freeing work.

Douglas S. Hardy *has been on a lifelong journey of learning to relate to others in uncontrolling ways, while welcoming the uncontrolling love of God to guide his life with his wife and three children, and his work as a professor of spiritual formation at Nazarene Theological Seminary, a spiritual director, and a leader of retreats and pilgrimages.*

4

Immanuel Journaling as a Simple Tool to Experience God's Uncontrolling Love

John Loppnow

The Immanuel Journaling process is a concrete practice to experience the uncontrolling love of God.

"Don't ask what the world needs. Ask what makes you come alive and do it. Because what the world needs is more people who have come alive"

Howard Thurman

God's love is what drew me to being near God. His Presence of care and support for me in the painful and exciting moments of my life is what bonded me to God and continually inspired me to be near Him and participate in co-creating the world of creative action, which is love in my perspective.

God's love, His presence of care and support, did not stop the most painful event of my life, my parent's divorce. Rather, God's love was present and active within me as well as surrounding me in His people. The experience of seeing myself through the eyes of God's infinite love enabled me to catch glimpses of what it might look like to live with greater freedom and hope during this very painful time.

I find the same powerful experience in the stories of my clients and the people I served as a pastor and a contemplative marriage and family therapist. The potency did not come from fixing the problems for people, but in helping them connect their wounded hearts to God's own heart. When people's shattered hearts are glued to God's heart of infinite love they begin seeing God's reality where everything belongs, and nothing needs to be abandoned or alienated.

Love Defined by Oord

Thomas Jay Oord defines love in the following way: "To love is to act intentionally, in sympathetic/empathetic response to God and others, to promote overall well-being." To say this in another way, loving actions are influenced by prior acts of God, others, and one's own actions. Actions we should regard as loving are those purposefully done hoping to encourage, create, or sustain something good."

In order for us to naturally become people who love, we need to experience love. In many ways I imagine we experienced some moments of love through our parents. Even as I write this I am well aware that all of us have moments we did not experience that love. This is not to blame our parents for the outcome of our lives, but rather to acknowledge the human experience of pain.

It seems to me that the strong love bond between God and people is developed when people repeatedly experience the presence of God's unseen stabilizing power in times of overwhelming events.

I am a parent and I intend to do my best to respond to God and my kids in order to promote the overall well-being of them and others. Yet, I fail in ways that I am not aware of. What gives me hope is that when I become aware I can repair and reconnect with them and with God. This belief and reality enables me to live with hope and energy to be faithful to this moment.

It is God's character of active and intentional care that empowers me to turn my attention toward Him. In simpler words, it is His Kindness that leads me to repentance. (Rom 2:4)

God's Character revealed in Exodus 3 + Jesus

The sequence of Immanuel Journaling is inspired by how God offers His children attunement. What is an attunement? Attunement is a concept that is used in the study of interpersonal relationships with families to examine how one person, for example, a parent, focuses attention on the internal world of another such as a child. In the context of parenting, attunement looks like this: mom or dad pays attention to a child's inner feelings, thoughts, and meanings of external behaviors and communicates in such a way that the child feels seen, heard, and understood.

We can confidently say that attunement is found at the heart of all strong and healthy relationships. When parents or therapists offer attunement, their children or clients feel less fearful and become more secure and confident. If human parents or therapists are able to offer attunement to their children or clients, how much more would God, our Good Father and Wonderful Counselor offer attunement to His children?

Immanuel journaling is based upon the conviction that God offers His children attunement. The sequence of God's attunement is found in Exodus 3:7-8a where God interacts with Moses at the burning bush.

The Lord said, "I have indeed seen the misery of my people in Egypt. I have heard them crying out because of their slave drivers, and I am concerned about their suffering. So I have come down to rescue them from the hand of the Egyptians and to bring them up out of that land into a good and spacious land…

God tells Moses that He **sees**, **hears**, **cares**, **is with** them, and will **do something** for them. God gives us a template for attuning. We can only imagine that the Israelites were experiencing the six big emotions (Sadness, Shame, Anger, Fear, Disgust, and Despair) in their suffering. By the time Moses arrives the Israelites were likely traumatized by their slavery, felt alone without God's help, and thus in deep despair. God reveals His deliverance plan to Moses but only after expressing attunement.

The Immanuel Journaling (IJ) process will take you through five steps from God's perspective as God offers attunement to you. Through this process, God brings healing to the broken interactions (misattunement) we all have experienced in life. It makes sense if what the psychological literature reveals as vital (attunement) to human development and formation is also core to God's character and presence.

In our book *Joyful Journey: Listening To Immanuel*, we take these elements and create an opportunity to use them as prompts to hearing God speak to us in our concrete situations. If God is a God of love, then we believe we have the opportunity to experience God's presence in caring ways (attunement).

We have taken the elements of attunement and God's character as revealed in Exodus 3 and created these prayerful journaling prompts.

23

1. I can see you

2. I can hear you

3. I can understand how hard this is for you

4. I am glad to be with you

5. I can do something about what you are going through

We have taken thousands of people through this process and can confidently share that the fruit of people experiencing comfort, hope and increased love because of God's care through attunement through the Immanuel Journaling (IJ) process. I invite you to try an experiment of using these 5 elements as a prayerful journal prompt and humbly sense how God might respond to you.

Personally, I was excited to see how the IJ process philosophically can resonate with God's uncontrolling love in relationships of healing both in and out of the clinical experience. My wife, Sungshim, and I are both contemplative therapists and coaches. We have facilitated individuals and entire congregations through these 5 prompts. It is my hope and prayer that you are open to testing it out with yourself and others you care about to see what the fruit might be within your local context.

People from all over the world, from the Netherlands, Switzerland, South Korea, the USA, Brazil, Mexico, Indonesia and beyond, have tasted and seen that the Lord is good using this simple tool God inspired us to co-create with him— Immanuel Journaling.

People suffering with anxiety, depression, and broken relationships have all experienced an increase of hope and self-efficacy when they know that God cares enough to see them and be with them.

I invite you to consider giving the IJ process a try. Experiment with it for 7 days and see what the fruit is from the experiment of interacting with God. Download the PDF with the IJ prompts here. https://www.presenceandpractice.com/immanuel-journaling

Brief IJ Process after I (John) completed the essay

I SEE YOU sitting on the couch reflecting on a fruitful and relationally full day. Your body is relaxed and calm after completing this important task.

I HEAR YOU saying how glad you are that you completed the essay and grateful for the quiet moments before you wrote this. You were also glad to get some feedback from some people and could really focus for a few hours. You are both excited to see how this may draw people into my presence and, at the same time, anxious that people may or may not like what you've written. You know this is natural, and you welcome these thoughts and feelings into my presence with me. You can hear Dallas Willard's idea of being faithful to your work and then *abandoning all outcomes to me.*

I UNDERSTAND HOW BIG OF A DEAL THIS IS FOR YOU. The Immanuel Journaling process is close to your heart, and you want others to experience the goodness of my uncontrolling love and you don't want to mess that up in any way. Part of you would rather play small and not release the essay so as not to feel anxious. You honor this part and bring comfort and understanding with my Presence to come alongside you. You really do not want to hinder people from the authentic experience of connecting with me because you know how much care and comfort and freedom being with me can bring.

JOHN, I AM GLAD TO BE WITH YOU IN THIS. You matter to me and what you are desiring to see happen here also matters to me.

I AM DOING SOMETHING ABOUT THIS. I am at work in your heart and mind, and I will bring about the right people and situations to help people partner with me to see the fruit of a "with God Life." John, I love you and I'm glad we did this together. I imagine your modeling will invite other people to experiment with this way of living. Thank you for co-operating with me in your everyday tasks.

John Loppnow is a Contemplative Therapist and Coach. Along with his wife, Sungshim, they coach couples and individuals in transformative brain-based skills to experience greater hope, joy and vitality. John enjoys conversing with interesting people on his podcast **Presence + Practice**. *See www.loppnowrelationshipcenter. com and www.presenceandpractice.com*

5

A Client's Reflection on Uncontrolling and Relational Therapy

Janyne McConnaughey

How can counseling that's not about God restore a client's trust in God?

*E*ight years ago, I walked through the door of an old Victorian house for my first therapy appointment. The therapist I had come to see was on a list of psychotherapists recommended to the students in the counseling program at the college where I taught. I wanted advice about signing my faculty contract for the following year. Surprisingly, when asked what my goal was for therapy, I found myself writing the word *peace*. Little did I know that this longing for peace was due to surfacing memories of childhood abuse. The subconscious protective strategies built as a small child had stood the test of time and were collapsing.

Unlike the church-based myth that therapy that is not spiritually focused will draw people away from their faith, I found the exact opposite to be true. This reflection follows my quest to understand the reasons why my faith grew stronger—against all odds—while healing from early childhood, childhood, and young adult trauma, including religious abuse. The therapeutic healing process included EMDR (Eye Movement Desensitization and Reprocessing). My growing understanding of Open and Relational Theology and God as uncontrolling walked alongside the trauma-based therapeutic process of healing.

In hindsight, I realize that my therapist's therapeutic methods modeled the uncontrolling love of God. We became partners in the quest for healing layer after layer of my traumatic story. As a therapist, she was always working for my good but could not change the harm inflicted on me in the past. Nor could she control my actions and choices or the actions of some who, unaware of the impact of trauma in my life, unintentionally continued to cause additional harm while I healed.

Instead of controlling, her role was to empower me. This role did not involve rescuing—something I often wanted her to do and had hoped God would do for a lifetime. Her role was to help me recognize my strength and develop the resources and tools that would enable me to weather future storms in healthier ways. The idea that I possessed everything I needed to do this was counterintuitive to the teachings of an all-powerful God who controlled all aspects of my life. The lifelong teachings in the church about my identity being in Christ, having no strength without God, and never trusting my feelings or choices walked right in step with trauma-induced patterns of learned helplessness that caused me to second-guess every choice.

During the healing process, I realized how deeply the idea of God as controlling had permeated my spiritual life. Though I did mention God during sessions, that *did not mean* I wanted to talk about God. It was simply a fear-based response to being told to keep God at the center of everything. I quickly realized that the spiritually simplistic platitudes had never helped me and would never provide an answer to my inner turmoil. It was not a spiritual problem.

When I stopped looking for a spiritual answer, I recognized a deep-seated belief that God had caused my pain for the purpose of using me to help others. I believed the only reason to heal was to be used by God for this purpose. There was nothing in any of this that involved a relationship with God. My trust in God was as fleeting as my trust in my therapist. I now see that the process of learning to trust her eventually helped me to trust God. Therapy needed to *not be about God*. It instead needed to focus on building relational trust—the only path to this was an uncontrolling relationship.

Sometimes, when I mentioned God during the first two years of therapy, it was more about trusting my therapist than God. *Would this person I was paying to help me give me the same answers as the church?* After sixty years of receiving spiritual answers to what I was beginning to understand as the effects of developmental trauma, receiving spiritual admonitions would have been a deal breaker. It would have been evidence that another person placed spiritual answers above a relationship, disregarded my pleas for help, and attributed the problem to a lack of faith.

Those with a history of spiritual abuse often exhibit strong distrust for a God who appeared to abandon them along with the religious leaders and often the church in general. Those who are trying to keep their faith intact often believe that will only happen if they work with a Christian therapist, unwittingly seeking help that may add another layer of pain—usually due to a lack of understanding of the impact of trauma—especially when it is religious trauma. The therapeutic relationship cannot help but be intertwined with distrust. Focusing on a client's relationship with a God they may feel abandoned them adds a layer that can stand in the way of developing the trust necessary for healing relational trauma.

How did trust develop in my therapeutic relationship? Some days I tried to take control and needed boundaries set that were appropriate for the relationship. On other days I fell into a pattern of helplessness and longed to be told what to do. The thing I longed for on those days—for someone to tell me what to do—was the very last thing I needed. I believed God required blind obedience and had been told what to do by parents, teachers, pastors, and bosses for over sixty years. I both fought against and longed for control. What I needed in every session was relational care. Being asked, "What do you need?" was a foreign question and certainly not something I thought God cared about. I needed the care of an uncontrolling God to be modeled.

My work as a survivor advocate allows me to observe many who have bravely chosen to seek therapy. Their success or failure depends on the principle of "good fit" which is dependent on the relationship. A therapeutic relationship is a dance that depends on an uncontrolling therapist and a client's growing sense of empowerment. This is much like how God works in our lives—with uncontrolling love that leads us to self-reflection and builds confidence in making choices in line with that leading. This process moves us from powerlessness to empowerment.

In my advocacy work, I have learned that attempting to either push or control the healing process of others is most often useless and often damaging. Many trauma survivors want someone else to be in charge and dictate the direction and steps of their healing process. When this happens, they will often give a false sense that the work is successful when they may only be reenacting compliance from previous control-based relational abuse. I often tried to appear healthier than I was to please my therapist or help her feel confident in our work—she recognized this immediately.

Spiritual counseling is especially susceptible to this because the goal is to be more spiritual. The result is compliance, not empowerment. It is the exact opposite of what is needed. It is easy to fall into a controlling relationship with someone who was trained to be compliant—almost always true of those who have experienced religious abuse.

In conclusion, it was my therapist's uncontrolling approach to therapy that allowed me to forge my personal path to finding answers to my spiritual questions. These spiritual questions were wound up with trauma but were not the core problem. The empowering care I received allowed me to understand the relationship God desired to have with me. The purpose of therapy was not to help me trust God. It instead provided a model of what relational trust feels like. For me, trust was the sense of felt safety for which all survivors long. Felt safety is what I attempted to ask for when I wrote *peace* on the intake form. God could not have modeled this trusting relationship without partnering with a therapist who empowered me through uncontrolling relational care.

Janyne McConnaughey, *trauma-informed author and speaker (www.janyne.org), has authored four books including* Trauma in the Pews: The Impact on Faith and Spiritual Practices. *She earned a PhD in Educational Leadership from University of Colorado—Denver and retired from a forty-year career in education. Janyne currently serves as Board President for the Attachment & Trauma Network (ATN). She and her husband live south of Seattle.*

6

UNCLENCHED FISTS AND OPEN HEARTS

MELODYE PHILLIPS

Words for those afraid to step into the fears of new belief.

A week ago the world forever changed.
How can one moment impact everything?

How can a moment have the power to undo an entire life's way of knowing and being?

Sometimes it happens in one single moment. Sometimes in a series of small moments that seem insignificant.

Then it's over.

All that is will never be the same again.

And all that was hoped for will never awaken.

In a moment, my understanding of God falls from the shelf high on the wall. It was packaged so neatly, in its sacred ceramic box.

I watch it fall. Slowly. Then at a horrifying speed as it meets its own death.

The echoing shatters ring in my ears and shake my core.

I stare. In this tragedy upon tragedy, what do I do?

I should run from this broken boxed God.

But I can't.

I'm called to the pieces. There's a beckoning pulling my entire being, though I desperately want to flee.

So I kneel. My shaking hands begin to sift through the shards of smooth ceramic. Now rough and jagged.

The pieces cut and my hands bleed.

I keep trying to fit the pieces back together. They won't fit. The harder I work to fit them together, the deeper they cut into my palms.

Through the tears and panic, I try to put God back in that box. I need God back in that box.

If God is out of my pretty, safe box, all bets are off.

My world has already unraveled. But this box cannot unravel.

The tears course harder down my hot cheeks as I realize my box, and the God that belonged in it, cannot be saved.

I hold the broken pieces to my chest as I weep. I feel the pieces dig deeper into my hands, into my chest as sobs rip from me.

But then.

I look closely at the pieces. I realize the pieces that were cutting me are gone. There are still pieces left from the broken box and from the God of the Box.

But there are new pieces.

Pieces that can't fit into any box. Nor would I ever want them in a box.

They glow and pulse with life.

The colors of these pieces are an unknown mixture, wild and inviting.

Uncertain and safe.

The fragrance of these new pieces is one I've never known, but one my soul knows is home.

These pieces are bringing new life into death.

These pieces become the voice of God. Simply saying "stand up. I am here."

So I stand. Unsteady and terrified.

What if I fall? Will these pieces shatter too?

I look at the pieces and know they can't be shattered.

These pieces have withstood all of eternity and will continue to stand.

I can't put the pieces together. But I don't want to.

I begin to love the pieces and want them with me. In their unbridled mess, I want these pieces close to me always, reflecting bits of themselves as I navigate this new unknown world. I want these pieces close so I continually hear "I am with you."

Now I walk slowly. Bent over and fragile from my undoing. Deeply wounded. My hands bandaged and scars from the God of the box. I walk with my heart forever broken.

But my soul. Oh, my soul.
It is home.

If you allow yourself… if you close your eyes and breathe in… if you make space for the questions to surface… you'll see yourself in my story. You'll hear your own questions bubble forth.

Because it's all our story.

"I used to pray when I felt anxious…it doesn't help anymore." She whispered as the tears fell down her downcast face.

Before the heaviness. Before the miscarriage, before the traumatic delivery of her child, before the eating disorder, before the sickness of her beloved father, before the death of her precious friend, this incredible woman had found comfort and refuge in prayer that led her to God.

Before.

Before all her world slowly fell apart, she could find refuge and trust in the God that worked all things for Good.

Tears continued their steady descent down the gentle curve of her quivering cheeks, soaking all in their path.

Sobs that only come when that wall within your soul has finally broken began to echo against the beige walls of the office. She felt broken.

The trust she once held was slipping away as her desperate plea was swept away in the night to be unanswered.

Like a piece of paper being blown away in the wind, she watched as her comfort and foundation began to disappear, further and further from her grasp. No matter how high she jumped or how fast she ran, she couldn't catch the paper to tuck back into her soul.

She feared she had lost her faith along with everything else.

If God isn't who she'd been taught… who is God?

If God isn't controlling, if God isn't all powerful in the traditional sense, how did she navigate life without feeling an overwhelming sense of anxiety?

Is God *really good* to allow such tragedy?

Tears continued to free fall as the questions nestled in her soul found a path to spill forth. All the world was crumbling as she knew it and because God and prayer were now unknown and fear invoking, she felt completely lost in the freefall.

This moment was pivotal. To name the doubts and questions that Christians are not allowed to experience was a burden that she needed to no longer carry.

To discover that doubt wasn't an indication of her own moral failure or even the failure of God was… earth shattering and redeeming.

There is freedom in the release.

Exploring the idea that maybe God doesn't control us and the events of our lives for our good or even God's own good began to shift something deep within her.

Her anxiety didn't magically disappear.

However, her relationship with God is deepening as she is now allowed to draw near, despite questions and a budding new understanding of God. She regularly utilizes somatic coping skills to manage her anxiety.

This deepening is wild and messy. This deepening is building a new, more solid foundation in her relationship with God.

She has Hope. Her hope isn't the white knuckled logical hope of all she had been taught through her life. This Hope is living and breathing. Moving and fascinating. This Hope is embodied.

Instead of drawing from God, she draws near. As God and the Spirit beckon her into their tender care and fold, she now relaxes into that fold. She found she is not also losing her faith amid grief and anxiety. She learned that God meets us when we feel broken.

As a therapist/spiritual director, I knew how to hold space for these questions and make room for every question and fear to pour onto the floor in between us and come to life.

As a Christian going through my own deconstruction, I saw myself in those tears. I heard my own heart and soul cry as she purged herself of all the things she thought she wasn't allowed to say out loud.

The idea of God's controlling love is sold and packaged to us from the moment we step into a traditional, evangelical church. We must not question the idea that God doesn't control everything.

Believing that tragedies, traumas, loss, and all suffering happen for the glory of God makes us question that glory. Allowing ourselves to face this question feels threatening and wrong.

We miss something beautiful and deep when we put those questions inside a ceramic box, high on the shelf.

We fear these questions because questions are full of uncertainty. Uncertainty lacks a sense of safety.

In sessions I often hear "I have control issues." My response is to reframe the idea that control is a negative thing. Our desire for control is often linked to a desire for safety. *A sense of safety is natural desire linked to survival.*

There's a sense of safety in believing that God is controlling everything.

Even when that belief feels dismissive and is harmful, sometimes it's safer. It feels safer to believe that someone is the puppet master, controlling the world that's spinning at a frightening speed around us.

It's a pill we can swallow and use to push the questioning thoughts and emotions down.

To open our clenched fists and let our hearts lose, tenderly exploring the texture and smell and taste of this belief is downright terrifying.

If God isn't controlling, who is?

Am I safe if God isn't controlling me and the world?

Are my loved ones safe?

These are the questions we need to explore. No question is off limits for a God that lives outside of the limits.

Let them come.

Join God, the Holy Spirit and Jesus in this liminal space of tension and uncertainty... of beauty and Love.

I promise you; God will show you a new depth of life and faith that rocks your world and explodes it with a color and fragrance that the Spirit is waiting to unleash into your being.

No matter how threatening and terrifying, step into the chasm and find you are not alone.

You are welcome here, friend.

Melodye Phillips is a therapist and spiritual director and specializes in maternal mental health, food and body image issues, as well as parenting struggles. She lives with her husband and their three precious children. Melodye's passion is to integrate spirituality and mental health. She occasionally blogs at faithfoodandfreedom.com

7

NOT OVERPOWERING BUT EMPOWERING PEOPLE

DAVE ANDREWS

The Spirit challenges us not to exercise control over people, but to encourage people to exercise control over themselves.

When the Spirit came during Pentecost, this helped people create a liberating society of small, local, self-organized communities that were centered around empowering those who were marginalized and disadvantaged. These spirit-inspired communities worked to help others realize their potential as men and women made in the image of God.

Paul says (in Gal. 5:22–23) the 'fruit' yielded by the Spirit is 'love, joy, peace, patience, kindness, goodness, faithfulness, gentleness and self-control. Against such things there is no law' and that in any community open to the Spirit will yield the fruit of the Spirit.

I see this fruit the Spirit yields on different levels. On a personal level, there will be love (passion and compassion), and joy (awareness and appreciation) and peace (trust and tranquility). At a relational level, there will be patience (persistence) and kindness (sweetness not bitterness). At a social level, there will be goodness (generosity) and faithfulness (fidelity). At a political level, there will be tolerance (non-violence) and self-control (self-management).

Paul stresses 'against such things there is no law.' In 'spirited' groups, agencies or organizations, there should be no laws that discourage the development of these qualities. All the structures, processes and protocols should be specifically designed to facilitate the development of these characteristics—especially self-control.

The Spirit of God is committed not to overpower people but to empower people—not to exercise control over people, but to encourage people to exercise control over themselves.

Traditionally our idea of power has been defined as the ability to control other people. This idea of power emphasizes the possibility of bringing about change through 'coercion'—an approach that tries to make others change according to our agendas.

While the traditional idea of power means taking control of our lives by taking control of others, Jesus advocated an alternative idea of power—taking control of our lives, not by taking control of others, but by taking control of ourselves. This alternative way of viewing power emphasizes bringing change by 'conversion'—is a spiritual approach, which embodies the noncontrolling Spirit of God. This view does not try to make others change, but encourages us to change ourselves, individually and collectively.

The traditional idea of power is popular because it often brings quick, dramatic results, but it is characterized by short-term gains for some, and long-term losses for everyone else. Every violent revolution has betrayed the people in whose name it fought its war of liberation.

The alternative idea of power is unpopular because it is usually a slow, unspectacular process, but it is the only way for groups to transcend their selfishness, resolve their conflicts, and manage their affairs in a way that can do justice to everyone.

The essential problem in any situation of injustice is that one human being is exercising control over another and exploiting that relationship. The only solution to this problem is in the alternative Spirit-inspired approach. This approach emphasizes controlling ourselves, individually and collectively, through self-managed processes and structures.

We can create space for a new movement of the Spirit by cultivating what Harrison Owen calls 'Open Space,' where the Spirit is free to operate. We can do this by encouraging people to consider something they really care about, something they really want to do something about, and we encourage them to identify it, name it and own it for themselves. Then we encourage them to extend an invitation to meet with others who care about the same thing. Those who respond to the invitation come into a circle that they hold open, as a host, for mutual conversations. We encourage the host not to control these conversations, but to let people come and go as they please, trusting the Spirit to bring order out of chaos, clarity out of confusion, conviction out of concern. We encourage those who are hosting multiple conversations to welcome any expression of passion, compassion and responsibility as signs of the Spirit's prompting in a particular direction. Then we encourage people to organize processes and structures that will support the activation of this critical mass of spirited interest.

When my wife Ange and I became involved in our neighborhood we hoped to create an open space for developing a Christ-like life in the community where we would model a lifestyle characterized by the radical, non-violent, non-dominating compassion of Christ. This is a community distinguished by a commitment to love and justice. This is a community where it is normal to work from the bottom up to empower people (particularly the marginalized and disadvantaged) and enable them, through self-directed, other-oriented, intentional community processes and structures to realize their potential, as men and women, made in the image of God.

We called ourselves the West End 'Waiters Union' (waitersunion.org) because we wanted to be 'waiters' in the West End. We did not want to set agendas for people. We wanted to be available, like 'waiters,' to respond to people's needs, and to do what we could to help. We wanted to develop a therapeutic sense of hospitality in the locality, so all people, especially people usually displaced in the inner city, could feel at home in the community.

The Waiters Union is not a high-profile network. As 'waiters,' we keep a low-profile. None of the activities we are involved in carry our name. They all carry the names of the groups that organize those activities—which we contribute to—but we do not control. As a result, a lot of people in our area may know us as people but may not know that the network we are part of exists. Which is fine, because the network exists to promote the community, not the network; and the network can function more effectively as a catalyst in the community if it is prepared, to be more or less invisible, rather than attract attention to itself at the expense of local groups.

However, we are not secretive. We welcome enquiries and answer questions as freely and as fully as we can. And we are inclusive. We invite anyone who is interested in our work to with work us, alongside us, as partners in the work together.

The work we do is 'self-directed' and 'other-orientated'. Each person has the right to shape every group they are a part of and being part of a group depends on participation. A person becomes a part of a group simply by participating in the group. Once a person is a part of the group, they have the right to manage the group. We believe people should have the right to shape all the decisions that have an impact on their lives and we believe the best way for us to shape the decisions that impact on our lives, individually and collectively, is through the process of consensus. So, all the groups nominate rotating facilitators for their meetings in order to 'be careful to do what is right in the eyes of everybody.' (Rom.12:17)

As the groups work from the bottom up to empower people, we especially include people who are usually marginalized and disadvantaged in the decision-making process of the groups. All the groups work with the people that they work for, and, in so doing, seek to enable the people they work with, as partners, to realize their God-given potential.

Through one group, we seek to promote the aspirations of the displaced original inhabitants of our neighborhood, for whom Musgrave Park, in the middle of the neighborhood, is still 'sacred ground.' Through another group, we seek to support refugees by sponsoring their settlement and the settlement of their families, working through the anguish they go through as 'strangers in a strange land'. Last, but not least—though they are often considered 'last' and treated as 'least'—through a whole range of groups we seek to relate to the people in our community, who are struggling with physical, intellectual, mental and emotional disabilities—not as 'clients', nor as 'consumers', still less as 'users'—but as 'our friends'!

Typically, when we meet with our friends, we emphasize the personal and relational, keeping the tone generous, gentle, and easy going. This allows the interaction to move back and forward from light humorous superficial exchanges to heavy heartfelt in-depth conversations.

We start with check-ins and pick up on any personal concerns people have and then focus on one of these points of pain while reflecting on what personal challenges they are facing and what personal approaches they have found helpful in overcoming these challenges. Throughout all of this we discourage people from trying to fix one another or give each other advice, but instead encourage the person (who is the focus of concern) to trust the Spirit to be an inner guide to lead them into truth that others can affirm and confirm in their own experience.

Dave Andrews *and his wife Ange have worked in therapeutic communities with marginalized groups of people in Australia, Afghanistan, India and Nepal for fifty years. He earned his M.S.W.A.P. at the University of Queensland. He is the author of twenty books, the most recent is 'To Right Every Wrong' www.daveandrews. com.au*

– 8 –

SELF-EMPTYING STORYTELLING

MICHAEL JOSEPH BRENNAN

*Educators foster learning for students who are co-creators of
the future through story-telling and deep listening.*

I have to admit, I like being seen and heard. I find it difficult to shrink so that
other people can flourish. I have a big personality and an important title. As
the Dean of Students, I have power to edify or ignore students, teachers, and other
faculty. It would be easy to ride a power trip and I have met many people in disciplinary roles that do exactly that. It is also easy to be dismissive because teenagers
usually find ways to get into similar kinds of situations whether they get in trouble,
break-up, or get a bad grade. My daily prayer is that my own words and actions are
reduced, and anything that I say that is good or loving or wise will be amplified.

In my school, I supervise the school counselor and the Diversity, Equity, and
Inclusion Coordinators, so I find myself having to step-in to listen to stories from a
counseling perspective rather than a disciplinary perspective, and many situations
require empathetic redirection or conflict transformation.

Teenagers respond to me differently than they do to other adults. Sometimes
this is because I'm weird and say weird things that they find funny, which is dis-
arming—but more than that, it is intentional. Deans cannot be trained for every
situation or every aspect of the job, and I was an English teacher, so my training
mostly comes from books. It is really easy to admit that I make mistakes because I
can say with confidence that I have no idea what I am doing quite a bit of the time.
This is funny because it just seems self-deprecating.

But through it all I found that my belief in an uncontrolling God has deeply affected my own uncontrolling discipline. Some people believe they are coerced by God (or fate or the universe), and then they become controlling and coercive themselves. The fatalists often respond to situations in black and white and right or wrong. But there is another way. A way that allows for a plethora of possible responses and requires wisdom to respond lovingly with physical, mental, and spiritual well-being and safety at the forefront. A way of uncontrolling love.

I remind myself to allow for awkward pauses. I shrink. I try not to give hints that I agree or disagree so that they do not feel the need to tailor the story for me in fear that I might judge or dismiss too early. I just try to get them to tell the story—usually for more than five minutes. After that, I ask a bunch of questions, but mostly I try to empathize. Sometimes I even say weird things, like today, as I write this essay, a girl walked by when I was talking to two other girls, and she said she was sick this week. I asked why she was at school if she was sick. She responded, "you know how you sometimes vomit during that time of the month?"… and of course I said "yes!" Even if this is only theoretical knowledge because I teach Women's Literature and not experiential knowledge. Basically, staying weird is my personal secret to offering uncontrolling love.

Uncontrolling love also pushes me to ask: What if students were treated with dignity? What if they have something to offer the world now rather than after college? Maybe we would not feel the compulsory need to push college on young people. Maybe they would not rebel if we were transparent about the decisions we make.

They say it is a dangerous thing to let people with underdeveloped frontal-lobes become co-creators in the world. But Paul says, "but God demonstrates his own love for us in this, while we were still sinners Christ died for us" (Romans 5:8). So, while we were still messing up, Jesus invited us to follow Him. Perhaps we can do the same for youth in our uncontrolling love.

I have seen other male disciplinarians dismiss female conflicts as "girl drama" and then sometimes those situations have resulted in one of the students talking to the counselor about suicidal ideation. That is not uncontrolling love.

How many LGBTQ+ students feel safe at their schools and how many feel safe enough to "come out" to their Dean? Students of color also tend to fear their Deans because they are often disciplined at a higher rate than white students. This is not uncontrolling love either.

If disciplinarians do not zoom out in these situations to see that different people need to be cared for differently, they can miss opportunities to build relationships. And we should be asking whether the rules are more important than the students because the students often feel like the rules matter more, especially if we don't take the time to explain our reasoning.

Here is a recent example of how I brought uncontrolling love into the hallways of school. Four students were given detentions because they took their plates out of the dining hall and allegedly threw the plates in the bathroom trash according to the housekeeping staff. When confronted, the seniors explained to the Assistant Dean they gave their plates to a girl going back to the cafeteria because they were going to be late for class. Initially, they talked themselves out of the detention and were told there would be no consequences. However, when I weighed in I pushed the fact that they are seniors and should know better.

Angrily, they asked for a meeting (not knowing that I was the one that changed the detention). I explained to the students that if they had better time management as seniors, they would not have given their plates to a girl who would then throw them in the trash. They agreed that one detention should be served. However, what about the other? I agreed and said, "you already have the one and I'm too lazy to take it away, but we'll play rock, scissors, paper and if I beat both of you, you serve it, and if either of you win, they don't." Of course, the students didn't like it, but it was funny and therefore it seemed fair enough. They won.

The point is, this was a disciplinary meeting that resulted in all-around better relationships with every adult and student involved and this is how we invite people to change. We stay weird, humble, funny, open, and uncontrolling.

If I had told them "Because I say so," they could have easily lost respect for me. In this case, they understood the importance of managing time, talking to people for understanding, the importance of cleaning up after themselves, and likely other important lessons that are more difficult to measure.

We can hardly control ourselves all the time, so I argue it is time to let go of the reins of control for others. It is time to stop trying to control outcomes. People will change because they are invited to participate in the outcome. Trust is risky and people are messy, but God alone draws us closer to reciprocating relationships and stewardship. I know that for myself, I do not need anyone to criticize me more than I already criticize myself. When I apply that to the teenagers I work with every day, I find ways to offer an uncontrolling love.

Michael Brennan is the Dean of Students at Oxbridge Academy in West Palm Beach and an editor for The Weight Journal. He is working toward a Doctor of Ministry and Theology at Northwind Theological Seminary.

– 9 –

GOD WANTS TO BE YOUR MIDWIFE

BECCA DE SOUZA

*Meeting a God who brings comfort rather than control allows
our pain to give birth to joy.*

J sat in my therapist's office, moments after a panic attack, staring at the floor
feeling surprisingly calm in my body, which had been absorbed in terror only
minutes earlier. My therapist asked, "can you hear the birds chirping outside?" I
could and I soon heard, "I think that's enough for today. I'll see you next week."

I had worked in pregnancy support for many years without realizing the impact of my own traumas on my body and mind. A PTSD diagnosis in late 2016 was
welcome news as I lived with sometimes debilitating symptoms for over a decade.

I spiritualized my symptoms so wholeheartedly without knowing the nature
of trauma or how we carry it in our bodies. I worshiped them away (briefly), I
repented of fear, asked Jesus where he was in my darkest moments, and forgave
everyone I could think of, even God. My spirit was free, but my body was still
terrorized.

The concoction of hormones and chemicals that had kept me alive through
multiple experiences of trauma continued to haunt me. Hyper-vigilance, catastro-
phizing, traumatic anxiety, and sleep disturbances were completely normalized
in my life with three small children. The upheaval of motherhood disguised my
undiagnosed mental illness and I convinced everyone that I was ok until it was
clear that I was not.

A decade earlier I was in a populous West African country volunteering in
mother/child healthcare with a small team of skilled birth attendants. Working

alongside local midwives and doctors, we supported laboring women in a government maternity hospital. We saw the strength of mothers as they brought their babies into our beautiful and terrible world. For three months we rubbed their backs, monitored contractions, encouraged them in their power, and did what we could to ease some of their ache. Again and again, insurmountable pain gave way to ecstatic joy.

Our time there ended tragically as a van accident took eight lives and sent nine of us to hospital. Many who survived would live with significant physical injuries. I woke up in a tiny clinic in the bush, doctors and nurses rapidly working to care for those most in need. Fast moving vehicles and physics can be devastating to hopes and futures.

I was flown back to the US to recover and quickly found myself under the weight of grief—my own and everyone else's. So many dear people I loved died that day and the theological wound was as undeniable as my broken bones.

The notions of God as Powerful Hero, Controller of Life and Death, Protector of the Righteous—those illustrations I had heard so many times in my evangelical upbringing completely failed me. In the following months my broken heart was wide open to encounter God anew: First One on the Scene, Hands Covered in Our Blood, Weeping with Those Who Weep, and One Singing Songs of Hope.

The groaning and labor pains of all the women I supported had found a place in my own body. The only picture of God that made any sense to me, the only words that resonated true with the new world I found myself in was God as Midwife. If our mothers had named the Holy One, would God have firstly been midwife, continually welcoming new life in even the most excruciating circumstances?

Birth can be the most powerful experience of a woman's life—when the variables align as they should, when body and baby and mind and circumstances cooperate, there is possibly no more brilliant picture of redemption. Endless hours of intense waves of pain, a woman moving her body and groaning intuitively, the beautiful cocktail of oxytocin and endorphins and just as she declares the end of herself, the light breaks through. She brings her precious baby into the world, screaming glad deliverance cries on her chest, the sweetest surrender of pain to joy.

In John 16, Jesus uses birth imagery to describe the hopelessness and loss that those who love him would soon feel and yet, their sorrow would turn to dancing, like a mother with a fresh babe on her chest.

Birth's power for joy and redemption is entangled with its unpredictability. Labor and birth can be as magnificent, or as devastating as the ocean itself. Most women left undisturbed would birth safely and beautifully, but within nature there is spontaneous need for interventions as well. The World Health Organization says 10-15% of women will need cesareans or other interventions as they give birth in order for mum and baby to stay safe. 99% of maternal suffering and death in childbirth occurs in the majority of the world, where global inequity leaves some countries with less than half of their births supported by a skilled birth attendant. When midwives are present at a birth, they can make all the difference.

Birth trauma is much less about how the labor and birth progress and much more about how the mother feels while it's happening. If she feels alone, afraid, ignored or disempowered in decision making, she's much more likely to feel traumatized by her experience of birth. A woman well-supported even during an emergency can experience less trauma than a woman with a normal physiological birth who perceived abandonment or disdain by her care providers.

Highly skilled midwives attended all three of my births in Australia, on Dharawal Country. My first full-term labor was one that needed life-saving interventions. My midwives used their deep wisdom, resourcefulness, intelligence and compassion to support me to do what only I could do. They could not give birth for me. They could not miraculously extract the baby from me in a painless way. But they could be with me, in the truest sense. Their presence gave me confidence and courage, their quiet voices comforted me deeply. Their watchfulness and skill gave my son the care that he needed to survive.

Another midwife was present through one of the longest and most desperate nights of my life as I labored with my daughter. When she was born my midwife laid her on my chest, sharing deeply in my joy and my relief.

In my third and most endorphin-filled birth, it was not until I saw photos later that I realized how quiet but close my midwife was as my son was born. In the depths of transition though I felt completely alone, her presence was giving my body courage in my life's most vulnerable moment.

God is not in control of what happens in our lives, in the same way that a midwife is not in control of how a birth unfolds. And yet, her presence can make all the difference: she brings a multitude of comfort measures, deep knowledge of normal physiological birth, and that which might need interventions. She spends endless hours keeping watch, reminding us of our courage and strength, and tenderly showing us that we are not alone. How much more is God eternally resourceful, utterly creative and wise, understanding all there is to understand, and bringing the most possible good out of every moment by moment by moment?

We join God in confronting long-standing systemic injustice, subverting the destructive plans of the empire as midwives Shiprah and Puah did in the Exodus story. More often we hear the groaning of Romans 8, the labor pains of all creation that find reverberation in our own bodies as well.

God is with us; families, neighborhoods, people groups and nations, this whole wildly spinning planet are all promised that the dreams of God will indeed, one day, be born alive.

I work with pregnant women who lack the support they deserve in this tremendous rite of passage which is birth and motherhood. If I relied on an all-powerful God who always brings miracles to those who pray, I would be irrevocably disappointed. For example: Why didn't the baby turn enough to avoid the cesarean for the mother who already had suffered so much trauma in her life? Why hasn't my client been rescued from the addiction that's now seen her baby removed from her care? How can God fail to provide housing for a single mother who has experienced enough instability for a dozen lifetimes?

Fortunately, that's not the God I'm looking for anymore. I know the God who sees disappointment and enters in, who accompanies us to the psychologist's office, a God who leaves a meal at the door and offers to hold a fussy baby.

God is a midwife named Emmanuel. God with us in our most catastrophic pain. God with us as the devastation one day surprises us with new life. God with us in all the days and nights in between.

I have never found God absent in my darkest nights, even when the pain has threatened to swallow me, and the future has felt completely chaotic. God has always stayed close, putting pressure on my lower back, whispering truth to my inconsolable heart, hands covered in my blood, tears falling with my own. She hasn't been in control of or responsible for my pain but is always present, always welcoming the most possible good, the healing, the new.

Becca De Souza lives as a guest on Dharawal Country (Wollongong, Australia) although she grew up in the US and is a proud Shawnee descendant. She works as a trauma-informed doula and birth educator and graduated with a BA from Messiah College in 2004.

10

ANXIETY AND CONTROL

TAYLOR QUALLS

It's hard, if not impossible, to live a life of love when we live out of anxiety.

*I*t seems to me that there is a direct link between our anxiety and our attempts to control our world. For so many of us, the more overwhelmed and afraid we become the more we try to do the impossible, controlling everyone and everything around us so that we can feel safe.

If it is true that God does not control, then it follows—at least in my mind— that God must be perfectly non-anxious. To be present in love and the gift of freedom, God's presence with us must be completely lacking in anxiety.

As a therapist, I believe it is my sacred task to emulate this uncontrolling, all-loving God by engaging those whom I encounter with loving, non-anxious presence. It is this presence that provides the space for healing. Sometimes however, it is easier said than done.

The Millers were incredibly loving and caring, anxious parents. They actively sought the best for their children, but they became anxious when their children deviated even slightly from the course they had charted out and understood to be best for them. At least that was how I understood their family when their son Dean entered my care in long-term residential treatment. His parents' incredibly high anxiety and well-intentioned high expectations had created something of a split in Dean.

Dean had a greater desire to be and be seen as good than anyone else that I have entered into a therapeutic relationship with. He did all the right things, he opened doors for old ladies, served on school and youth group leadership teams—you get the idea. Sometimes he would even risk his social standing to call others out on their bad behavior; he wanted to prove that he was *the* good kid. Until he wasn't anymore. Like a boiler building up pressure, Dean's denial of his own darkness would result in an explosion of some truly outrageous acting out.

Dean had internalized his parents' anxiety and their attempts to control him into their image, and by the time I met him he did the exact same thing to himself. His acting out was not the result of him being some wild, out of control kid, but quite the opposite. His attempts to control his image created a comfortable lie that he told himself—that he was completely good with no darkness inside of him. It also created a dangerous split within him because what we don't allow ourselves to see can never be healed.

So here I was, doing my best to bring a loving, non-anxious and non-controlling presence into the Millers' lives. I would offer my observations, hoping to help them see the pattern that they were in. I would teach them different ways to communicate so that they could really listen to each other. These are often the things you do in family therapy. The problem was that it was not going fast enough for them. As the months passed by and the Millers were not getting the results that they were looking for, their anxiety level rose higher and higher, and with it the intensity of their grasping for control.

This reached its apex one day in family therapy when Dean's parents said, "If you would just let go of your thoughts and feelings and accept that we are right, your life would be so much easier." On the outside I like to think that I was calm, cool and collected, but on the inside, I was outraged. I knew they were afraid, but this felt like an attempt to deny his very personhood, his individuality. On top of that they were shutting me down every time that I attempted to help. With every attempted intervention I felt more and more like they were telling me to go sit in the corner while the family worked this out on their own. The session was completely out of my control.

I now appreciate the irony of that last statement, but it took me entirely too long to figure out what was going on that day. For all of my desire to bring a loving, non-anxious presence into the room, I got lost somewhere along the way. I became overwhelmed by the Miller family's anxiety, and I joined them in it. While Dean's parents were saying that everything would be fine if he just abandoned his own self and did as he was told, I was doing the exact same thing to his parents (albeit a bit more subtly). I had joined in the control-fest. We were a trifle of control (a trifle is a layered cake, right? I've been watching a lot of *The Great British Baking Show* lately). This was far from my best moment as a therapist.

At this point I ended the session because I knew that I was lost, and we were not going anywhere good. Then I had a choice to make. I made a mistake and joined in the chaos and attempts at control, now what was I going to do with it? I wish I could say that I devised a brilliant plan going forward because I am brilliant, but if I'm being honest, I sort of stumbled on the answer as I went. I joined in with the family's mess, and I was now in the unique position to show them the way out.

It did not take long for anxiety to kick into high gear for everyone in our next family session, including me. Instead of following it and grasping for control, instead of shaming myself as a bad therapist or pretending that it did not exist, I offered the same grace to myself that I wanted the family to offer to each other. Then I extended it to them. Instead of being an outsider offering a non-anxious presence, I was now an insider who knew and understood the anxiety they were feeling, who had engaged the very same desire to control that they were experiencing now. I did my best to show them the way out from the inside.

When Dean's parents said something that struck me as outrageous, I checked my own anxiety and desire to control and turned it into curiosity and a non-anxious presence. I did my best to help them do the same, translating their anxiety and attempts at control into the language of relationship and hurt, something that Dean could engage with and connect to. Dean's walls of defensiveness came down as he could see his parents as people who were hurt, not out to get him.

Let me be totally clear, my choosing to be a non-anxious, loving presence with the Miller family was not the magic bullet that solved everything. It did, however, bring about a shift in them and in me. I was able to once again do my best to emulate the non-controlling, all-loving God that I know, to embody that presence to them. They were able to see and experience what it is like to escape the trap of anxiety and control, even if just for a moment, and they knew that they could do it again.

When I think about these sessions, I am reminded that I am always human in all of my beautiful messiness. I bring my training and experience into the therapy room, but I also bring my own brokenness and quirks into the room. I'm also reminded that that's not a bad thing. I may have never gotten through to the Miller family as an outsider to their anxiety and attempts at control, perhaps it was only as one who had sat in the muck with them that I could help them find the way out.

Isn't that what Jesus did and still does for and with us? The perfectly non-anxious God took on our anxiety, took on all of the brokenness and quirkiness of being human to show us the way out—the way of the cross rather than control. Perhaps sometimes, in order for our non-anxious presence to mean anything to those whom we walk alongside, it has to be tested. This doesn't just apply to therapists but to all of us. Perhaps it is only when we risk genuinely entering into one another's quirky brokenness, taking on one another's anxiety, when we feel the full weight of it and come out the other side choosing to be present as non-controlling love rather than fearful control that we become the hands and feet of the crucified God in the world.

Taylor Qualls is a Licensed Professional Counselor living in Lee's Summit Missouri. He earned his Master's in Counseling from MidAmerica Nazarene University and his Masters in Theological Studies from MidAmerica Nazarene University. He loves hiking, traveling, and is a nerd about the Eastern Church. He is not a good dancer, but that's never stopped him.

11

HELPING THOSE WHO HELP OTHERS

TARA H. WEST

*Changes in my perspectives and choices to grow have enabled
me to help others in their choices to grow and change.*

*I*n my work as a Wellbeing and Goals Coach, I use client-directed coaching. This connects beautifully with the concept of God's love being uncontrolling as it is all about our ability to choose our own path, our mindset, our habits, and beyond.

My clients are the providers and administrative operations team members of our counseling and coaching practice. I work with counselors, social workers, psychiatric nurse practitioners, medical assistants, dieticians, and office support staff. We are a practice owned by a Christian man, but he has never felt that we should be called a "Christian Counseling Practice." Therefore, our employees come from a variety of faith backgrounds and current faith practices.

When the practice owner and I dreamed up my position, his hope was that I could provide an outlet for all the practice employees that would include an opportunity for them to vent if needed, to help them with self-care so they could be their best for their clients, and to leave an open door to discuss spiritual matters if they wanted. He felt a need for this but did not feel he could offer this outlet for fear it would not come across in an objective and optional way.

Since my approach to coaching is meant to help the whole person, covering six areas of life (emotional, social, mental, spiritual, vocational and physical), it seemed a potentially optimum approach to meeting the practice owner's desires to provide this open door for growth and ongoing conversation to all his employees.

The coaching I offer is optional, completely confidential, and an employee bene-fit without cost to them. They can freely participate in sessions with me at their choosing, with no strings attached, and on their terms, to cover whatever they most need or want to address.

A number of my clients do want to discuss spirituality to one degree or an-other, mixed in with a variety of other topics in the other five areas of their lives. These individuals represent a spectrum of faith journeys. Several come from a Catholic background, one or two still practicing while others left the church but are searching for something that will work for them. One client was raised by one Catholic parent and one Jewish. She leans more towards simply finding the spirituality in nature, serving others and meditation. A few other clients grew up in very conservative religious circles and are trying to find their way forward as adults, with one of these few continuing in their more conservative denomination. Another client follows his higher power, and his sobriety is his top priority in life next to his family. Other clients have a much more open belief system. One follows practices from most major world religions while another uses crystals and seeks guidance from a medium. The third simply lives by doing good and helping as many other people as she can. I can only think of one client who never addresses anything of a spiritual nature.

Believing that God is love, gives us free will, and desires for all of us to flourish in this life has enabled me to work with each client, no matter where they are in their faith journey or how they are choosing to address their spiritual nature. I would not have always been able to meet people where they are like I am now able to do.

My upbringing in a conservative Protestant denomination taught me more about judging others and comparing them to the rigid standards my church told me mattered the most to God. I would have been little help to most of my clients if I had not experienced my own faith transformation over the course of my 30's and 40's. Because of quite a few writers and speakers, my studies in spiritual for-mation, and God's work in my life, I came to a place of being able to hold space for my clients, whatever they share with me.

I learned, over time, to invite God into my questions, my doubts, and uncer-tainties, even my secrets and dreams. Somehow, I came to realize that I needed to allow God to love me in the midst of all these parts of myself, and to believe God's heart towards me is always for my good, filled with love and empathy for me in my humanity, as well as coming to recognize that God hurts with me in those times when bad things happen to me or my family. I now see that God's intentions towards us are good, even when other humans do things that God doesn't desire for us or when we are affected by sicknesses or tragedies that are simply a part of living in this fallen world.

Experiencing this reality of God's love in this way has in turn brought me to a deeper love and empathy for all others which enables me to be present with my clients in whatever they share with me in our sessions. Some have needed me to simply listen and be objective. Others have revealed enough to me that I have seen their stories resembling parts of my own, and this has opened the door for more in-depth discussions about their spiritual searching and questions.

I am able to speak freely of God's love with a few of my clients, and I've had the opportunity to encourage them to ask God into their struggles and to allow God to love them there. For some, this has helped them with grief over losing a child, others with their marriages, still others have found help navigating through their hurts and frustrations with conservative faith upbringings or parents.

As I work with these dear people (who are essentially my colleagues in this counseling and coaching practice), the truth becoming more and more apparent to me is that everyone is searching on some level, has questions and is trying to make the best choices for their lives. Their choice to sign up for sessions with me as their coach is representative of this desire. Every part of the client-coach relationship is ultimately determined by the client. We do not go anywhere in our conversations that they do not choose to go.

As I stated initially, the idea of God's uncontrolling love fits wonderfully with coaching that is client-directed. My hope is that each person who allows me to journey with them via the avenue of coaching will come to know that the choice to grow and become rests with them. When given the chance, I convey to them that they are loved in the midst of all their choices. When they question negative things that have happened in their lives, I open the idea to them that we all have the same freedom to choose and sometimes other's actions affect us, while our choices may often affect others.

Not all clients are interested in God's heart towards them, but for those who are, or those who might be searching for that security and confidence of knowing they are loved and truly understood for who they are, then it makes a huge difference to be able to bring in my own experiences of how God has loved me as I am and how God has carried me through difficult times of hurt, abandonment, grief, disappointment, etc. When given the open door, I can share my story and serve as an example that can assist them in moving forward in their own faith journeys.

Tara H West *has her Master of Arts in Spiritual Formation with a Bachelor of Arts in Christian Education and minor in Psychology. Besides being a Wellbeing and Goals Coach, she is a writer, speaker, teacher, small group leader, and a wife with three adult, plus two in-law, children. You can read about some of her journey on her website at: fittingthepiecestogether.com*

12

THE BUTTERFLY EFFECT
(OR THE EFFECT OF BUTTERFLIES)

ROGER BRETHERTON

The mystery and wonder of life guide us towards an open and relational view of psychology and theology.

I'm not in clinical practice anymore. I used to work in the British National Health Service as a Clinical Psychologist, but fifteen years ago I moved into academia. And now, every year, I guide undergraduates through the maze of theories and formulations commonly known as 'abnormal' psychology. Each year I neatly set out the numerous approaches: the medical, the social, the behavioral, the dynamic… and knock them down like dominoes. All of them, it turns out, are imperfect, and all of them are partial, but as long as we keep that in mind, it seems that all of them are useful.

Over the years I found that the pressing questions that slowly steered me towards an increasingly open and relational theology were the same ones that changed my understanding of psychology. The old sureties that underpinned the therapy and spirituality of young adult life collapsed simultaneously. Initially I thought that a higher-education setting was a sure route to certainty, but the more I lectured, the more difficult I found it to believe that any one perspective in psychology was the final word. It seems to me that any theory of mental illness that lacks curiosity and closes itself to revision gives off a pungent whiff of fundamentalism; it becomes a bully in the playground of ideas.

Maybe I'm still hung over from my ten-year binge in clinical practice. I have too many doubts. I'm still shaken by the number of beautiful theories that shattered when applied to my clients in the real world. After a decade of being exposed to the unimaginable suffering of clients with trauma, maybe the radical openness of theology leaked into my psychology. One of the main tenets of open and relational theology is that the future is open, unspecified, and yet to be determined. No psychological model can ever sum up the complexity of human existence in a way that dictates inevitable therapeutic progress. The most appropriate attitude I could adopt to my clients seemed to be a loving attentiveness, with no attempt to control the outcome on the basis of a prespecified model. It was my experience of the clients themselves that pushed me in an ever more open and relational direction.

Mary was one such client. She didn't have cancer, but she feared she did. Over the past year, she'd exhausted every test and scan the National Health Service (NHS) could justifiably offer, and she emerged with a unanimous clean bill of health. But this wasn't enough. When one scan was completed, she wanted another... because any reassurance given was short-lived. There was always the chance they'd missed something, always the possibility an aggressive tumor had sprung to life in the days after her last test. She wanted to be certain—absolutely sure—that she would be healthy for the foreseeable future, so she chased down the final stubborn possibility of cancer until it was zero. Almost.

It was the *almost* that bothered her.

Twice, sometimes three times a week, she appeared at the local clinic with yet another bodily omen of impending death. Her leg ached. Her eyes hurt. There was blood in her stools. She couldn't catch her breath. Her fingers tingled. Her shoulders were stiff. Each time, her family doctor did his best to reassure her that, as far as he could tell, she didn't have cancer. Each time, she'd retreat from the office pacified, only to return a few days later with a further complaint. She was driving her doctor, a man renowned locally for his gentle bedside manner, steadily 'round the bend.'

So, with some reluctance on her part, he referred her to me. From her perspective, being referred to a clinical psychologist was a mistake—an unwelcome distraction, even—from the serious business of finding a life-saving medical intervention. Mercifully, however, she indulged me for a few sessions.

She'd been scared of dying since childhood, so our work together ranged across a broad spectrum of concerns: from the cognitive-behavioral understanding of health anxiety to the existential meaning of death. One week we weighed up the pros and cons of anxiety medication, the next we discussed the work of Viktor Frankl. And then, in the final session, we talked about butterflies.

Butterflies were visiting her kitchen, far out in the local farmlands, more often than usual that summer. One after another, they fluttered in through the open door and circled the scullery. She was captivated by them, and so was her young son. They joked together that they were angels sent to comfort her, to let her know that all would be well; someone somewhere knew she existed.

My office was on the first floor, looking out on an ancient weather-beaten wall, strewn with ivy. It was only when she mentioned the butterflies that a glimmer outside caught my eye. And there, as I looked out of the window, were dozens of brightly colored butterflies resting on the ivy, gently opening and closing their wings in the sunshine. In the ten years I'd occupied that office, I'd never seen a single flutter, let alone a flurry like that. I jerked upright in my chair and gestured to Mary, and we stared out of the window like a pair of wide-eyed toddlers gazing into a rock pool.

After that, any further conversation seemed superfluous. We said our goodbyes and finished the session. Over the course of the afternoon, the butterflies slowly vacated the ivy outside, and by the next day they were gone. They'd never visited before, and they never came again. It was almost as if they'd been waiting in the wings to put on a show.

Why did they come at that moment? Was it just coincidence, a delicate plague of crimson and black confined to the thirty mile tract of land between her home and my office? Or were they angels dispatched to reassure her that her pain mattered and was known? Or was it some strange quantum phenomenon, whereby our consciousness called them into being?

I don't know. It seems too bland to call it coincidence; too grand to call it synchronicity; too lazy to call it a butterfly effect. Perhaps *serendipity* best sums it up. It certainly made me wonder if the world was much more open and interrelated than I had previously allowed.

This year, during my annual round of mental health lectures, there will inevitably be an eager undergraduate student who, in reviewing the models I presented, will ask which of them I endorse.

I'll struggle to answer.

Of course I have my favorites. I tend to prefer the psychological theories that view 'madness' as an extreme version of everyday experiences, but ultimately, I have as much certainty regarding my knowledge of insanity as I do the reasons butterflies alight on ivy.

I won't say that, of course. I'll probably mumble some high-sounding excuse for an answer. After all, it didn't take me long to learn that pretending to know the answers is part of the lecturer's job description.

Or maybe this year things will be different. Perhaps I'll find the courage to share my uncertainty. Maybe I will be open and allow the student to impact me, as I once allowed my clients. And who knows, maybe this year, my teaching will sail a little bit closer to sanity.

Roger Bretherton is a Clinical Psychologist and Associate Professor at the University of Lincoln (UK). He studies Character Strengths and is the writer and presenter of The Character Course (www.thecharactercourse.com).

13

A LOVING THERAPEUTIC RELATIONSHIP

ROB GIANNAMORE

A therapist cannot control the outcome of their clients sessions.

*T*herapeutic rapport is the most important element of a therapeutic relationship; the therapist must cultivate an attitude of acceptance regardless of who is presented that day. Without this, you will never establish trust, and the work cannot go on.

"Welcome, my name is Rob, and I will be working with you today" is an example of establishing this from the get-go. One might even say: "Before we get started, I want to let you know that I love you, but I don't care." Let me explain, in Buddhist thought, it is believed that we suffer because we cling. If this writer clings to the outcome of a session or the plight of the client and does not consider the agency that the client has exhibited in their life prior, then no work will get done. In this therapeutic relationship, it is established that regardless of the choices made by the client, they will always be welcomed back the next week. The limiter, then, is that this writer can only care about the person in a limited, uncontrolling way. For kids, especially teenagers, it is emphasized that this love is different: a love that is open to the possibilities for the client's life.

We are creatures attached to our clan and when we lose that attachment, many negative behaviors can be created as we long to re-secure that attachment. Have you ever been told by your minister, well-meaning Sunday school teacher, or even a parent that God is "emotionless," "controlling," or "knows all the plans?"

How about the classic, "all things happen for a reason," or "I can do all things through Christ who strengthens me." Mental health and trauma don't work like that. Sometimes things do happen for a reason, that reason being that humans make really poor decisions and treat each other in really negative ways. A God who is seen as *withholding God's love with a sense of condition* has alienated a whole generation of young people who have been parented and preached from an authoritarian model.

There is a now famous video of a mom playing with her baby. In the video, the mom and baby are sharing in interactions, both reciprocating each other's expressions. About mid-video, the mom turns away from the baby and turns back with a flat face. The baby plays along for a second but soon begins to make bids for attention, reaching out and squeaking and ultimately beginning to cry and fuss. This takes place in a matter of seconds. We are creatures with great sensitivity to the love and attention of the caregiver, so that in a matter of minutes, our demeanor can change. If this love is withheld for a lengthy period of time, we internalize that something is wrong with us, producing anger or frustration that is often projected onto others.

Seventy-one years ago, a theorist named John Bowlby turned our world upside down by showing how constant loving care by a mother figure impacts parenting. We are learning now that the old style of authoritarian parenting ("I am the parent, you are the child") does not work for the growth and independence a child needs for healthy development. Should it not be considered that our views of God are similarly hazardous to our spiritual health? I feel it should be.

God loves you, but God also allows you to think about what is going on. God does not want endless suffering; God does not create your endless suffering, or those long nights where you can't sleep thinking about all the awful things that could happen to you. This writer often tells his clients that it is not their job to love their parents, it is *their* job to love *you*. If you love your parents, it is because they established a solid bond with you and allowed you to express your humanity in the fullest manner possible. This writer would challenge that our relationship with God is the same way. It is not our job to love God. If we love God, it is because God loved us first. With no strings attached, no shoulds, no coercion.

There is a story in the bible that illustrates this. In this story, Jesus one day is in a village, and he is looking for some water at a well. He approaches a woman, a Samaritan woman—someone society casted as an outcast—and asks her for a drink of water. Jesus then goes on to point out to this woman that she has had five husbands, and the man she is with now is not her husband. Despite some of her less than positive behaviors (contextually), Jesus sends her forth, suggesting that Jesus is a loving and accepting God.

Person-Centered Therapy is an approach to therapy founded by Carl Rogers in the 1940's and focuses on a non-authoritative approach, allowing clients to have agency in sessions such that, in the process, they discover their own solutions. As this writer is a trained minister and a trained clinician, it is often important at the beginning of the relationship to establish if there is any spiritual/religious trauma. Oftentimes, there is, and often in the form of authoritarian parenting but also disengaged parenting or absent parenting, as well. In assessing the clients' religious experiences, the majority report an authoritarian God dictating their religious upbringing.

Person-centered therapy and person-centered faith allows one to begin to see the loving movement of the parent and God through surrogacy in the session. Often, a client will present with a report of some calamity between the current session and the last... self-esteem and self-worth being pretty low. If God talk has been established in the first few sessions, the conversation is brought back to love, asking the client to consider what *they* want to do about the current situation and how a *loving, patient God* would respond. This writer then models the surrogate parent by asking open ended questions, affirming statements, reflective statements, and summarizing statements with no judgment towards the client. Too often, this writer has been asked why this notion of God is not talked about in church.

Communities can begin to encourage the need for exploring an uncontrolling God by looking at their statistics. In 10-15 years, maybe up to 65% (or more) of their congregants will no longer be sitting in the pews. If this writer had a seat in church for every time an interested listener asks why the idea of an *uncontrolling* God is not taught in church and that they would come and hear this message, this writer would have a fairly large congregation. We are in the midst of an evolution in consciousness. Our youngest millennials and Gen Z'ers are hungry for relationships. Our current congregations that adhere to biblical literalist, authoritarian interpretations have lost their relevance in an age where young people can find meaning elsewhere. The time is now.

Rob Giannamore is married to his college sweetheart; they have four children together. Rob is an endurance athlete, and holds a black belt in American Krav Maga. He received his Master of Divinity from Methodist Theological School in Ohio and a Master's of Science in Mental Health Counseling from Cappella University. You can find his blog at shalemconsulting.com

14

WHERE IS GOD IN HEALING OUR WOUNDEDNESS?

TAMBRY HARRIS

Ignoring emotional and psychological pain stunts us; a holistic approach is required to heal and live life fully.

"Let the past be the past."

When memories and intuition brought forth the fact that I was sexually abused as a child, this is what I was told. It's clearly the easier answer and is certainly the most socially acceptable: silence the pain and push down the hurt… and I couldn't do it. My survivor-self knew repression would only keep me stuck with woundedness festering inside my body.

Strong evidence has proven that ignoring past trauma is not the healthy approach. I would even say it is not the life-giving approach. When I was introduced to the book, *The Body Keeps the Score,* by Dr. Bessel Van Der Kolk, I finally found an ally. Dr. Van Der Kolk gave scientific data to what I intuitively knew: I needed to take healing steps for my mind, body, and spirit to thrive.

We all have choices to heal or not heal, to grow or not grow, to ultimately bring good or harm from difficult situations. Being in charge of your life and knowing you have some ability to shape your circumstances starts with awareness of subtle sensory, body-based feelings. The greater the awareness, the greater our potential to control our lives. Knowing ***what*** we feel is the first step to knowing ***why*** we feel that way. Believing we have control over the direction of our lives is critical. I may not have had control over what happened to me as a child, but I have control over how I move forward. I have control over whether I stay stuck in survivor-mode or if I move into a thriving life that God would want for me. My internal GPS is saying, "recalculating," so I can get back on course.

Dr. Van Der Kolk states, "The greatest sources of our suffering are the lies we tell ourselves." My abuse left me with the belief that I was unworthy. In my work, I find that this is true for many survivors of abuse. It took two things to break my belief: first, examining the woundedness with the guidance of a therapist, and second, allowing God to support me and love me unconditionally. That was the healing combination I needed to find and claim my truth… and my intended path.

"Where do you think God was when the abuse was happening to you?"

I believe God was there, crying for his beloved child. I believe it broke God's heart. However, God's nature of uncontrolling love means that God could not single handedly prevent the abuse. God could not stop the abuser from passing on the abuse he experienced as a child. My abuser did not choose to do his own healing work and instead allowed his woundedness to harm others. Instead of transforming his pain, he transmitted it. I believe God cried for him, as well. While I believe God's nature could have guided my abuser in choosing a different path, God could not force him.

This knowledge was critical to my healing. There was no malice or over-sight by God. I was not less important to God and my sense of unworthiness was false. My trust in a loving God kept me close to the One who is the ultimate comforter. I could feel God's spirit supporting and loving me, even when I didn't feel lovable.

As a child, I always had a sense that God was with me. I would stand outside in the backyard looking up into the stars believing God was somewhere out there. I felt God's presence, and in some ways, I thought he might be smiling down on me. It took years for me to believe that God would actually draw near to me, but God became so near—his spirit within me—that I just needed to acknowl-edge it.

Knowing that something better awaits and that God is present, wanting each of us to know peace, love, and kindness, is the foundation for my healing. Combining the knowledge of God's uncontrolling, unconditional love with our own will to heal and take control of our lives is what enables us to take steps to-ward healing and thriving.

"The brain may forget but the body always remembers."

My therapist told me this as I struggled to understand what was going on within my healing journey, which highlights the critical importance of mindfulness practice in trauma recovery. By nature, trauma shuts down our inner compass, skewing our ability to know our truth and navigate our way forward. Somatic therapy, which recognizes that a person's inner feelings and trauma impact their physical form, was an essential step for me. By releasing pent-up trauma from the mind and body, healing occurs from the inside out. This unique approach combines mindfulness, grounding techniques, and traditional talk therapy.

Allowing my body to **release**, allowing my body to **know**, and learning to be **present** to my pain was essential. Releasing this pain and learning to be still in my body opened me up to mindfulness, meditation, and the ability to feel present and centered.

Therapists will tell you that the brain seeks to protect your well-being and that memories come when you are ready. I believe God protected me until I was strong enough to process my past, and my therapist partnered with God to support me as memories were revealed. Slow, intentional healing is critical. Examining our woundedness and allowing our relationship with God to grow can free us from the limiting box of trauma.

"God invites us to cooperate with God's work to promote healing, goodness, and love."

One of the core beliefs in Thomas Jay Oord's book, *God Can't*, is that because there are things God **cannot** do, God needs our cooperation and "participation…to make our lives and the world better." It is not God's fault that over 35% of women worldwide have experienced sexual abuse. It was not God's fault, nor mine, that my childhood innocence was stripped away by a pedophile.

What I **can do** is be a voice bringing truth into the space of secrecy, silence, and shame that surrounds this topic. I can encourage each survivor to sense a God who wants them to thrive and to see the "Going-Forward" chapter that awaits them. Trauma and abuse are often surrounded by shame, and as a Spiritual Director and Transformational Coach, I see many people stuck at the point of seeking to understand their worthiness and other limiting beliefs.

As we invite God in, we begin to do the healing work to overcome the emotional, spiritual, physical, and mental pain. This approach took me to a new level of meaning in my life and brought about the desire to be a wounded healer, understanding to some degree the wounds and pain of others. I bring what I know. I create safe space for individuals to be still and bring their questions and their pain to God where a deep level of healing happens. I invite others to open their hearts to know that God is with them, always ready to be drawn into that sacred space. Mindfully inviting God into the healing process and listening deeply to God's discerning voice will bring increased peace and direction.

Henri Nouwen, in *The Wounded Healer,* states, "Those who can articulate the movements of their inner lives, who can give names to their very experiences, need no longer be victims of themselves, but are able slowly and consistently to remove the obstacles that prevent the spirit from entering. They are able to create space for the Spirit whose heart is greater than their own, whose eyes see more than their own, and his hands can heal more than their own." We are allowed the opportunity to choose healing, growth, expanded space and collaboration with God's spirit.

I have come to believe that all of these broken pieces in our lives can come together to create a beautiful mosaic that is uniquely *us*. We may need the help of others to know how the pieces fit and even which ones to release. By allowing God to shine through our mosaic, we bring beauty and hope to those around us. As wounded healers, we align with God and act as sources of healing, helping to overcome some of the negative forces that exist in this world. We can be encouragers for those needing support, and we can be the light on God's intended path for them.

If you are interested in stepping into your healing growth, expanded space and collaboration with God's spirit, I would love to **share a free chapter of my book** which frees you from deeply rooted limiting beliefs created by trauma and nurtures healthy, life-giving beliefs to open you up to a whole new chapter in your life. Contact me at tambry@survivorstothrivers.com. I also welcome the opportunity to work with you to claim your exciting next chapter by transforming unhealthy patterns into life-giving ones that manifest your thriver self.

Tambry Harris is a Spiritual Director, Transformational Coach, Speaker and Author of Awakening the Light: A Survivors to Thrivers Going-Forward Story *(American Bookfest 2020 Best Book Finalist). Tambry helps others claim their best selves and lives by examining limiting beliefs and unhealthy patterns that get in the way of attaining their deepest desires and embracing their whole self. Tambry earned her Master's Degree in Applied Psychology from University of North Carolina at Charlotte. She blogs at survivorstothrivers.com and loves all things nature.*

– 15 –

UNCONTROLLING LOVE GOES TO PRISON

TYLER J. PARRY

In an environment where trauma is leveraged for control, the experience of uncontrolling love can prove transformative for incarcerated persons.

*P*at was one large human being. Stout and thick-limbed, it was not difficult to imagine that he was what he claimed to once have been: the muscle for the Mob. Pat was born into organized crime; from his youngest days he recalls family by blood and family by oath. He engaged in what outsiders might consider ruthless criminal behavior but seemed to him a natural way of life. "It was in my blood," Pat would say, "I had no choice in the matter." Even when serving the family went against his very nature and moral convictions, Pat did what he was told. He understood power and he understood respect and he understood that while love was constantly mentioned, it was loyalty and obedience that truly counted.

I met Pat when I served as a chaplain in a state prison. Pat had served more than two decades of a life sentence for murder. He was a lifer's lifer; he knew how to jail. Pat understood the power structures of prison, visible and invisible, written and unwritten. Pat knew who the bosses were and where he stood with them. He understood the trauma that had led him to prison, the trauma that was inflicted upon him in prison, and how both were leveraged against him almost every moment of every day.

What I was keenly aware of before meeting Pat was most, if not all, incarcerated individuals were survivors of trauma. Many grew up in family situations that harmed rather than nurtured within communities in which power was wielded to oppress and control. Certainly, the process of arrest, trial, sentencing, and initial incarceration inflicted further dehumanizing trauma. The incarcerated environment is one of fear and violence, exceedingly limited privacy, and the arbitrary and capricious enforcement of petty rules. All of this is designed to create a cowed population, one that could be controlled at any cost.

Pat opened my eyes to the utter cruelty both on the part of corrections staff and fellow incarcerated persons. Personal preferences were routinely and intentionally ignored. Trauma reactions were met with force. Traumatic wounds, often evident to all, were salted for the amusement of others and, above all, to reinforce the control of the panoptically-enabled authorities. "I came in here with wounds," Pat said, "and every day they are opened up again and again not to help me get better, but to keep me in my place."

As a chaplain, I strived to help create a safe space within the violent and trauma-inflicting world of prison. I wanted the chapel to be a place where persons could allow themselves to relax, to draw in deep breaths, and to find the comfort of the Holy. Pat helped me to understand that while such an environment was indeed helpful, it was not sufficient, especially if the theologies presented within the chapel implicitly or explicitly reinforced a model of coercive power and love. Pat sought comfort in his faith, but what he found was yet another power structure seeking to control him.

"I came to Mass as often as I could," Pat recalled, "I came to Bible study and small group classes. I was here in the chapel as often as I could be." Pat found a message grounded in obedience and faithfulness, a gospel that called for full submission to the demands of holiness. This resonated with Pat; it is what he had heard all of his life! He dedicated himself to beating his body and making it his slave. His dedication to physical and spiritual fitness blended together as he trained himself to be a soldier for Christ. The driving force was loyalty, loyalty to the divine monarch who demanded unwavering and unquestioning obedience.

"I bought into it 100%," Pat remembered. "Every day it was a matter of training my body and training my soul. I didn't question what the teachers told me. I didn't question what my fellow brothers told me." Little if ever was the topic of Divine Love discussed. The Kingdom of God, from this point of view, closely resembled the informal power structures of the prison. There was one who had power, and all who wished to live under the Powerful One's protection did so by demonstrating their loyalty and obedience. This worked for Pat for a while, until one day he found himself in the same moral situation he had found himself in on the outside.

"I'm in prison because someone who said they loved me and would protect me told me to do something, and after I did it, they let me hang out to dry. The same thing happened here," Pat recalled through tears. "I thought that we were brothers in Christ, that we were following the law of God, but it was just a sham. They were running stores, and when a store had to get broken up, they came to me. I didn't like it, but I did it, and as soon as I was in the hole, I was *persona non grata*, you know? Anyone in the bucket was a sinner, and sinners weren't part of the Kingdom."

Pat's time in solitary confinement was devastating. Cut off from nurturing relationships, Pat retreated into himself, reliving the trauma that brought him to prison, and the trauma that brought him eventually to solitary. That is where I met Pat, and where our relationship first began. There we would sit, with our backs leaning up against the cold steel of the cell door and our heads resting mere physical inches but also miles apart. The chaplain's role was to listen, and Pat's role was to speak. The chaplain's stance was one of transparency, trusting that the presence of an Other, of the Holy, might emerge from the emotional space that is created when two meet one another sincerely and openly.

Pat was in need of love. His restless heart would not find rest until it found love, but not the "love" of his family or the "love" of the gospel he had heard. The love that brought Pat peace and introduced to him an experience of liberty was one that refused to control and coerce, one of pure invitation and, thus, of pure vulnerability. This was not the agenda-laden love that was his experience in every other context of life.

Ironically, it was not for months that I ever saw Pat physically. Our conversations ranged across similar topics and our posture was always the same. I often wondered whether such conversations were bearing any fruit. I warred against my own natural leaning towards setting goals in order to focus on the relationship we were building, moment by moment, in that awful place of isolated suffering. I recognized that not being able to see Pat was an impediment to me, but a tool for him. He knew what I looked like. I did not know him. In Pat's mind, that gave him a sense of control, a way of reversing the power dynamic that was always present when staff and incarcerated persons connected.

Eventually, Pat was granted release from administrate segregation and returned to general population. Pat wrote to me, asking to talk, but not in the chapel. We met on the block, sitting at the bolted down, stainless steel tables surrounded by tiers of cells. Pat was not ready to return to the chapel, and he probably never would, but he had turned a corner in his spiritual journey. In the darkness of solitary, with every sense assaulted and by his thoughts battered, Pat had come to see that the love of the Holy was not one of demands, but one that empowered by working-with. Pat had discovered a new sense of love and power one that could saturate his way of being and give him the strength to resist.

Uncontrolling love was the love that stood apart. Uncontrolling power was the power that stood apart, and now Pat would be one who, in his own framing of his life and environment, would stand apart. He could endure and journey forward. He could live.

Tyler Parry is a chaplain and priest in the Episcopal Church. Tyler has a background in military, prison, and hospice chaplaincies, with a focus on aiding trauma survivors. Tyler earned a BA in philosophy, an MA in historical and theological studies, and a ThD in restorative theology. Tyler enjoys competing in Highland Games and cheering at his children's soccer teams.

– 16 –

OPEN AND RELATIONAL CARE

CHRISTY GUNTER

*Three key concepts of Open and Relational Theology apply
clinically in a therapeutic context and to how the church relates
to caring for the vulnerable.*

*I*n the last few decades of my adult life, there were several times where I
needed extra help. As many single moms do, I turned to the church for those
resources.

One of those times I was in need of a box of extra food, so I drove up to a
church that was advertised by my kid's school. The entry signs were easy enough
to follow, but once I arrived, I had no idea where to proceed from there. I went the
wrong way and felt incredibly humiliated. Especially when I tried to turn around
and ran over a curb.

I sat in my car for a moment trying to gain composure. I had a one-on-one with
the divine begging to just run away instead of going inside for more embarrassment.

Then I saw someone outside my car window. I cursed internally and smiled
as she asked some questions I did not hear. I followed her inside. Teens lined the
exit and entry way, so proud of the service they were doing for the Lord.

They mixed up my name, gave me a Spanish form that I couldn't read, and
then led me into the main room. Nothing was open. Nothing was relational, and I
felt absolutely no uncontrolling love.

Every fiber of my being wanted to flee when I perceived what was coming.
I could see, like the others before me, I was about to be sat down, talked to, pros-
elytized, and prayed over.

By this point I was talking *AT* the divine with a few choice words that would bring shame upon my grandmother. I did not want to do this. But I sat down like a Nazarene quizzer about to jump in question recognition anyway.

A man in a matching red shirt, like all the others, looked at me. I pondered if death would be more fun.

"Christy?"

Yep. That's my name.

"Welcome back," he cheerfully said.

"Thanks. I've never been here," I said.

He asked me two more times, convinced I was unaware of my ability to recall driving and walking into places, until finally, he said, "Oh. Well. Welcome."

Great, I thought. Let's get it all over with and let me out of here.

He asked me if I was married. I hate that question. There have been very few times in my life where my answer was positive. But, you know, it's a church and he made me answer. It was a required field. Nothing was open. Nothing was relational, and I felt absolutely no uncontrolling love.

Red shirt man asked how many and how old my kids were. He asked all sorts of questions that were invasive and embarrassing. He asked if I went to church and if I went every Sunday. He even asked the cross streets of the location of this church I attended. The cross street convinced him I really was a churchgoer, but he was concerned that it might be Catholic. I wondered if I could facepalm him right there.

He asked if I had anything he could pray for, and I shook my head no. He asked if he could pray for me anyway. But this question was not asked in a way where "no" was a possible response. I felt I had no choice in the matter. I would be prayed over.

I sat there as he petitioned the divine on my behalf, staring at the floor, eyes wide open. Teenagers on the sidelines continued to be so proud of their work. I thought starvation might be better than this. Nothing was open. Nothing was relational, and I felt absolutely no uncontrolling love.

When his prayer was over, I asked if I could walk forward. Such a question for permission to exist in space reminded me of domestic violence.

Finally, the light of day became visible, and I followed a young teenage boy out to my car. But not before some man, without asking permission, grabbed me and hugged me. I did not hug him back. He called me by name and thanked me for coming. I stared like a deer in headlights. Nothing was open. Nothing was relational, and I felt absolutely no uncontrolling love.

We got to my car and the teenager decided the shape of the box would not fit in my trunk, so I opened the side door.

"Do you live in your car?" he asked. I replied I did not. "Oh, then why is there so much garbage in your car?" he responded.

That's when I died, and my ghost now writes this chapter.

Kidding!

I don't know about you, but when my life is in chaos, my car reflects it.

And although I do not expect a kid to choose perfect words, his behavior reflected the church environment I was just experiencing where nothing was open. Nothing was relational, and I felt absolutely no uncontrolling love.

So, why do I tell this 'death by embarrassment' story?

Because it demonstrates the exact opposite of what I needed. I was vulnerable and needed a church that acted like the Open and Relational divine this book seeks to describe.

Three of the core foundations of Open and Relational Theology set a framework for how we believe the divine behaves and creates a context for how we can behave, too.

In Open and Relational Theology, we assert:

1. The future is open and unknown,

2. The divine is relational while affected by our actions, and

3. The divine loves us in uncontrolling ways.

In this essay I want to work with these three foundations to propose how these concepts relate to what I refer to as Open and Relational Therapy which can be applicable clinically in therapy or in how the church relates to the vulnerable.

I now work as the Director of Client Services in an agency that works to provide safety, healing, and opportunities for survivors of domestic and family violence in the North Texas area. Every day I put my heart into empowering five client services teams (the clinical team, rapid rehousing, the legal team, advocacy, and our two shelters) to be trauma-informed and survivor-centered in how we approach our community.

But here is my secret: I do this with an open and relational framework. I lead, guide, advise, coach, and interact with clients in the way I imagine the divine connects with us.

The people who come through the doors seeking help with domestic violence situations are as vulnerable as I was that day in the church waiting for a box of food.

When we are vulnerable, we often experience a world shaded by violence. A world that seeks to control us, is forceful with its demands toward us, takes away our agency and autonomy, and we feel the imposition of someone else's will on us. That's what violence is. Or, as I explain it in my book *Survivor Care*, violence is dehumanization, objectifying a person, and demanding a person is less than a meaningful human.

Clients come for therapy and advocacy having experienced a dehumanization of being that stripped them of agency and autonomy, and often the church's response encourages further dehumanization, just as my introduction story illustrates.

What is needed is NOT more control, forceful pushes, required fields, impositions of someone else's will, and a loss of agency. What IS needed is:

1. An approach toward humanity that believes the future is open and unknown and acts like it,

2. A relational worldview that believes the divine is affected by our actions and thus we also are affected by another's actions, and

3. The type of love for others just like the divine loves us in uncontrolling ways.

So, what does this look like in the therapy room or in church expression to the community?

It means instead of having a set agenda and required fields that embarrass people, we are **open**. Just like the divine is open to an unknown future, we too might be prepared with tools and training, but we are open to what is before us. We do not act like we know the future any more than the divine.

It means that instead of pretending like we are the experts who know best, have access to the absolute truth, and act in a way that approaches humans with an all-knowing power, we are **relational** like the divine and believe that clients—people—are the experts in their own lives. It means we may offer a lot of options and resources but ultimately it is their choice, and we believe with them they are capable of making decisions for their life.

It means that instead of imposing our will on the client, we set up ways to help develop their confidence in agency and autonomy. It means instead of forcing them into prayer or an agenda that may not help, we ask if they want to sit or stand, question if they want this chair or that chair. It means we set up the whole time with us in a way that communicates they do not need to ask permission to walk forward. We approach them in **uncontrolling love**.

It means that Open and Relational Theology applies to therapy and community care.

Dr. Christy Gunter, LMSW MDIV is the Director of Client Services at an agency that serves families of Domestic and Family Violence in DFW. Christy is the author of "Survivor Care: What Religious Professionals Need to Know about Healing Trauma" *that was released in 2019 from Wesley Foundry Books. She has an earned doctorate in Global Health and Wholeness, a Master of Divinity, and a Master of Social Work (Phi Alpha Baylor) and has over 500 additional hours of specialized training in violence, assault, trauma-informed care, and other related topics.*

17

A Journey of Love from Addictions

Hugh Leroy Thompson

For those who feel lost, helpless, and unloved, being or living with an addict, there is hope.

*H*e was a likable guy with excellent skills as a custom home builder. He took pride in his work. He never drank on the job, and he would fire any worker who did. He was a high-functioning alcoholic. At first, he only drank on weekends for relief and rest, but at other times it got worse. When family members confronted him, he responded, "I have it under control, no problem!"

This person was my father-in-law. My wife dealt with his problems since childhood. After we married, her mother often called us in tears, "He's blacked out again. What should I do?" She was unable to set boundaries.

Our family met with an intervention counselor to prepare for a supportive, loving confrontation. Prayerfully we hoped for treatment. Our sessions were emotional, at times, draining, but we were committed to following through. Unfortunately, dad got sick before we were able to complete the intervention. He was diagnosed with liver cancer which had spread throughout his body. It was inoperable. Sadly, he died six weeks later. His doctor said his alcoholism was the major contributing factor.

I share this story to show the tragedy of countless people who experience this turbulent river flowing through their life and family. Understanding the disease and finding help is possible. Ultimately, this is a journey of love, but loving someone with an active addiction means facing brick walls, dead ends, repetitive nightmares, broken dreams, and hopelessness. You feel powerless and defeated. Love alone has no power to change anyone—not even God's love has this power, according to relational theology.

The term *addiction* comes from the Latin word *addictum,* meaning "held in bondage." In Puritan and conservative thought, an addict is considered a victim of moral failure or a *sinner.* However, in Scripture, *sin* is also considered a "broken relationship." Some theologians suggest it is the "failure to love."

God loves every addict; the addict *can't* return love to God, much less to others. Why? The drug(s) of choice has trapped the person in a prison of powerlessness and delusion. The first step of Alcoholics Anonymous confesses, "We admitted we were powerless over alcohol—that our lives had become unmanageable." This is the core belief in an uncontrolling self and an opening to experiencing God's uncontrolling love.

We read Romans 7:19-24 where Paul admits that his *affliction* controlled his behavior.

> *"For what I do is not the good I want to do; no, the evil I do not want to do—this I keep on doing. Now if I do what I do not want to do, it is no longer I who do it, but it is sin living in me that does it. So I find this law at work: When I want to do good, evil is right there with me. For in my inner being I delight in God's law; but I see another law at work in the members of my body, waging war against the law of my mind and making me a prisoner of the law of sin at work within my members. What a wretched man I am! Who will rescue me from this body of death?"*

Paul's confession is the same cry of desperation as the addicts.' The addict, like Paul, acts in their own best interest.

Regrettably, certain drug counselors or therapists treat alcoholics as poorly as they do LGBTQIA+ persons. They believe in conversion therapy based on moral principles to change their minds and hearts; confessing and praying to a "higher power" that their "sin" of alcoholism or LGBTQIA+ identity be forgiven. They offer a "silver bullet" as a promise for sobriety. The addict is given another level of delusion (and so is the LGBTQIA-identified person!)

Where to begin? Accepting drug addiction (*not* LGBTQIA+ identities) as a *disease* is vital. The late Dr. Meg Patterson, a Scottish doctor, successfully treated Eric Clapton and members of the rock band *Rolling Stones.* Later, Boy George.

Her approach primarily treated the brain. She discovered that through medical treatment, addicts had a primary *drive* or desire for God.

For many years studies and research have maintained that drug addiction is a *disease* and that drug addicts' brains are different from the *typical* person's. They experience a void or deficiency of certain chemicals requiring balance. Some addicts need alternative chemicals to balance brain function. Certain ones need a depressant. Others require a stimulant or pain suppressant to cope with daily life.

Therefore, the addict must be medically and socially detoxed. They must be isolated from all enabling factors, including external support systems. No constructive therapy is practical or possible until the addict's brain and mental capacity can respond. Abstinence is absolute! This process will feel confusing, confounding, and agonizing, which can result in deep despair. The reality is, "You only see the stars in the darkness." The uncontrolling God is revealed, and recovery begins, but not before the addict and their family experiences "emptiness/darkness."

Addiction is a relational dynamic. No one goes down this winding, twisting road alone. God's uncontrolling love partners with your uncontrolling love bringing hope and serenity. Warning! This is a bumpy road.

Any treatment or therapy for addiction cannot succeed without the participation of significant others. God created us for relationships. The Garden of Eden was not complete without Adam and Eve. God wants to love and support us daily. This happens through the relationships interacting with us each sunrise and sunset. God is interactive, according to theologian Thomas Oord. The Holy Spirit is God's *persuader*. Persuasion happens through prayer, meditation, Bible study, and spiritually filled individuals. We know God through others, who are *angels*, meaning "messengers" of God.

To appreciate this reality, you must explore the nature and creative attributes of an uncontrolling God. God seeks to heal addicts and anyone who is sick. God did not design human life to suffer disease or disaster. Well-known author, Jean Houston of the human potential movement, teaches that God's infinite wisdom and creative genius designed all of life, especially humans, with natural *tropistic* growth. *Tropism* is the theory that every living organism has a natural movement to stay alive, be healthy, and grow. Psychologist Abraham Maslow stated that all humans are created to actualize their potential. God *can't* be an enabler or a co-dependent; otherwise, one's potential is limited.

Famous author and psychologist Muriel James was asked, "What must one do to change?" Her discerning answer: *"**Stop** doing what you're doing!"* Like an old saying, "*If you want to dig a new hole, you don't dig the same hole deeper!*"

Long-time actor Will Rogers agreed: *"If you find yourself in a hole, the first thing to do is stop diggin.'* Appears simple. Nope! It is a complex and trying manner for anyone. Everyone involved with an addict must cease repeating fruitless actions.

Addicts and their loved ones need to medically and socially detox. This is called *abstinence*. The addict begins this process by letting go of any substance used to survive personal misery and admitting to being "powerless over alcohol" by accepting help in "stopping" one's death trap. Ironically, one such trap is Step Two of AA/NA: "Came to believe that a *Power greater than ourselves* could restore us to sanity." The fact is that the uncontrolling God cannot "restore" your sanity. Instead, God claims, "I can't," but you "can!"

What is needed for the addict is equally valid for the dysfunction and disease of the family. Every person in the family system needs "social detox." Why? Living with an addict becomes toxic. Your false sense of power to control or change the alcoholic is futile. You need to "stop" the unhealthy habits destroying relationships. Discovering your *uncontrolling love* can restore your sanity but not the addict.

The irony is that addicts *can't* recover in solitude. They need love and care from significant people in their life. In turn, this support system participates in treatment, learning of God's *uncontrolling love* and theirs. Blame, shame, and guilt are forgiven. Over time, healing and sobriety happen when the addict practices the steps and behaviors necessary for healthy relational and spiritual wholeness.

Beneath the drugs, an addict is seeking God. Spiritual principles and practices are essential in treating addiction. Spirituality affirms that God has created human nature with natural healing. Our souls and body are interwoven. Healing is primarily a spiritual process.

Hippocrates, the great Greek physician, claimed that doctors don't heal. He concluded, "Natural forces within us are the true healers of disease." Bill Wilson and Dr. Bob Smith, founders of AA, declared the alcoholic cannot "self-will" oneself to sobriety without a "higher power." However, God has no controlling power to change the alcoholic. The innate gift from God is your free will to make decisions for good or bad. God forgives your unhealthy, self-defeating choices. There is no punishment!

Although you are responsible for the decisions and actions that are taken, your life is open and free. Be filled with gratitude and humility for God's grace (uncontrolling love and power). The freedom to decide is like a two-edged sword. You have power no other organism has: the ability to say "yes" or "no." The Bible states, "…make sure your statement is 'Yes, yes' *or* 'No, no;' anything beyond these is of evil *origin*." (Matt 5:37).

Boldly saying "yes" is trusting the uncontrolling God of love. God is "showing the way even if you don't know where you are going!" Remember: being "lost in the world of addictions may well be a way to new beginnings." Let the journey begin!

Hugh Leroy Thompson has more than 30 years of experience in the field of addiction. He earned his M.Div. from Candler School of Theology. He was the executive director of a hospital chemical dependency unit and a counselor, trainer, consultant, and developer of addiction programs. Thompson is the author of Unwrapping the Gifts of Recovery (CreateSpace Publishing, 2014).

18

THE WATERFALL

JOHAN TREDOUX

*An exploration of the uncontrolling love of God in a clinical
chaplain patient encounter.*

*J*remember a carefree upbringing as a pastor's kid in a town called Rustenburg, 60 miles from Johannesburg, in apartheid-era South Africa. I remember looking forward to my dad's day off, as it provided me with an opportunity to go up and swim in the mountain pools on a nearby kloof. I recall the exhilarating experience of free falling with a waterfall between two standing pools of water. I also remember yelling my name into the mountains, only to have echoes come rumbling back… Johan, Johan, Johan…first strong and then weaker as it faded off into the distance. Unfortunately, this free-flowing movement with a waterfall between two pools did not translate into my spiritual and religious world. My childhood evangelical world brought with it legalistic mores, prejudices, and theological norms that were confined to a specific pool of water. I was baptismally immersed in this pool and the only echoes I was interested in were my theological echoes of religious certainties.

My carefree world changed when my dad felt pressured to resign as senior pastor. As is usually the case in these separations, scapegoating practices and spiritualizing formulas were alive and well. In this early, literalist stage of my faith journey, my ears picked up phrases like: "God is in control!" or "everything happens for a reason." Unbeknownst to me, these phrases were hardwired in my body and became part of my embedded childhood theology.

Tom Malone brings deeper insight on this metaphorical idea of swimming in a religious "stagnant pool." He describes it as building a "set" in a play. In this set, we "know" what is "true" and how things *should* be. We "know" who we are. We "know" who the other is. Unfortunately, according to Malone, it is a "knowing" almost always about the other, the outside, or about me. *It is never about the connection itself.* The "waterfall" between the two pools was nonexistent. This set me up to fall into the trap of prejudgment... that devilish state of "already knowing" and "pre-constructing" opinions about others without real relational connections.

Gradually, over three decades of pastoring and teaching, as a life-long student, my BA in Hebrew, M.Div., and Ph.D. in Pastoral Theology caused me to deconstruct the boxed-in faith that was handed to me. Fundamentally, as a "rebel in the ranks," I struggled to free myself from "pack thinking." Mentors like Thomas Oord (*The Uncontrolling Love of God*), Mildred Bangs Wynkoop (*A Theology of Love*), Peter Enns (*The Sin of Certainty*), and Bradley Jersak (*A More Christlike God*) helped me to realize that God is not into control, but rather approaches, awakens, or woos us through uncontrolling love. This truth has become front and center in the last 4 years as I shifted away from pastoring in a church setting to becoming a Board-certified Clinical Chaplain.

The shift from being an evangelical senior pastor to becoming an interfaith chaplain was hard and thrilling all at the same time. The expression of my lived theology through the lens of the uncontrolling love of God brought a significant expansion of my worldview. I learned to get out of my bubble and become culturally sensitive to the meaning-making systems of Buddhist, Hindu, Jewish, and Muslim patients (to name a few). As I encountered the meaning-making systems of these patients, I discovered that it was not so much about "bringing God into" the room but more about "bringing God forth." It was as Oord described his belief, that divine love is tailor-made for each creature and never coerces, withdraws, overrides, or fails to support the freedom, agency, or self-organization of others. For me, this meant the expansion of "witness" to the rich idea of "withness."

As a CPE-trained Chaplain, this "withness" meant entering the world of patients with a "listening presence" and the constant hope that the process of "active listening" can facilitate inner dialogue, which would allow patients to become compassionate witnesses to their own painful experiences, ultimately leading to self-healing. I have learned that the practice of presence includes a focus on emptiness, and self-emptying, to make space for being fully present. "Withness" is about the relational connection that occurs when I become attuned to the body language, voice, and nonverbal communication of the patient.

In a word, it is to experience
the Uncontrolling Love of God
as Resonance…
that
"Beautiful waterfall"
between two pools.

Resonance describes the desirable state of interpersonal empathy. It is to experience the feelings of others within oneself as if those emotions are one's own. Physiologically, this empathic process is said to be processed by a network of *mirror neurons*. This network involuntarily resonates, or mirrors, the feelings and thereby establishes an empathic connection between two individuals. I have found that if I can stay in this "active listening" mode, there is a strong likelihood that the patient can experience the love of God in an uncontrolling way.

However, that is a big *if*, and it's one of the biggest challenges in my role as a professional clinical chaplain. The temptation to control the conversation or try to "fix" the patient by giving advice is ever before me. Voices from my embedded childhood theology of a "controlling" God is ever present in my inner dialogue tempting me to control the conversation. The temptation to pre-construct opinions rather than to construct them in the present shows how difficult it is to be a true active listener.

These struggles with control will be demonstrated as I invite you to consider the raw humanity of a patient I visited in a Level I Trauma Center. Through the process of reflective listening and being attentive to her facial expressions and body language, this patient entrusted me with her story. The patient was a 60 y/o female who, because of a stroke, was left with speech deficits and left-sided weakness. On this admission, she was found to have an acute brain bleed which required an immediate procedure to reduce swelling. At the point of this encounter, her strength and speech were improving. This patient had to carry the burden of feeling socially disconnected through a stroke and being insecurely attached to her family because of her sexual orientation as a gay person.

I encountered the fight and flight parts of her traumatized brain as she shared the suffering caused by her family who severed ties with her when she came out as gay. She shared the following verbatim:

The severance with my family will always be with me. Early on, after coming out, I lived with the fear of expanding rejection. I have dealt with unending critical voices and shaming, and at times, I felt the pain was so acute I could not bear it anymore. But when I finally came out, I experienced a freedom I had never felt before. I recognized as much as possible there would be a cost, my cross to bear. (At this point the patient turned her head; She then showed me her surgical incision behind her right ear). *Chaplain, do you, see this incision... it saved my life. For some of my family and previous church friends, however, this incision is seen as God's punishment for the lifestyle I have chosen.*

The impact of her startling revelation was a jarring moment for me. The stark nature of the brutal sentiment shared created a deep holy silence in the room. Flashing in front of my eyes were images of my younger brother who came out 30 years earlier. I felt an emotional shift within. It was sympathy to profound empathy. And yet, I did not share my inner thoughts (in self-awareness, through a great tug-of-war, I was able to manage the counter transference welling up within me). Had I done so, I would have only demonstrated my own need and/or internal urge to move quickly to a more comfortable place of a cognitive solution-seeking role. I would have moved into a posture of control.

Instead, I held her pain in *silence* for a while, followed by a simple open statement, *"how is this going for you now?"* I was able to stay with the feelings that underlie her story. In doing so, the patient was able to mimic me (through the mirror neurons system) by staying connected to her own emotions, and that in turn helped her to self-empathize with her painful feelings. As a spiritual care provider, I had to return and re-return my focus to stay in tune with the patient's pain and suffering by using paraphrasing, summary, and open-ended statements. In turn, I experienced the patient feeling comfortable to return and re-return to feel her own emotions by retelling her painful story in greater depth and detail.

Through empathetic listening, genuine compassion, and attunement to the patient, I was able to extend God's embrace. And there, in between "stagnant pools" of family expectations, outdated theology, and broken bodies, we experienced a "beautiful waterfall" of uncontrolling love. This encounter affirms Oord's assertion that God's actions originate in love, shifting and turning in all its various expressions as God promotes overall well-being without control.

*Rev. **Johan Tredoux, Ph.D., BCC.** resides in Lenexa, KS. Johan is a Board-Certified Chaplain (APC), presently serving as a chaplain for St, Croix Hospice in Overland Park, KS. Johan earned his MDiv. from Nazarene Theological Seminary, KC., MO. and his Ph.D. from the University of Manchester, UK (2015) in the discipline of Wesleyan Theology.*

– 19 –

LITTLE WHITE LIES

JO-ANN TRINER

Distortions of truth are a control tactic of the powerless with damaging, dangerous, and even deadly consequences.

*T*heology and therapy intersect at a place where love faces off with all forms of illegitimate control. In this combat zone, the opposing forces of good and evil engage in a great confrontation. They spar, not on a battlefield of bloody contention, but in the combat zone of the heart. Armed only with weapons of mass compassion, they go to war in a way that undermines all of our assumptions about winners and losers. In this scenario, everyone wins, and one eternal principle is proven: Love and truth are inseparable twins. One without the other constitutes a power play and form of cloak and dagger control. Clothed in cunning disguise and with intent to deceive, untruths lead many astray, often into grave danger and death.

Sharing common ground, theologians and therapists walk hand in hand, working to undo the damage of a culture spinning out of control. Both operate in resistance to manipulation tactics that have sickened far too many and sent others to their graves. Operating under the bedrock beliefs that love heals, they labor on the front lines of reform. In their respective roles, they see that the absence of authentic love and trust reduces us to participants in a vast theater of the absurd where retaining our humanity and controlling our fate is perplexing.

Evidence abounds. People are regarded as less valuable than the products they create. They are thought of as property, used for pleasure and personal gain, their talents wasted in the rush for profit. Persons of soul and substance are bought and sold into slavery. Others live in terror and tyranny under the dictates of oppressors. Millions have unjustly gone to the gas chambers and perished in genocides. Others have suffered enslavement, persecution, and a litany of other atrocities. What leads human beings into such dark places often seems innocuous at first.

Power of the Little White Lie

Imagine forced deportation from your home and a government order to pack a suitcase with your valuables. This might include documents, money, mementos, a blanket, and perhaps a teddy bear. Such is the memory etched in the mind of Holocaust survivor, Paula Gris, whose childhood ended at age three on her family's mandatory transport to Transnitria, one of the vast killing fields of the Holocaust.

The simple mandate to carry suitcases served a function of mind-control unknown to the deportees. It provided a sure and easy way to suppress rebellion. This control tactic kept the oppressed on the move from place to god-forsaken place: on cattle cars, in forced labor camps, even on the death march. As long as bags were packed and carried, there was an anticipated arrival at a place called home, however humble that might be. As long as deportees held onto their suitcases, there was hope. Such trickery brought them, suitcases still in hand, to the very doors of the gas chambers where they died.

The full moral weight of this must seep into us at a soul-deep level if we are to become conscious and committed advocates for the innate freedoms of the human family. Illegitimate control is our undoing, taking us down into Danté's Inferno. Until we admit this, we are all at risk for the unthinkable in forms sadistic and grotesque as any we can imagine.

If a mere suitcase can become an instrument of mass control, or a hijacked plane an instrument of terrorism, anything can be used in the arsenal of evil.

Thousands of these suitcases are now on display in a state-of-the-art protective storage room in Poland's Auschwitz-Birkenau State Museum. It is better known as The Wall of Suitcases memorializing those sent to concentration camps during World War II. In post-Nazi history, the suitcase became a symbol of the incomprehensible damage done to human beings by something so seemingly innocent as a little white lie.

The correlation between small sins, such as "little white lies," and mortal consequences brings us face-to-face with the problem of deceptive control and the solution an uncontrolling God models for us.

The Sliding Scale of Control and Other Slippery Slopes

Between total control and total freedom is the sliding scale of everything in between. It's a vast and murky gray zone where the purity of good intentions or evil intent is anyone's guess, and that's the problem. Discerning the degree of innocence or deception is often next to impossible. The ill-intentioned use this to full advantage.

As seen from the opening narrative, control accomplishes outer compliance but seldom inner compliance. People may be marching to the drummer but ready to bolt out of line in the blink of an eye. While their outer person complies, their inner person rebels. This is the morsel of freedom the well-intentioned have to *their* advantage.

What we know with certainty is that manipulative control of any kind represents a felt moral oppression. We may not protest outwardly for a variety of reasons, but we protest inwardly in the silence of our inner selves. Holocaust survivor, Victor Frankl, calls this state of inner silence "the last of the freedoms—the freedom to choose our attitude in any given set of circumstances, and to choose our own way." While prisoners were forced into death marches stripped of everything that made them human, they retained this inner freedom. In this respect, their captors never obtained full compliance.

Behind Artificial Smiles

Depraved forms of control give rise to rage. Behind the artificial smiles of the compliant, real persons dwell who often seek to avenge their controllers. In this way, evil begets evil in the form of revenge. Those who don't rebel suffer a stifling suppression of their true thoughts and feelings. This can result in depression and other disorders. Others react in the opposite extreme and become aggressive or passive aggressive. The Reverend Dr. Martin Luther King is often quoted for saying that riots are the voice of the unheard. He refers here to the chaotic energy within seeking expression, as victims of coercive control yearn to be seen, heard and respected as the sovereign beings they are. In this vicious cycle, evil begets evil.

Control takes so many forms. It morphs into power wars, dictatorships and authoritarian regimes, sadism, emotional and physical abuse, and all manner of societal and personal suffering. Victims hunger for relief from these forms of oppression having suffered intimidation, false imprisonment and brutality in their many disguises. In the name of country, religion, and all that is sacred, we have persecuted others, misaligned with the very love we teach and preach.

Conversely, real power is used to introduce compassion into the world, address hunger and housing needs, alleviate affliction, guide each other in a positive direction, and teach true leadership skills to future generations. Thoughts, words and deeds are potent and consequential in the power equation. This chain reaction begins with the sheer power of intention. With the intention to help or harm, we create either a hellscape or a heaven.

The concept of Uncontrolling Love informs us in all walks of life. Attention to it holds the potential to release us from the ever-increasing list of subversive controls that keep us captive.

The God of Uncontrolling Love brings out the superpower in each of us. Much like the original televised Superman, we "come to earth with powers and abilities far beyond those of mortal men." This is what working in the Soul Zone does for us. We become enabled to help others in ways mere mortals only dare to dream.

The evolutionary clock is ticking on the control paradigm worldwide. Ways of life that have dominated society for centuries are losing momentum. When the right moment arrives, the masses will cease unconscious compliance to all that runs contrary to their essence. We can thank technology for this.

In concert with our technologies, we are creating a thinking membrane, hovering above us like a giant rainbow reaching across the globe. This organically grown meeting place is the sphere of reason, a kind of communication channel, forming gradually and growing in importance. Pierre de Chardin predicted it over a half century ago. Today, it evolves further into the study of cognition in a place commonly called the noosphere. If we are lucky, we will launch further into the ethereal, above the realm of mind, into the realm of heart where knowledge bows to wisdom. Perhaps from this holy of holies within we can end our preoccupation with control.

In the new world waiting to be born, the dress rehearsals are over. The puppets have cut their own strings. Players have put away their costumes. Tricksters have taken off their masks. At long last, the red carpet is rolled away and the lights are out. The theater of the absurd is closed. Some linger in their seats.

Jo-Ann Triner is a dual career professional. She holds a Doctor's Degree in Educational Administration with thirty-eight years of service in non-profit leadership roles. She is founder and President of Soulful Work LLC and serves on the Board of Directors, The Institute for Research on Unlimited Love. She is the author of an upcoming book entitled SOULFUL WORK 2.0: Powered by Inner Person Potential.

20

IS GOD'S WILL SOMETHING WE NEED TO FIND OR SOMETHING WE HELP CREATE?

JULIE EXLINE

God might be leading us in a divine dance, one where we actually get to improvise.

*A*ren't Christians supposed to seek and obey God's will? This is what I was taught, growing up in a fundamentalist Baptist church. Our faith leaders taught us to see God as the Creator, the ultimate authority—one with a good, specific plan for our individual lives. So we should seek God's direction for everything in life.

And we tried. I mean, we really, really tried. To be sure, we turned to God for guidance about right and wrong, but we also wanted to find God's path for our lives: what our roles were as men and women, who we should marry, where we should live, and our life's work. After all, if God has created us for a specific, special purpose, then we should try to find out what that purpose is: our own personal mission from God.

And it's important to get it right. Because not only is God's guidance the best guidance, but you certainly don't want to be OUT of God's will. Not only would you be wandering around lost, but you might disappoint God. And if you're actively resisting or rebelling against God, you could be punished—maybe even be tossed into Hell for eternity!

But how are we supposed to know what God's will is? How do we get it right?

My church looked for answers through the Bible. Of course, the scriptures gave tons of direction on moral issues, and much of it was helpful. But I also saw how people could use the Bible as a bludgeon—a way to keep themselves and others in line. It was natural to feel self-righteous if we followed the rules and fearful if we did not. Plus, it was all too easy to use the text to judge and vilify others who seemed to be committing obvious sins: drug use, divorce, sexual impurity, abortion, and following "false" religions were some of the big ones. Was this focus on rules really leading us to follow Christ's loving example?

And what about the literal interpretations of this infallible text, said to be "God's Word"? Messages in the Bible didn't seem as straightforward as leaders said they were. I remember hearing things like, "The Bible's message of salvation is so simple. Even a child can understand it." I wasn't so sure. Have you ever read Leviticus? What about Revelation? Was I really supposed to pluck out my eye if it offended me? I didn't see people doing that. And besides, how could we trust our own interpretations of the Bible, much less our own moral compasses, if the devil is running around, spewing lies and corrupting people's minds?

Not only was the Bible confusing and even contradictory in places, but a lot of it was just plain *scary*. Was God really going to send people to Hell for eternity simply because they didn't believe in Him or understand Him? We also lived in great fear of the Rapture: Jesus could come back at any moment and take those who were saved back to heaven, but the rest would be left to suffer the horrors of the Great Tribulation. So when I would come home from school and no one was home, I had that little flutter of fear: Had I been left behind?

These experiences left me with a fair amount of religious trauma and a lot of baggage around the Bible. Now my goal is to help others who are having similar challenges. I work as a psychology professor, and my colleagues and I have spent several decades studying the struggles that many people have around religion and spirituality, including issues with God. My colleague Ken Pargament and I have written about how therapists can help clients work through these spiritual struggles. And in my own case, therapy definitely helped. Just having that listening, supportive ear made a huge difference. Even though neither of my therapists had the same religious affiliation that I did, I felt a true spiritual bond with each of them. Their love and care were key parts of my own healing.

My beliefs continued to shift, too. After a long spiritual-but-not-religious period and some church hopping, I joined a charismatic church about 20 years ago. All in all, my experiences there were positive. The environment felt warmer and more loving, more open, and less judgmental than what I remembered from my childhood church. I was still trying to figure out God's will, but there was more flexibility in how divine messages might come through. We talked a lot about hearing God's voice—through Scripture, of course, but also through signs, words of prophecy, and even the occasional miracle! God's love seemed more alive and accessible now, more exciting.

Later, I went through training at a Jesuit university to become a *spiritual director*—someone who talks with people about spirituality and helps them try to hear what God might be saying to them. Echoing themes from the charismatic church, we talked about how God speaks in many ways—not only through Scripture but also through life events, other people, or our own reason—and maybe even through physical sensations.

What's more, this spiritual direction training introduced me to some new ideas about God's unconditional love—views that included a genuine hope that all people might ultimately "be saved" and end up in heaven together. Internally, I breathed a huge sigh of relief. I now felt like it was possible to be a Christian without worrying so much about hell. I didn't have to abandon my Christian faith. I could seek God's will with more joy and passion, as part of a more intimate relationship. Still, though, I saw God's will mostly as something to be discovered.

Around 2016, my spiritual director lent me a sermon series by Martin Smith, a Bishop of the Episcopal Church, entitled "Co-Creators with God." Smith introduced the idea of a more dynamic view of God—one in which God is continually involved in the process of creation. It's not just "one and done;" it's still going on! Also, to add an inspiring twist, Smith suggested that we are actively engaged with God in the ongoing process of creation—one that includes the unfolding of our own destinies. So God's will is not just something we discover; we may also help to create it.

Over time, I started to see my relationship with God as a dance. Yes, God may be leading, and always leading us in the direction of love and wisdom, but perhaps God also takes pleasure in giving us freedom to improvise. While doing our best to keep our eyes on God and stay in step together, we also get to add our own flourishes, our own beauty, our own style... and God is PLEASED with all of this. God WANTS us to make meaningful choices, to follow our deepest desires, and to be the most authentic and alive people that we can be. We can do all of this and still stay close to God. It's all part of the dance.

In a recent survey of adults in the United States, we found that many people see God not only as a source of safety, security and love; they also see their relationships with God as exciting and energetic, spontaneous, passionate, and sometimes even playful. Importantly, when people see their relationships with God in these energizing ways, they feel more grateful to God for their blessings and express more desire to pass on kindness to others.

But what about those times when we feel confused or enraged about suffering or evil in the world—or when we feel mad at God? We've found that when people face these kinds of spiritual struggles, they often do better if they see God as a partner who collaborates with them to solve problems. And when people are angry at God, it usually helps if they can recognize, accept, and perhaps even express their negative feelings, instead of just keeping them bottled up inside. I'm starting to wonder whether these ideas about co-creation and energy—about seeing God as our partner in the dance—might also help us to work through problems in our relationships with God. I'm not sure, but I'd like to find out.

How have things changed for me? I do still seek God's direction and listen for God's voice. I look for signs, and I try to follow God's lead, but I've lost much of that fear of being out of God's will. Why? Because I believe that God's love is within us—and all around us. It moves and sustains us. It's where we live and breathe and have our being… and we can learn to awaken to it, to see it, to let that love light radiate into us and through us, then guide it out into the world. We each get to do this in our own unique ways, with our own style, our own palette, our own spice. These are our beautiful acts of creation—of co-creation with God.

Julie Exline, Ph.D., *is a Professor in the Department of Psychological Sciences at Case Western Reserve University in Cleveland, Ohio, specializing in spiritual and religious topics. She is a licensed clinical psychologist in Ohio and has been certified as a spiritual director through the Ignatian Spirituality Institute at John Carroll University. Her research focuses on spiritual struggles and supernatural beliefs.*

21

THE IMPROVISING CHAPLAIN

MARK A. FELDBUSH

*An improvisational approach to pastoral care allows
the chaplain to provide support in line with the patient's
own spirituality.*

Clinical Pastoral Education (CPE) is a ministry training program that is frequently offered in hospitals. Students who enroll in CPE include congregational clergy, seminary students, and lay people interested in pastoral care ministry. I am a Certified Educator and I coordinate a CPE program in a pediatric hospital.

Hospitals are disorienting places. Consider the patient who feels like a foreigner in a strange land. Due to their illness or injury, they have to leave home. They sleep in a strange bed. They wear odd clothing—a thin cotton gown that closes up in the back. And the food they eat is nothing like home cooking. It is hard to get sleep. Nurses and other medical team members barge into the room to give medicines or take vitals. In this disorientation, the patient often asks spiritual questions. Why is this happening to me? Did I do something wrong? Where is God?

Hospitals are also disorienting places for student chaplains in CPE. They, too, are like foreigners in a strange land. They have to learn to find their way through the maze-like halls of the hospital. Understanding the new medical terms is confusing. The soundtrack beeps and whirring sounds of the IV pumps and ventilators is a strange musical score. Then the student encounters people with diverse religious beliefs, ethnic backgrounds, sexual orientations, gender identities, and socio-economic statuses. In this disorientation the CPE student also asks questions. Can I do this? How do I provide spiritual care to someone who holds different beliefs than I do?

As the student chaplain learns to navigate this disorientation, they "want to get it right." They do not want to "mess up" during the ministry encounter. In this disorientation, students often assume that a controlling approach to spiritual care will be the right way to minister. This directive approach often includes reading scripture, praying, and sharing their faith. These practices function like a script that says, "If you want to have peace with God, you should believe and practice your faith like I do." This script approach is supported by a theology with a controlling view of God.

This drive to be "perfect" often comes from a "fear of falling short of an impossible external standard," says pastoral care professor Edward Wimberly. One of my students wrote a weekly reflection about the fear of going into a hospital room to visit the patient and not knowing what was going to happen. This student chaplain wished for a script to tell them what to say and do at the right moment.

The improvisation website PeopleandChairs.com shared a Venn diagram in 2014 that describes theatrical improvisation (improv) as the place where joy and fear overlap. Chicago improv pioneer Del Close understood the value of affirming fear. He "always said to follow the fear in your work. It is good to be uncomfortable; otherwise there is no danger, no excitement, no growth," writes Charna Halpern. This improv principle of "following the fear" is consistent with the pastoral formation process of CPE.

CPE students are typically drawn to the work of ministry for the joy and satisfaction it gives them to serve God by helping people in need. The clinical context of working in a hospital and facing trauma, death, and crisis can be a scary experience as it takes the pastoral care student out of their comfort zone and challenges their skills and competence. An improvisational approach to pastoral formation in CPE invites the student pastoral care provider to be present with their own fear and anxiety, to follow it and to listen to it as an ally in their formation journey. By following their fear on the path of pastoral formation, the CPE student will learn how to be present to the emotional and spiritual needs of the care recipient and to allow the appropriate spiritual care to arise out of the pastoral relationship.

My experience as a chaplain and educator is that there is no script for pastoral care ministry. Rather, I understand pastoral care as an improvisational process. This improvisational approach to pastoral care calls for being with people in the *here and now*. Through conversation, the chaplain assesses and understands the needs of the patient. Then the chaplain offers empathic support by helping the care recipient to draw on the practices and beliefs of their own spiritual orientation.

This improvisational approach to spiritual care is informed by an uncontrolling view of God's love. It recognizes that God is already present in the spiritual tradition of the patient, no matter what that spiritual tradition is.

The art of improvisation is a creative act. While it may appear that improvisers engage in *creatio ex nihilo (creation from nothing)* or simply making it up as they go along, they actually participate in what I have called *creatio ex materia (creation from existing material.)* Theologian Peter Heltzel uses the language of *creatio continua* to describe this phenomenon while discussing jazz music.

> *"While driven by spontaneity, freedom, and innovation, improvisation is never so unstructured... that it could be considered creatio ex nihilo.... Rather, it is a creatio continua, a continual creation drawing on existing materials to make music in new ways. Improvisation is the creative deployment of traditions and forms that are at hand; the dynamic involved in improvisation therefore can be understood as a constant negotiation of constraint and possibility"* (p.18).

Improvisers work in relationship with the ideas and emotions (the material) presented by their stage partners to create a scene. Improvisation is about discovering what exists in the context of a relationship and allowing the relationship to become something more. The art and work of improvisation is guided by several maxims, the first of which is typically: "Yes, and..." This maxim comes from a place of hope and courage. It opens a world of possibility and action to the improviser as they develop relationships among the other improvisers. This sense of building relationship is key for those developing the art of pastoral care.

In my work of improvisational clinical pastoral supervision, I begin with the relational nature of the God of Hope (Romans 15:13). As a Christian, I understand that the one God exists in the community of the Trinity. Because I believe that the God of Hope exists in community, I also believe that hope flows outward into God's interactions with humanity. Andrew Lester says, "Since hope is rooted in God's love, and love implies relationship, then hope must happen in community whether between human beings or between human beings and God." Because I believe that we are people created in the image of God, I also believe that our human relationships can be sources of hope for one another in the midst of our brokenness. We experience this kind of hope and support in community.

This theology of improvisational hope does not require each pastoral care encounter to move through pain and suffering to hope. What it does mean is that because I have hope, grounded in my own experience of suffering, I can be a hopeful presence. When someone experiences disorientation and struggles, I can be with them. In my improvisational pastoral care, I can be a visible demonstration of God's uncontrolling love for that person.

Mark A. Feldbush is an ACPE Certified Educator and APC Board Certified Chaplain serving at Nationwide Children's Hospital in Columbus, OH. He earned his Doctor of Ministry degree at Ecumenical Theological Seminary in Detroit. His dissertation is titled The Improvising Pastor: Following the Fear on the Pastoral Formation Journey. *Mark is an avid listener of spiritually informed rock-n-roll.*

22

THE ENCOUNTER

TORI E. OWENS

Therapy is a relational encounter.

𝒯he skittish mom of three entered the office smelling of a combination of coffee and stale smoke. She had dark, swollen circles under bloodshot eyes. Eyes that never settled and darted at each unfamiliar sound or muffled voice. She wrapped herself up with arms in oversized sweater sleeves. Maybe she could cocoon herself up and away from every unexpected sound, sight, smell, or touch. She was exhausted and could not remember the last time she had slept through the night.

The skinny girl in pink leggings and a t-shirt couldn't stand quietly or sit still. She moved around the office in fits and starts, unable to stay in one place for more than a few seconds, touching everything whether she should or not and without asking permission. Relentlessly compelled to move without limits or boundaries, her mouth, too, spoke every word or thought unfiltered and unabashed.

The teenaged young man, shrouded in a black hoodie, Vans, and ripped black jeans, hid his eyes behind long, unkempt hair. The weight of loneliness and deep sadness pressed him into the chair. He moved slowly, imperceptibly, as if limbs and torso and head were made of lead and his reservoir of energy had already been spent.

The beautiful, wispy teenage girl born a boy. Struggling less with her own identity and more with callous Bible-quoting peers, high school teachers dead-naming her, and the oddity and spectacle of walking solo—and for all to see—to the single faculty bathroom two halls over.

The small boy barely waist-high made eye contact without blinking, chin jutted out defiantly and with teeth clenched. He cussed a stream of words he must have heard time and time again, threatened to remove his belt, and slowly walked forward. He had been engrossed in play and just realized his mom had stepped out of the room without notice.

The young woman in college with raised pinkish-white lines peeking out from under the edge of her sleeve cuffs did not say a word. She wouldn't say a word for months. Sitting with feet firmly planted, hands grasped in her lap, and head bowed. No sound. No movement. No emotions. Yet she always returned, deliberately and promptly.

Each person's story is unique in the complex layering of personal hurts and traumas, family history, and perceived inherited generational "curses," yet so much the same in their courage, vulnerability, and intention in showing up for therapy, often for the very first time.

It begins the same for most everyone: introductions after having emailed or texted or briefly talked on the phone, sometimes in person, but these days, most times via telehealth. Then I say something like, "Tell me a little bit about what brings you here," or "What's on your mind?" or a gentle "Talk to me." Sometimes it's a quiet: "I'm here."

There are different responses depending on how many times we've been in session, such as a sheepish smile and a glance away, saying "I've never done this before, "or a shrug accompanied by, "I don't know how to explain it." Other times, it's words like, "I'm just so hurt," or "I'm afraid that you will be disappointed in me."

Even with all this difference, in some ways, it's the same. Two humans. One encounter.

I don't even remember my first impression of therapy. I recall sitting in classes listening to lectures on Freud, Jung, or some other person of privilege in psychology, reading about another theory or model and wondering how I would explain my *own* approach to future clients.

I stopped thinking in those terms when I met the woman in college who remained silent for months. I started out talking, asking questions, stumped, and confused, and probably even exasperated at times. She did not say a word. I would offer up breathing exercises, coloring, Play-Doh, Legos, puzzles, stress balls, origami. Nothing. Zip. Zero. Nada.

One morning on the day of one of her sessions, before she promptly showed, I sat there flummoxed, "What am I supposed to do? I have no idea what I am supposed to do! She can't keep NOT talking!"

But… what if she did? What was I going to do then? What if I stopped hoping and wishing for her to talk, and instead just accepted her? Instead of trying to come up with "things to do," forcing a battle of wills, and seeing who could hold out the longest in silence… what if I intentionally held space, relational space, and we just were…together?

Trust me, this had to be Divine inspiration. I was at my wit's end.

She arrived. We went into session. I told her, "I'm going to try something a little bit different today. We're just going to sit here together if that's okay with you?" She nodded.

She nodded. I think it was the first time she acknowledged something I had said. The therapist finally got a clue.

I wasn't dictating the terms. I wasn't assuming what she needed. I wasn't trying to fix her or change her. I wasn't expecting anything from her. I wasn't just filling space. I wasn't telling her what she was doing wrong. I wasn't telling her what she was doing right. I wasn't coddling her. I wasn't talking to be talking. I wasn't assessing for a diagnosis. I wasn't developing a plan of care. I wasn't even determining her symptoms.

I wasn't controlling the session; therefore, I wasn't controlling her. I just accepted her for who she was and what she brought into the therapy space. Finally.

I believe she had been waiting for this from me for a very long time. I am still ever grateful for her patience.

Therapy became more about energy and holding space, not words, not theories, not models, not privileged men's (or my own) beliefs or diagnoses. None of that mattered in the end. It still doesn't. It was and is the relationship, the encounter, the intentional space, the open acceptance.

We sat together for hours. Not waiting, not assuming, and not expecting. Just being. She taught me to hold the space with Love, to listen with my heart not just my ears, to see with my spirit and not only my eyes.

In time, we developed a routine. We would sit. I would breathe and listen with my ears and my heart. Sometimes, I would say what I felt I was receiving from her energy—a few words, a random thought—but only with her expressed permission. I did nothing without her permission.

At some point, she began to email me after sessions. She was a beautiful, intelligent, and thoughtful writer, expanding on whatever word we had exchanged earlier, and revealing, bit by bit, her story. I was honored to bear witness to her journey, the past and the present.

I don't know if she knows how much she changed me with each encounter. Most days, in the mornings or when I walk the dogs, I will breathe in Love and breathe out thanks and well-being for my clients. But, sometimes, still, I will breathe in Love and breathe out thanks and well-being for her, especially.

Tori E. Owens is a licensed professional counselor in private practice and a domestic violence shelter in North Georgia. She is also a registered neutral/mediator. Tori earned her M.Div. from Nazarene Theological Seminary and her MA from Argosy University. She recently completed the Living School (Center for Action and Contemplation) and is currently training in Child Parent Psychotherapy (ages 0-5). Tori was recently accepted to study under Dr. Thomas Jay Oord in the Open and Relational Theology doctoral program at Northwind Theological Seminary. You can find her at: www.toriowens.work or

23

THE DIVINE CHANGE WE NEED

JOSHUA ANDREWS

God is not a God of trauma, but a God of love, joy, peace, and unity.

*Y*ou do not have to be a clinical counselor to see the effects of trauma in people living within your community. If you have walked upon this earth then you have experienced the human condition of grief, pain, suffering, and also love, peace, and joy. Clients who sit down with a mental health professional do so because they experience emotions that, to them, are beyond the norm and life has become very hard and even unmanageable. When life becomes unmanageable due to grief, pain, or suffering, you start to experience a drought of love, peace, and joy.

Clients discuss life situations that they desire to change so that they don't feel bad anymore or make others feel bad by their negative actions and thoughts. Clients, and I dare say all of humanity, simply want to live a better life with better relationships so that tomorrow will be a better day. Sometimes we all need to change our structure of life and start to perceive with a different vision than what we have been handed growing up.

Most, if not all, clients enter into a therapeutic relationship because they have lost vision of how today, let alone tomorrow, could possibly be better. Clients hear the voices of their past and present screaming that they are no good and will never amount to anything in this world. Traumatic events of their past creep into their present as a self-fulfilling prophecy of worthlessness. These traumatic beings of the past (parent, grandparent, uncle, aunt, sibling, teacher, et.al.) take on a ruthless force in the person's mind, body, and spirit. Some give in to these lies and view ending their life as the only viable option as they cry out to God but only hear the voice of a perpetrator and not the voice of our loving creator.

In my own personal life, I have experienced the highs and lows of life and I used to believe that God was in control of all of my experiences, if not in control then allowed them to happen. I received scripture spoken out of context as the only truth but the only thing it brought to me was confusion, chaos, and a lack of understanding of the true nature of God. I can remember time and time again people quoting Billy Graham's wife Ruth, "If God doesn't punish America, He'll have to apologize to Sodom and Gomorrah."

This idea of a perfect God only accepting perfect people who live perfect holy lives was engrained into me and frankly scared me half to death. I viewed God as a monster who not only killed his one and only Son for the sins of the world but, I guess, it wasn't good enough because he was coming after me and needed more pain and sacrifice to satisfy some deranged pleasure. I viewed holiness as a burden to constantly bear knowing I would never be enough for this domineering and angry God. I can't tell you how many times I asked for forgiveness and for Jesus to be the Lord of my life all to feel not good enough the next time any guilt revealed itself.

Life experiences have a way of truly making you think about cause and effect, power and control, freedom and determinism, and how God fits into all of it. I have come to understand God differently over the years of my journey on earth because I believe change is necessary. Change is necessary because humanity never stops developing, growing, thinking, or experiencing emotions. All of humanity, even the most reclusive, experience life changes that affect their individual understanding of self and community. Change should not be thought of as a proverbial "four letter word" to be avoided but an evolutionary reality that can benefit the collective whole for better future possibilities. Change of behavior, change of emotion, change of knowledge, change of beliefs, and change of perception within relationships; all these changes contribute to a change of life.

I have come to embrace Open & Relational Theology as a way to see life and God with an improved vision. I believe this vision enables me to see God as an all-embracing love that engages with creation in a moment-by-moment existence. I view God as guiding and encouraging creation to cooperate with God's essential nature of love. This loving nature enables me to say God never wills for any evil to occur, in fact, God never allows any evil to occur because if God had the power to stop evil, God would stop it. What loving God would allow trauma, wrath, evil, homicide, genocide, violence, etc.…to occur when it could be avoided?

I see God as a divine dance partner, as Richard Rohr has written and spoken about, who genuinely desires to be involved in every aspect of our life with the fullness of love. Clients who receive this view of God no longer have to accept God was punishing them, hating them, or teaching them a lesson through a violent event. Clients can now see God as one who desired none of the pain and trauma to happen but is a God who suffers and experiences all the emotions with them. God is our dance partner that never guides us wrong and is always available to help us up when we do fall after rejecting God's divine guidance.

I see God as the one who will never leave us or forsake us, especially during the darkest valley of our life. A God who never predetermines a future action and never forces us to choose one possibility over the other, yet a God who desires all to walk in God's love and experience the peace that passes all understanding. I see a God who desires good mental health for all of humanity and seeks to help us overcome familial, religious, financial, and societal traumatization. This is the God that I have chosen to accept, worship, serve, and proclaim to all in hope and I am glad that there is one less trauma-inducing being to handle.

Clients who receive this new type of vision can appreciate that what they were once labeled in the past is not carved into stone in order to label them in the present. The future is yet to be realized and the only event we will know for sure is God will be with us and love us in the present to make tomorrow a better day. God is not a God of trauma, but a God of love, peace, joy, and unity.

Joshua Andrews is a Licensed Professional Clinical Counselor and an Ordained Elder in the United Methodist Church. He earned his Master of Arts in Clinical Counseling from Ashland Theological Seminary with additional Master of Divinity & Doctor of Ministry classes. Josh is currently a Doctor of Ministry and Theology student at Northwind Theological Seminary focusing on overcoming religious trauma through Open & Relational Theology.

24

UNCONTROLLING COUPLES THERAPY

LON MARSHALL

Resolution to couples conflict is a better fit if it comes from them.

Several years ago, Consumer Reports came out with surveys measuring customer satisfaction for individual Psychotherapy, and Couples Therapy. Those who reported about their experiences in individual therapy were very satisfied. A high percentage of individuals found Psychotherapy helpful and would recommend it to others. Couples Therapy was a different story; a majority found it unhelpful and would not recommend it.

This troubled me. It did not match what I was witnessing in my practice, where over half of my caseload is with couples. I have worked with eight to ten thousand couples in my 30 years of practice. I generally have found that couples are reaching their goals for therapy and are happy with the outcomes.

I thought about this for a long time. Why were couples not finding therapy helpful in most settings, and why was I getting different results?

What I decided is that individuals were finding therapy helpful because they were affirmed, accepted, and encouraged. Mental health professionals are trained to do individual therapy. I decided the problem was that therapists were using individual therapy skills to do couples therapy. Couples Therapy is a different animal. There are two people with differing opinions. Therapy intensifies if you allow them to express their feelings and describe what they see as the problem; specifically, the other person, who is sitting there.

I think there are two elements that are important to successful Couples Therapy. One, the therapist needs to be very active and involved with the couple. There needs to be intervention, involvement between and within the interaction. Two, that interaction must be uncontrolling, persuasive, invitational, making sure to allow the participants to use their own resources to resolve the conflict.

I want to take a moment to reflect on the purpose of this essay and those in this book. These essays are about the intersection of Therapy and Open and Relational Theology. As I understand it, Open and Relational Theology has the view that God is active in our lives, partnering with us. There is intervention, and action on God's part. God is close not distant; involved, not passive. At the same time, God is uncontrolling, persuasive, and inviting us into relationship. God is a Spirit. We have bodies in time and space. We are to use our resources to be free agents of peace in this physical world.

Over my years of practice, I have called this an incarnational therapy. This is how God revealed in Jesus is present to us, and works with us, and through us. My attempt is to imitate Jesus. And this does not take the form of teaching or telling couples what to do. It is through a process of questions imagining new possibilities where couples are invited to create their own resolution.

My experience has taught me couples come to therapy with similar expectations. I believe it is universal to anticipate the opportunity to tell the therapist what your partner is doing to contribute to the problem and to articulate what you want from your partner. This is what couples have been doing before seeking help from an outside source to no avail. That does not work before coming to therapy and it will not work in therapy. What it does is set up a debate between partners. One person describing how the other is at fault and the other defending their position and returning accusations.

The therapist must understand what does not work and seek to intervene in this pattern of interaction. Early on the therapist can do this with invitations to imagine different outcomes or patterns of interaction, but couples are often determined to tell the therapist what their partner is doing to cause the problem. The therapist must intervene to prevent this type of interaction. This can be done graciously. It is primarily done by invitation and persuasion. It is very important for the therapist to be vigilant and active in this way.

The couples who have resolved their problems and achieved satisfaction in their relationships have done so by making a subtle shift. I have learned by watching them for 30 years. The shift is simple but not easy. Successful couples can move from "this is what I want my partner to know I need," to "I wonder what I could do that my partner would like." When both partners can do this simultaneously, then something special can happen.

Therapists can encourage this process by asking helpful questions. Twentieth Century philosopher Ludwig Wittgenstein has said, "It is a mistake to look for an explanation, when a description of what works will do." Some questions are better than others. Therapists must craft the most helpful questions. Good questions help couples describe what works or might work. Wittgenstein also said that "All we have is misunderstanding... there are just more and less helpful misunderstandings." As therapists seeking to be active and involved, yet uncontrolling, persuasive and relational, we seek descriptions over explanations and encourage the most helpful misunderstandings.

One of the most helpful types of questions is exception-finding questions. This is where the therapist asks about past success. "When was the last time you got along a bit better?" "What are your better days like?" "What was it that attracted you to each other?" "What percentage of the time are you able to resolve differences?" All of these questions can be followed up with curious questions about how that happened, and what it would take to replicate these unique outcomes.

Another helpful type of question is future-oriented questions. "Describe the kind of communication you would like in your relationship." "Suppose when you leave here you talk together about how helpful this meeting was. What would need to happen for that to come true?" "What if a Miracle happens tonight while you are sleeping? The miracle is that the reason you have come here is fixed, taken care of... When you wake up what will be the first thing you notice?" These questions can be followed up with more questions like, "And what would happen next?" "And what difference would that make to your partner?" and, "When your partner is doing that, how will you respond?"

Scaling questions are another type of useful tool for helping couples with active intervention and uncontrolling invitation. Percentages or Likert scale questions can often be helpful. "On a scale of 1 to 10, how ready do you think you are to hold empathy for your partner and begin the healing process?" "How much of this miracle is already happening on a scale of 1 to 10?" "What needs to happen to go from a 5 to a 5.5?" What would your wife notice about you when she thinks it's improved from a 3 to a 4?"

You have probably noticed that the location of expertise has changed places in this model. Instead of the therapist being an expert that dispenses knowledge to the couple, the couple becomes the experts about their own relationship and what is needed. This again is modeling Open and Relational Theology. God is not singlehandedly rescuing us when we are in trouble. Instead, our creator and suffering servant is cooperating with us to bring about Shalom.

Lon Marshall is a Licensed Marital and Family Therapist. He is the architect and founder of Cornerstone Brief Therapy in Coralville Iowa. His caring methods have been recognized for their ability to bring about positive change. He has a master's degree in Counseling Psychology from the University of Missouri in Kansas City. He also is a peacemaker with his conference Mennonite Conflict Transformation team.

– 25 –

THE POWER TO CHANGE

MARNI PERSCHNICK

We're all motivated by fear and love, but only one is healthy long-term: uncontrolling love.

*M*y name is Marni, and I'm a recovering legalistic Evangelical. I'm also a clinical social worker and have worked with clients addressing their mental health with psychotherapy since 2014. I'm a 1 on the Enneagram, so I'm a perfectionist, and having structure and rules, and checklists make my heart happy. I naturally applied these ideas to God and found a lot of comfort in literal perspectives of God, including God's control over the world. "God's will" was something I was constantly chasing, and this informed how I saw people for a long time.

I attended Christian Universities for my undergraduate and graduate degrees in social work. I prayed for my clients and prayed for God's will for them. I observed great loss and suffering, and I looked at it all through the lens of it being part of God's plan. There is a comfort in accepting that "God is in control" and that pain has a purpose. And it's a quick answer to quote Jeremiah 29:11, "For I know the plans I have for you," declares the Lord, "plans to prosper you and not to harm you, plans to give you hope and a future" (NIV) and to not get into the deep, nitty-gritty of how suffering is painful and harmful.

When I was in grad school, I grappled with what I believed about humans and change. Could humans really change their lives, their behaviors, and their circumstances? And if I believed that, where was God's will and power in that? I wondered what the purpose of prayer was. If God knew me and all of my desires and what I struggled with, and God was all-powerful and had a plan for my life, why did I need to pray? If everything were already planned out, and I couldn't change it, why pray? These questions, and how God's power interacted with people's ability to change really challenged my belief structure (and remember, I like structure!).

I thought about how I drove by accidents and prayed for comfort, peace, and safety of those involved. And I also prayed a prayer of gratitude that God had kept *me* safe from the accident. I started to question if that was a good prayer to pray. Didn't God love the people in the accident the same way that God loved me? Why would God protect me and not them? Had I been more faithful, disciplined, and worthy of that love? That didn't feel right. God's love is unconditional and given to all equally. And what about babies who had cancer when they had literally not had a chance to sin or be faithful yet?

I struggled with these questions and found a breakthrough when I thought about how my parents love me. I thankfully have very loving and supportive parents. I thought about how they would respond if I got into an accident. The scenario went like this—I was in a car accident. I was ok, just shaken up. But the other person had died. I imagined that my parents responded with love and "oh my goodness, we're so glad you're ok." Then I switched the scenario, I was the one who died, and the other person was ok. I imagined my parents responded with grief and sadness. Perhaps God's love was similar to this. Perhaps God weeps with those who weep and feels gratitude with those who narrowly miss tragedy. Perhaps God's love is this, *and* that. God doesn't love those who escape accidents more than those who die in accidents.

The client I sit with who experienced horrific abuse as a child and now suffers trauma as a 50-year-old adult, and the client who just got the "all clear" regarding a cancer diagnosis are both loved and accompanied by God through their experiences. God isn't asserting power and control over the cancer diagnosis and leaving the abused victim in the dark. God is sitting with both clients and desiring for them to both move toward wholeness.

This brings me back to the question of *can humans change?* If God desires wholeness for all people, I believe that God has given us the ability to move toward that wholeness. And sometimes, we need help to access those abilities inside of us because our life experiences have covered them or led us to believe that they no longer exist. And this is where therapy can be a healing and sacred practice. I work from a person-centered approach to therapy. Both Carl Rogers and Fred Rogers influence my work. I believe that people can change because God gives us the ability to change. God loves us without controlling us by forcing us to align with God's will or a plan already lined out. God's love is a true love.

I've worked with clients who have a controlling partner. The "love" they experience from these controlling individuals doesn't *feel* loving. It feels fearful, insecure, demeaning, and hurtful. While someone may assert control over another person and think they're motivated by love or just trying to help someone, they are slowly whittling away the personhood of the individual they are controlling. My clients who have left controlling relationships have almost always had to recover their sense of self. They have been gaslit into believing they can't be trusted, and they often struggle with knowing who they are. God made us who we are. God doesn't want us to lose ourselves or our ability to trust ourselves out of devotion to God.

Because God doesn't control us or force us into a predetermined plan for our lives, some power rests in our hands. We have the power to change ourselves, our behaviors, and our circumstances. I want to clarify that this power can be limited for specific groups of people by societal injustices and institutional discrimination. And it is the responsibility of those of us with more power to work to dismantle those barriers to wholeness in others.

When someone steps into my office, I no longer believe that they are power-less to the ever-powerful will of God—that their pain and suffering is just part of a bigger story that will glorify God in the end. I believe that their pain and suffering is awful. I believe that what they are going through has completely turned their life upside down. I believe that they are beyond what they perceive as their ability to change. And I see my job as showing them God's love—weeping with them and celebrating with them. I aim to help them notice where their power does lie and what steps they can take to regain a sense of personhood. I aim to help them find their skills and resilience and help them find their wholeness.

Just as God's love is uncontrolling, for therapy to be loving, I also need to be uncontrolling. Control doesn't help someone grow; it only gains compliance through fear. I have found that in working with people, we're all motivated by two things—fear and love. Both are effective, but only one is healthy long-term: love. I see my job as loving my clients by demonstrating compassion, empathy, and validation. When they can do this for themselves, they grow exponentially.

Therapy isn't always successful, and people don't always grow. People have to choose to change. Sometimes we stay in unhealthy patterns of behavior because they work. Humans tend to stick with what works for them. There has to be some kind of benefit to a behavior (even if the benefit is just the comfort of knowing the behavior) for it to be sustained. And so, to not be a controlling therapist and show God's love to my clients, I also have to accept that sometimes they won't choose to change or grow. Even if they choose to remain unhealthy, I choose to remain in uncontrolling love because I know this is the most loving thing I can do.

Marni Perschnick *is a licensed clinical social worker and spiritual director in private practice (www.wellnesswithmarni.com). She also leads Forest Therapy walks in the Sierra Nevada mountains. Marni is in seminary to be an interfaith minister, and enjoys helping people connect with God in nature.*

26

EFT AND ORT ARE A MATCH MADE IN HEAVEN

ELISA JOY SEIBERT

Emotionally Focused Therapy and Open and Relational Theology are a perfect fit.

*H*ave you ever had two friends you really want to meet each other? That is how I feel about Open and Relational Theology (ORT) and Emotionally Focused Therapy (EFT). They are perfect for each other! If you are reading this book, you are likely already sold on ORT and see its deep value. Allow me to introduce you to EFT, what it is, why it is such a great fit for religious practitioners and therapists who embrace ORT, and how it is so powerful in helping people heal.

Relationship and Attachment are at the Heart

Both ORT and EFT embrace the core values of relationship being at the heart of all that is and love being "our ultimate ethic," in the words of Thomas Jay Oord. They additionally affirm the value of science and that deep transformation can be realized. Dr. Sue Johnson, the originator of EFT, states it this way: we are created for connection.

To understand EFT, we must see relationship (and I would add, the relational nature of God) is woven into the universe through the science of attachment. British psychiatrist John Bowlby's theory of attachment puts into words what many of us instinctually know: we humans (and many animals, like the cats and dogs we love!) are wired to connect at a deep level. We need at least one other person to be there for us, to hear us when we call, to soothe us when we are in distress, to help us know we matter, and to be there completely for us. In Western cultures, we tend to acknowledge babies have attachment needs. We concede they would not survive if they didn't have someone completely there for them. But most people don't realize attachment covers the entire life span. We all have those same needs. Yes, even as adults. Attachment, at its core, is about survival. Our brains were made to cope relationally, not individually as the culture dictates. Load-sharing is the path to a healthy life.

The revolutionary and empirically validated Emotionally Focused Therapy flows from attachment science. There are vast implications for attachment theory and EFT. For example, EFT is the *only* therapy proven to help people actually change their attachment style from birth (such as from anxious or avoidant attachment) and *earn secure attachment*. In turn, secure attachment impacts our view of ourselves and others, helps us cope with stressors and trauma more effectively, parent from an attuned place, and experience greater relationship satisfaction. Secure attachment and EFT also correlate with improved mental health, more resilient immune response, lowered perception of pain, and reduction of heart attacks, among other benefits. Secure attachment and EFT are powerful!

For our purposes here, as we keep the lens of attachment and EFT, I want to focus on the way God's love has positive ripple effects in how therapists can help people experience that same love in their most important relationships, starting with the therapy process itself.

What Does God Have to Do With It?

One of the most fundamental beliefs in the Christian faith is that God is love (1 Jn 4:16). The very essence of love is that it is uncontrolling, in Oord's words. That love has led God to reach out in connection to humans over the millennia, seeking to connect with us, the created ones. Not only does God reach out to us, but God made us, down to the neurotransmitter activity in our brains, to be wired for connection—with God, others, and ourselves. We were made to reach back. Perhaps you have experienced the mystery and beauty of a newborn baby instinctually grasping your finger with their tiny hand. That is attachment at work.

For us to have secure attachment with God, we must see God as a safe haven and secure base (John Bowlby's phrase). Uncontrolling love is key. Uncontrolling love says, "I am here for you, no matter what. You are allowed to have all of your feelings. You may have your protest come up, your fear, your deep longings. I can make space for them all. No feeling will be shut down, and at the core I will stay with you, present, open, engaged, responsive. I will be real with you as you are real with me, and I will stay connected with my primary (soft, vulnerable) emotions even if you go to armored secondary, reactive emotions like anger and numbing out. I am here for you... no matter what." You can hear in these words a calm centeredness and openness, a warmth that gives space for the other to be authentic. It is safe. All of this is the opposite of control. Control is fueled by anxiety. Anxiety restricts the possibilities and can be experienced as repressive, even violent. That is not God! God is not anxious and does not pressure us, only invites us with welcoming love.

The Role of the Therapist in EFT

Part of the delightful privilege of being a therapist is that we get the profound and sacred opportunity to live out that love as a safe haven and secure base with the clients who come to us. There is a beautiful parallel process that emerges. God loves us and provides a secure base for us as therapists. God is our Stronger Wiser Other (in Bowlby's terms). God reminds us of the secure base we are to be and how to show up for our clients as God does for us. We then take that experienced relationship with God and live it out with our clients as their temporary Stronger Wiser Other until they can walk into it with each other. Does this matter? Actually, it is almost the *only* thing that matters! Just as people are wounded in relationship, so they heal in relationship. In EFT we see that the deepest healing therapeutically does *not* come from merely changing our thoughts or behaviors but from deeply experiencing the loving safety, security, and acceptance of another human in our places of vulnerability. It is *all about relationship*. Emotions, "the music of the dance" and "language of love," as Johnson says, are the place where it all comes alive and where we must hover to help that deep healing happen.

God's uncontrolling love invites us to welcome our clients into their vulnerable journey. We start at the shallow end of the pool of emotion, building safety. We walk slowly to the deep end at a pace their nervous systems can tolerate. God's uncontrolling love invites us to compassionately see through their armor to the pain underneath. We do not force them to do anything they are not ready for (as control would do). We help them gently expand their window of tolerance and support them in noticing, distilling, and sharing their pockets of pain, to use Kathryn Rheem's words. In EFT with couples, this sharing helps their partner start to see the vulnerable places underneath that fuel the destructive patterns. If something is too hard, we slow down and validate, hover, and explore with supportive curiosity. We slice it thinner and help them name what is going on and what is so hard. Control would push, dictate a plan, fix. Uncontrolling love comes alongside gently, staying present, and not moving ahead until they are ready.

Attachment theory tells us that attunement is the fastest way to independence, not forcing independence as control (and Western culture) would do. We see this with toddlers. When learning to walk, they vacillate between excitement at the adventures ahead and fear of leaving their parent. They look forward and backward. If they return to their parent for reassurance and the parent smothers or leaves them alone (as control and non-attunement would do), they become clingy, anxious, dependent, or distant. If the parent tunes in, sees and validates their fear, stays gently present, supports them *when they are ready*, then they will become confident, secure, and more independent faster. This is called Interdependence, or Effective Dependence, as Johnson says. This is what God invites therapists to do with the clients who come seeking a new way of being with themselves, God, and their important others in the world.

If we take this slower attuning path of validation, hovering with emotion, and making space, miracles can happen in the therapy room. I see it all the time as couples take risks, reach, respond, show up for each other, grow safety they never experienced before, and discover love they never thought possible. This is what awaits us as therapists when we live out the uncontrolling, patient, attuning love modeled first by God. And EFT provides a powerfully effective roadmap and attachment-based process to help us get there.

Next Steps

If you are curious how to live out uncontrolling love in an attuning way, read Sue Johnson's *Attachment Theory in Practice.* Connect with other like-minded therapists through an EFT Community, like the Central PA EFT Community of which I am a part. And if you want to be transformed, get training in EFT (starting with EFT Externship). We can't learn this model alone, and through connection we can make a difference by living out God's uncontrolling love in this world!

Elisa Joy Seibert, Ph.D., M.Div., is a Licensed Psychologist, ICEEFT Certified Emotionally Focused (EFT) Therapist and Supervisor, Counselor Educator, former chaplain, and co-founder of the Central PA EFT Community. A graduate of Asbury Theological Seminary and Gannon University, she has a passion for equipping therapists seeking to learn and live out EFT with excellence (www.GrowingConnections. live) and specializes in helping couples transform their connection.

27

THE ART OF KINTSUGI AND THE FORMATION OF SELF AS THERAPIST

TIFFANY TRIPLETT

I am honored to sit with those who are mourning old conceptions of self, others, God, and the world.

*I*t was an early Fall morning, and I, a curious college Freshman, had just stepped foot in "The God Building," otherwise known as the School of Theology and Christian Ministry building on my college campus. On this day, we were going to receive back our first biblical studies exam and determine with our professor whether or not any questions should be thrown out of scoring. Now, being the good Sunday school student that I was…I knew I had aced the section where we had to write out the names of the books of the Bible in order…If you know the song, you know the song… "Genesis, Exodus, Leviticus"…I digress…but I did not know how I faired in other sections of the exam.

The professor addressed those questions most missed by students in the class and then made the "mistake" of asking if there were any objections to any of those questions. Of course I had an objection, but I scanned the room to see if anyone might speak on our behalf… silence… dead silence… so I decided to break the silence… with my hand raised, Dr. C.S. Cowles looked at me and said ,"you there." All of a sudden, I felt my cheeks flush and my question went something like this; "well Dr. Cowles, couldn't we say that God's love and Abraham's response to this love is the reason why Abraham no longer needed to sacrifice his son…that God in a way changed God's mind due to this relationship with Abraham?" Gulp…

silence…again. Dr. Cowles at this point peered over his lectern, which at this point seemed much bigger than it was previously; he then said, "that is an interesting question…what is your name?" I sunk down in my chair as I told him my name, and he briefly wrote something down on the sheet in front of him. I do not know what he wrote, nor do I remember if he answered the question, and I do not believe I scored the point for the class on the exam; what I do remember is the sheer fear that I had just said something blasphemous and would find myself in the Dean's office that week.

Thankfully, no such thing happened, but still, I determined that it was just a matter of time until my questions regarding the God of my youthful Sunday school years would come forward and I would find myself in the Dean's office needing to repent for my woeful ways—that I would be challenged to have more faith in this God with whom I was ultimately so angry with and had struggled silently to trust.

Why, you might ask, why was I, an 18-year-old college Freshman, so angry with this God? What could have possibly brought me to question the God of my youth? Growing up in the church we sang songs such as "My God is so big, so strong, and so mighty; there is nothing my God cannot do" and "The Lord is mine and I am His, His banner over me is love;" I had started to wonder where this mighty, loving God was and why, if He were these things, did He not do what was loving and mighty when I needed Him most?

You see, as a kid, I was ongoingly molested by a neighbor—I had experienced genuine evil. In the midst of experiencing this genuine evil, I would go to church on Wednesdays and Sundays, and I would sing the songs. and I would pray, and I would read my Bible; I would take part in the fellowship and life of the church, and I would enjoy doing so; but then, I would sit alone in my room and wonder why God didn't make my molester stop? Why would God not stop my molester from coming to church on the rare occasion that his child's orchestra played there? Where was God then when I was hiding in the foyer and calling my parents to come pick me up because I was not "feeling well"? If God was a just God as I had been told, why, when I broke my silence, was justice not served? Where was this all-powerful and all loving God and why, if he was these things, would this God not choose to step in and do something?

We would sing a song about Jesus being a friend of mine and I wondered what I had done that made Jesus not want to be my friend? Because certainly a friend who could, would stop such evil things from happening? Certainly, a God who was all powerful and all loving could and would stop evil things from happening? And yet, evil occurred, and evil continues to occur.

And so there I sat, an 18-year-old, pondering how a God could in one breath request of a person to sacrifice his son and in another determine that that sacrifice was no longer needed. I had heard the story before, but as I sat with it in this class, I imagined Abraham's pleas to God, his prayers, his faith, and his wrestling with the hard questions and it hit me that perhaps God was responding. Perhaps God does care. Perhaps God does love. Perhaps God *does* act, and perhaps as we exist in relationship with God, God changes, and God learns. And then in another breath, I wondered still, then why does evil still occur? Why do bad things happen to good people? Where is God?

Little did I know that my wrestling with the hard questions had only just begun. This time though I did not run from them. I did not hide from them. I faced them. My wrestling did not happen alone, but rather within a community of persons from professors to therapists to a wonderful Chaplain—people who opened their offices, a chair at a coffee shop, sometimes their homes and created safe, non-judgmental spaces to ask and to wrestle with these questions, these per- ceptions, and these assumptions. In these spaces, I processed the genuine evil that I had experienced. I questioned how God can be loving and all-powerful and allow evil to take place. I cried and wondered, on top of all this, why my Dad had to be diagnosed with cancer? I allowed myself to get angry at all of this, including the often heard excuses from well-intentioned people growing up when evil happened, such as "God has a purpose for all that we have been through, the suffering we have endured," or, "it's all in God's plan," or "evil exists because of Satan." And slowly, my anger turned to sadness. And I grieved. I grieved the God I thought ex- isted…and began grieving over the loss of the evil done *to* me…and kept searching for who God was and is.

Suddenly, the theological implications of the traditional views of God I grew up being taught—a God who was sovereign, all-powerful and in control, a God who was distant and who I "just needed to trust" because "His ways are beyond our ways and our knowledge." God, who was unable to stop evil things from hap- pening, but yet was somehow supposed to be understood as all-powerful and all loving, had crashed into my lived experience and shattered into pieces everywhere.

However, thankfully, much like the Japanese art of kintsugi, whereby an artist takes the broken pottery pieces and places them back together with gold to create an even more beautiful piece than once was, highlighting in a way what was once broken but is now made new, I sat in a variety of theology and philosophy classes, in church, in small groups and with these others mentioned above and be- gan to pick up these pieces and to look over them. As I did, I began to understand the centrality of love; more specifically I came to understand God as love. as om-nibenevolent or all loving; and everything changed, everything started to make more sense. Love became the gold that bonded the pieces that I picked up back together and, in so doing, it wrought about my well-being.

Knowing and receiving from the source that *is* love changes you. When I understood God's nature as love—as always loving—I understood that we can only respond to God's love if we are free; we can only have relationship with God if we have freedom. Abraham was free to love and respond to God, to wrestle with God, and to question God. God could not impose or stop Abraham, but rather through their relationship and Abraham's pleas, Abraham was changed, and so too was God. Like Abraham, I came to understand myself and others as free and *response-able*. I accepted the fact that my molester was also free and response-able. I chose to let go of blaming God for my molester's behavior, for not intervening, and to let go of my perception that God was uncaring and in-active; in doing so, I recognized God's presence—God's love—God's mourning and grieving with me during and in the aftermath of that genuine evil done to me.

Essentially, I came to know God as what Thomas J. Oord had defined as essentially *kenotic*, a God whose timeless nature is uncontrolling love and who gives of self in relation to others, a God who is *other* empowering and who seeks the well-being of all.[1] It is because of this timeless nature of uncontrolling love that we are necessarily free to have agency in the world to actualize potentialities available to us. It is also due to God's nature of uncontrolling love that we are self-organizing and have lawlike regularities in our world, which cannot be taken away. Furthermore, we, and those around us, have the freedom to act in loving and not loving ways both in ways that seek well-being and in ways that do not.[2]

And so, in response to this God of love, I choose to live a life of love with the intention of participating in the common good for the well-being of self, others, God, and the world. I do this both in my personal life as I participate in reciprocal, intentional relationships, but also in a professional capacity as a mental health therapist. When I go into each therapy session with a client, I'm aware of the all present, all loving God who sits with me; a God who sits with us and is present with us. I remember the experience of breaking my own silence, of sitting with those tough questions, of processing those emotions I tried to push down or away, of healing the trauma, of healing the parts that needed to know they were loved… and there but for the grace of God go I…

I am honored to sit with those who are going through their own process and who are mourning old parts, old conceptions of self, others, God, and the world, etc. Today, I get to take part in creating a safe non-judgmental space for people to sit in their silence, I have the opportunity to be witness to their breaking of this silence, to the processing of their emotions, questions, and attempts to make sense of the evil done to them or to another. I sit with them in their attempts at making sense of their relationships or making their relationships work, in their trials, and in their successes. I get to explore the bio-psycho-social-spiritual aspects of their selves with them; sometimes I even get the opportunity to offer up some cognitive reframes and wonder *with* them about God. Together, we pick up the pieces and, with the goal and intention towards well-being, we allow for love, connection, and attachment to begin to mend together a beautiful, potential-actualizing always evolving, new creation! Shalom!

Tiffany Triplett is a Licensed Marriage and Family Therapist in California. She is a Co-Founder and Clinical Director at Evolve Therapy San Diego. Tiffany is also an Adjunct Professor at Azusa Pacific University and is presently obtaining her doctorate in Clinical Psychology.

28

CAREGIVING TRIFECTA

TRACY L. TUCKER

*What might spiritual care in the face of death look like from an
Open and Relational perspective?*

"The most beautiful people we have known are those who have known
defeat, known suffering, known struggle, known loss, and have found
their way out of the depths. These persons have an appreciation, a sensitivity, and an understanding of life that fills them with compassion,
gentleness, and a deep loving concern. Beautiful people do not just
happen."

Elisabeth Kübler-Ross

*N*one of us has or will escape the experience of death, what lives ultimately
dies. Psychiatrist, Irvin Yalom refers to our awareness and the associated
fears of death as the "Mortal Wound." We carry that wound with us from our
earliest day to our final one.

Like a piece of a societal jigsaw puzzle, difficult feelings of grief, loss, longing, feeling lost, and even dread of death have become embedded components of
most, if not all cultures. Some will find ways of locating hope and even finding
peace in the face of death. The romantic embrace of death as an escape or something to be desired over a more difficult life can mask some of the pain, but it is in
our nature to struggle with facing death, especially first-hand.

The spiritual care provider will likely observe this struggle in their patients, patients' families, and even within themselves, often challenging everything they previously believed. Robert Dykstra was transparent as he wrote of his earlier experience in hospital chaplaincy, "The theological language I had relied on in 'safer' moments in my ministry seemed to grow increasingly flat and unable to sustain me in what I was witnessing in these overwhelming moments of ministry."

Consider this encounter from my role as hospice chaplain which challenged my personal beliefs and theological language. George (name changed) was in his mid-50s and very committed to his Hindu faith. George's husband, Frank (name changed) was slightly older and did not share George's faith. Frank would tell you that he, in fact, has no religious faith other than that he believes there must be some kind of god or supreme deity somewhere.

George had a painful form of cancer that was attacking his bones and had metastasized throughout his abdomen. Frank spent his day at George's bedside, knowing that the time for George's final transition was only hours away. George had not taken in any food or water for several days and had not spoken for the past two days.

During the last couple hours of George's life, Frank walked out of the room on the hospice unit and declared: "If or when I ever come face to face with God, he will have some serious explaining to do."

How does the spiritual care provider respond? How does our theory of God inform the type and level of care we offer to people in the face of death or the dying? What are the barriers to our own ability to provide spiritual care? What principles, theories, practices or theology might we employ as we provide excellent care in end-of-life crises?

How do we help hurting, angry people negotiate their pain and very natural feelings tied to their loss and grief so that they might become one of Kübler-Ross' "beautiful people"? I propose three practices for spiritual care providers to employ in the face of death: empathy, presence and relationship.

Empathy

Yalom wrote: "Empathy is the most powerful tool we have in our efforts to connect with other people. It is the glue of human connectedness and permits us to feel, at a deep level, what someone else is feeling." An authentic and meaningful spiritual care approach will be one of persistent empathy.

Educated through a conservative evangelical system and serving several decades in churches of that same ilk, my own first approach to spiritual care assumed a conservative Christian worldview. However, people in need of spiritual care are not necessarily sympathetic to that worldview. Within today's culture, that understanding of God, faith, and life is often thought of as dated, if not irrelevant.

Pastor, psychologist and founder of Stephen Ministries Saint Louis, Kenneth Haugk defines the role of the spiritual caregiver in the life of their care recipient. "When you enter another person's home, you know there are rules or customs of tradition, courtesy, and common sense. You are the guest. The other person is the host, and the host sets the rules, not you."

Consider the above example of George and Frank. George, a devout Hindu likely welcomed death, anticipating that he will have advanced even closer toward mokṣa. Frank's grief was compounded by George's spiritual conviction. Frank wanted George to fight for every last breath and to have that final moment as a shared experience with George.

Empathy necessitates the spiritual care provider share in Frank's desire for that fading moment with George. There is no room for commentary or judgment about selfishness, sexual orientation, debate about the existence of God, or how we should approach God respectfully. The spiritual care provider is the guest, not the host in this relationship. The host sets the agenda. And the agenda is empathy.

Author and sociologist Brené Brown wrote that "Empathy, the most powerful tool of compassion, is an emotional skill set that allows us to understand what someone is experiencing and to reflect back that understanding."

Presence

In the Old Testament story of Job there are four friends who respond to Job's claim to be a hapless victim of his personal tragic circumstances. My take on this story as it's written is that the fourth of the friends, Elihu simply sat with Job and waited while the other friends berate Job for his stubborn insistence upon his own righteousness. Reading this story I always wish that Elihu had simply remained at Job's side and kept his "helpful input" to himself.

Job was trying to make sense of his loss. Who among us would not have serious questions if our possessions and means of survival had been taken as well as our children and their families? Elihu had the opportunity to be simply present with Job and share in his pain. But instead, he opened his mouth to speak.

Being present with a person in pain and sharing in that pain, grief, loneliness, fear, whatever journey they are on, signals that their feelings are valid and offers the potential that they just might find a sense of well-being. This might be true even for those who may be transitioning from this life. Of all the items on Job's list of "Things I Need," critics and advisors were certainly not there.

Standing in the hospice unit that day, my presence with Frank gave space for him to have a shared experience in a relationship that could endure the differences in theology, ideology, lifestyle, and anger that represented his authentic feelings.

Relationship

Spiritual care is, if nothing else, relational. In his essay entitled, "Crossing the Ocean of Suffering, A Medical Perspective on Divine Impassability," Dr. Jonathan Kopel wrote about a relational God of the Bible who modeled a relationship with humanity in pain. Rather than a God out of Bette Midler lyrics where God is watching us from a distance, Kapel suggests that God is actually affected by our circumstances and present with us in them. "For God shows himself to be courageous and willing to be vulnerable by experiencing life with us. God opens himself to our pains and joins us on our journey. We do not feel alone or abandoned by God."

The authentic and effective spiritual care provider will embrace one in need through relational language and methodology. The spiritual care provider will be vulnerable, transparent enough to be relatable, and available enough to feel the pain of the other. Kopel adds, "Rather than a private affair, suffering [I would add 'grieving'] becomes a participation between our soul and God."

Frank was only part of my life for a few days, but that time allowed a relationship to form that provided for conversation and, I believe, effective care. Because my theory of God streams from an open and relational grounding, it made sense to choose a non-coercive and empathetic approach to both George's and Frank's needs.

In the conclusion to his work entitled *The Varieties of Religious Experience*, William James penned this statement, "Who knows whether the faithfulness of individuals here below to their own poor over-beliefs may not actually help God, in turn, to be more effectively faithful to his own greater tasks."

Applying the practices of empathy, presence, and relationship reveals a lived experience with God as I understand God to be at work within an open and relational context. We are co-participants with God in this life, co-creators in a relational dynamic that which empowers us to become the hands of God, touching others at their point of pain and grief. This belief and praxis align us with a loving and compassionate approach to spiritual care within the context of death and the dying.

Tracy L. Tucker *is a Senior Chaplain for Community Hospice and Palliative Care in Jacksonville Florida. He earned his MDiv from Nazarene Theological Seminary and is currently working on his DTM through Northwind Theological Seminary. Tracy is a Board Certified Chaplain through APC and has a Certification in Thanatology through ADEC. He enjoys a private cup of coffee most mornings while watching the hummingbirds at his patio feeder.*

29

THE CONSULTING ROOM AS A PLACE OF MYSTERY AND HEALING

MARGARET FIELD

Was Aristotle correct in saying that 'knowing yourself is the beginning of all wisdom'?

We live in an anti-intellectual culture where quick and easy answers for life's problems are sought. Based on an economic model, simplistic responses are pursued and quickly given, especially within the Church walls. The prosperity Gospel which flourished late last century is evidence of this; if you are unwell, you lack faith. If you are struggling financially, you need to give more money to the Church. Bang, all your problems will be solved! Current evangelicals, particularly those within the Calvinistic camp, likewise seem to avoid the complexities of life; whatever happens is God's will, and if we pray hard enough people will get well. But is life really this simple?

I suggest not! I would argue that we are governed by unconscious desires and motives. We act and think in ambivalent ways, causing deep internal conflicts because we do not know who we really are. The oracle at Delphi calls us to 'Know Thyself.' It is my belief that in trying to understand our inner core, the heart, which according to Jeremiah 17:9 'is deceitful above all things', we can more authentically be partners with God on this adventurous journey called Life.

As a psychoanalytic psychotherapist, it is my role to help make the unconscious conscious, or at least to assist with that journey. Praying with others can help. Personal self-reflection can also help, as can talking to trusted friends.

Exposing ourselves to the wisdom of poets, playwriters, philosophers and theologians can likewise play its part in our wholeness. But there are times when more is needed; when the skilled therapist is needed to listen in a multifaceted way making connections and therapeutic interventions that are beyond the skills of the ordinary listener. Would we expect to give a church leader a scalpel and expect him to carry out brain surgery on an ill patient? Of course not. They are not equipped with the skills to carry out such surgery. Why then do we often think that the Church has the skill to deal with deep mental health issues?

I often see my role as a remedial parent offering emotional nourishment to my clients as they work through issues often related to childhood trauma. My analytic work is primarily based on the understanding of the human mind expressed in the writings of people such as Freud, Klein, Winnicott and Bion, together with the philosophical and theological writings of Kierkegaard, Aquinas, and Aristotle. Each therapeutic encounter is different, and I, therefore, offer what can be termed as a bespoke service. We do not know where the therapy is heading since there is no route map to 'normal,' whatever that word means. As such therapy is 'open,' and I see my role to be a fellow traveler with my clients exploring unchartered inner territory which will influence their future thoughts and actions. The therapeutic relationship within the encounter is unique; it is dependable, reliable, confidential, and intense but above all very present in the moment. The style of therapy I offer could indeed be seen as open and relational, much like the theology I subscribe to.

My consulting room becomes a magical place where communication takes place on many levels; conscious to conscious, unconscious to unconscious and a myriad of other ways. Do I bring the terms 'God' or 'Jesus' or 'faith' into the room? No, not in an obvious way. But I listen with what Freud called a 'free-floating attention,' much the same as I do when I offer prayer ministry at the end of a Church service. Thoughts, impressions, and feelings surface within me. Are these promptings the result of the Holy Spirit? Or are they some sort of person-to-person unconscious communication? I do not know. And I do not think it really matters. What matters is that people are experiencing love and understanding in the depths of their beings, sometimes it feels for the first time. Perhaps the consulting room is more like a prayer room than we ever imagined.

Within each encounter, I see myself as partnering with God. I do not know where the therapy will take us, but I have learnt to rest in a 'not-knowingness,' a bit like Keats' understanding of 'negative capability'. My approach is respectful and compassionate, and I see each individual as being made in the image of God, whatever they are presenting me with.

Take Alex (not his real name) for example. He came to see me because he was wrapping his lower body in toilet paper, yelling at people to keep their distance. This 19-year-old man had isolated himself, worrying both his parents and the Church by his manic behavior, unable to hold down a job. The Church had spent time 'casting out demons' from him, praying 'over' him and 'for' him, to no visible effect. People were scared of him. His adoptive parents bought him to me in a desperate last-ditch attempt for help, knowing that I was a Christian psychotherapist. The initial phone call with the sobbing mother struck a deep chord within me as she said, 'I am losing my son, please help us find him again.' I gently replied, 'Perhaps Alex will first find himself, and then maybe he will allow himself to be found by you.'

A week later Alex arrived half-covered in unused toilet paper, and as he sat down in my consulting room, he asked whether I had any spare toilet paper. I realized that it was important for me to provide him with this, and every session I put two rolls on the small table beside his chair. This happened for almost two months. Initially wrapping his body was a frantic activity with little conversation, but as he learnt to trust me, he was able to wrap himself in a more considered and calm manner, and later he began to use less paper. I have come to realize in therapy that one does not ask 'Why are you doing this?' but rather 'Tell me your story'. Over time I came to realize that Alex's behavior was both a logical, clever, and considerate response to his inner turmoil. Alex believed that poisonous feces were protruding from the skin on his lower body and the only way to remain clean was to cover himself in toilet paper which would magically soak up the feces and the poison. He feared damaging others so yelled at them to keep away.

During the course of therapy it became clear that Alex had been physically and emotionally neglected as a child, often left in soiled and leaking nappies (or diapers if you are from the USA) for hours that went into days. He cried incessantly as a child, needing to have his nappy changed, and wanting to be held and comforted. He was left feeling dirty and angry, often getting infections, and fearing that he would pass those infections onto others. Wrapping himself in toilet paper as an adult was a way of protecting himself from a feeling of neglect, disgust, and repulsion which had its roots in childhood, and his yelling at people to keep away was a protective measure to stop him from infecting others. Alex's behavior was, in fact, to protect others.

One of the *tools* used in psychoanalytic psychotherapy is that of transference. Clients relive certain infantile conflicts by projecting onto the analyst particular feelings e.g. envy, guilt, anger, dependence, and in doing so healing, freedom and forgiveness of self and others can take place. It takes the *skill* of a trained therapist to work effectively with transference, but over time Alex was able to understand his behavior, and the use of toilet paper became less important for him. He was later able to replace wrapping himself in toilet paper by having a daily bath which ensured his skin remained clean. He no longer felt he was a danger to others and his yelling ceased. He currently holds a manual job in the city of London. Alex had started to understand himself, to find himself. In fact his Church members said he was now 'normal', but I again, wonder what 'normal' really means.

It is my belief that this type of analytic psychotherapy should be available to all, irrespective of social or financial status. As such I am an honorary psycho-analytic psychotherapist in a low-cost clinic in London, England. My dream is to see Churches offering analytic psychotherapy, as part of the pastoral ministry because perhaps like Alex, it is only when we have 'found' ourselves, that we can allow ourselves to be found by others. And perhaps our partnering with God will likewise become more exciting and radical as we allow ourselves to be continually found by God.

Margaret Field *chose to withhold her real name in the interests of her client work. She studied* Theology and Philosophy *as an undergraduate and then undertook an MA in* Political Theology, *before teaching in schools in London, England. Whilst teaching she went on to obtain a further degree in* Psychology. *It was therefore a natural move some years ago to fuse these subjects together, embarking on a clinical qualification in Psychoanalytical Psychotherapy. Margaret currently works in private practice as well as in a low-cost clinic in Central London. She is an active member of her local Church, with a passion to enthuse folks towards deep and adventurous thinking in their faith.*

30

WHERE GOD CAN'T, AGENTS CAN

RICHARD CRUSE

Perhaps the reason our prayers go unanswered is
simpler than we think.

𝓝o travel agent* could have predicted my long term "itinerary." I grew into my 20s in California, attended and graduated from the Texan flagship of evangelical dispensationalism in my 30s, and then served cross-culturally (four countries on three continents) for nearly a quarter century. When I returned to the States, I found myself in wildly different places **geographically** (Midwest), **theologically** (ex-evangelical), and **vocationally** (chaplain in a Level I Trauma Center and teaching hospital; Spiritual Advisor to a Gender Health Program). Each of these new locales contains its own unique story, but for my present purpose, I will focus on my *current* theological location.

In broad strokes, my foundational theological premise is this: the Gospel, or the good news announced by Jesus, is not simply a mechanistic formula for getting people into heaven. Rather, it is—above all else—the opening salvo and the culmination of the Creator's cosmic rescue plan. In the words of British theologian NT Wright, the Creator's plan is to put all of creation "to rights": in its original working order or reflecting the life of the age to come. Further, the accomplishment of said rescue plan not only involves, but also requires the responses of human agents and their participation in all sorts of redemptive activities, both consciously and unconsciously, from inside "the faith" and from outside. The proclamation of the Gospel is the Creator's call for human participation with God as active partners or agents in setting the world "to rights."

God's intention is not save people "*out of* the world system for heaven's sake," but rather to save them "*into* the world system for creation's sake." The good news, the true *protoevangelium*, emerges initially in Genesis 1:28-31. There we find those created in God's image and pronounced good being placed into God's "very good" creation. They are to oversee and care for creation in its entirety as they live in loving relationship with their Creator. All of humankind was (and is) invited into an amazing opportunity to be *active agents* for carrying out God's purposes. But, as we know, this mandate has not been fully carried out. Why? Because those created to be agents are always *free* agents: free to act responsibly and free to act irresponsibly. We see this reality lived out in the remainder of the Old Testament where we read about the centuries-long movement and growth of God's initially-called people (agents) from polytheism (worshiping many gods) to monolatry (worshiping one of the many gods) to monotheism (worshiping the only true God). This lengthy process reflects necessary steps toward the ultimate revelation and recovery of God's eternal purposes.

The cresting of this cosmic rescue plan takes us forward multiple millennia to John the Baptist, "a voice of one calling in the wilderness, 'Prepare the way for the Lord…and all people will see God's salvation.'" God's salvation, or deliverance, further and finally emerges as Jesus reveals himself as the *prime agent* of restoration and reconciliation:,

> *"The Spirit of the Lord is upon me,*
> *because he has anointed me*
> *to bring good news to the poor.*
> *He has sent me to proclaim release to the captives*
> *and recovery of sight to the blind,*
> *to set free those who are oppressed,*
> *to proclaim the year of the Lord's favor"* (Lk 4:18,19),

Humankind's shared agency in bringing the good news that God has acted on behalf of humankind, verbally and actually, is next hinted at in the Lord's Prayer: "…may [the Creator's] will be done *on earth* as it is *in the heavenlies*" [emphasis added]: not a physical or metaphysical location somewhere in the sky, but the life of *the age to come* lived out by God's agents now *on earth*. Jesus completed his task as the Agent of the age to come, but there is work yet to be done!

Jesus's good news was that he fulfilled through himself the promise of a renewed and restored creation, of which he is the first fruits. His method? The "capture and release of active and responsible agents back into the world system" (Mt 28:18-20ff), i.e., proclaimers and active agents in renewing and restoring the now-but-not-yet renewed and restored creation. They, and by extension we serve as witnesses and observable demonstrations of the life of the age to come.

As a hospital chaplain and one of these active agents, one stereotype I face (aside from often being seen as the "harbinger/angel of death") is that my primary, perhaps sole function is to pray for healing. More to the point, I am to pray for miracles. However, the reality is that I rarely offer to pray unless it's requested or it's absolutely clear that such activity is desired. Sadly, my track record for prayer-created miracles is pretty dismal. Consider the following encounter.

> *Unable yet again to bring myself to pray for a miracle, I left the patient's room feeling discouraged but far less bereft than the discharged patient herself: no home, the car (in which she had been living) towed away, no money for her life saving medications, no marriage (separated from her homeless husband), no (apparent) contact with her one adult son (and grandchild), living on a paltry amount of SSDI (Social Security Disability Insurance) that always left her running out of funds before running out of month. I had recognized the frailty and vulnerability behind her tough, stoic façade. As I had taken her hand, tears began to seep out and slowly make their way down her roughened cheeks. Angrily wiping them away, she mumbled, "I'm fine; I'll make it!"*

Pray for a miracle? What miracle should I have prayed for? Pray that the poorly-functioning housing authority might drop a housing voucher into her lap; that her confiscated car be found and repaired without cost; that she find an envelope with money adequate to buy her needed medication—and not just for a week or a month; that her husband show up at her bedside with flowers and guarantees for a better future; that her son graciously invite her to share his home? I could have, but I didn't because I actually could not and should not! But, one says, doesn't God promise to answer our prayers, all our prayers? Isn't the Bible filled with verses and stories of God's miraculous provisions?

> *"Ask and it will be given to you; seek and you will find; knock and the door will be opened to you,"* (Matthew 7:7).

"Again, truly I tell you that if two of you on earth agree about anything they ask for, it will be done for them by my Father in heaven," (Matthew 18:19).

"If you believe, you will receive whatever you ask for in prayer," (Matthew 21:22).

"Therefore, I tell you, whatever you ask for in prayer, believe that you have received it, and it will be yours," (Mark 11:24).

"Oh, wait," someone will say, "You can't just be a member of the Flip Wilson School of Prayer: 'I'm going to pray now, any y'all want anything?'"

"You can't just ask for something, you have to…

… be a Christian."

… fulfill God's requirements."

… have enough faith."

… be right with God."

… ask according to God's perfect will."

… ad infinitum, ad nauseum.

I've stood with countless families at the bedsides of their grievously injured or ill loved ones. They state with faith, hope, and authority: "Our God is a God of miracles. There's nothing our God can't do. Our God, who can even raise the dead, will heal our loved one!"

Where are all the answers to those prayers of certainty? Where are all the miracles, the ones that are not anecdotal, not learned from the internet, or the neighbor down the street? Where are the men and women, young and old, raised up from their deathbeds; fully restored from traumatic brain injuries; walking again after having their spinal cords ripped apart by gunfire; breathing deeply and without discomfort after their lungs were ravaged by COVID-19? Where are they?

"Miraculous," unexpected recovery does occasionally occur: a patient awakening with some return to baseline abilities following a lengthy coma; walking again despite significant spinal cord assault; returning to a full life following a

144

slow and seemingly certain descent toward death. When these happen, emails and Facebook posts abound with reports of God's miraculous intervention. God be praised! God has wrought that miracle. Now, I agree that God should be praised. I agree that miracles have taken place, but these miracles have names: EMTs, nurses, doctors, respiratory techs, creators of amazing medications and machines of all kinds and countless others. God's miracles are the **divinely called**, but also very **human** agents that demonstrate my premise regarding agency: those created in God's image and pronounced good are caring for God's "very good" but now broken creation.

Ultimately, I did pray for that dear homeless woman. After receiving permission, I took her hand and asked the Almighty to assure her that she is God's beloved daughter. As I gently wiped tears from her cheeks, I prayed that she might know God's nearness and tenderness. As I sat with her there in the comforting and uncomfortable silence, I prayed for agents to tear down the societal systems that keep her homeless and poor.

So, is the issue with unanswered prayer simply that God, because of sovereignly and predetermined outcomes that are beyond our understanding, **won't** answer these prayers? Or, is the issue that God, in love, **can't** force action from unhearing and/or unwilling human agents? How many answers to prayer do not come, how many miracles cannot come, simply because there are no willing agents of change?

*Agent: one who acts for, or in the place of, another (the principal), by that person's authority; someone entrusted to do the business of another.

Richard Cruse has served for six years as Lead Chaplain in a Midwestern county hospital that provides care for all but with special emphasis on the underserved and vulnerable populations. Prior to this, he spent 45 years in a variety of local church and cross-cultural ministries. He and his wife have been married for 49 years and have three sons and five grandchildren.

31

THEOLOGY, SPIRITUALITY, PSYCHOLOGY, AND STATURE

BRUCE EPPERLY

*Open and relational theology is holistic and
interdisciplinary in nature.*

*O*pen and relational theology seamlessly joins the often-separated disciplines of theology, spirituality, psychology, and pastoral care. Each of these disciplines shapes and informs the others, and gains insight in the interplay of theory, practice, and experience in a world in which our agency matters and our actions help create the future for us, others, and God.

As a pastor-professor for over forty years, I have observed that growth in theological insight transforms persons' spiritual and emotional lives. Conversely, psychological growth inspires new approaches to theology and spirituality. A new image of God inspires new visions of human possibility and behavior. When we discover that God is on our side and that God wants to help us and not hurt us, our lives open to greater energy and creativity. When we realize that our future and the future of our loved ones and associates is open, and that God revels in adventure and delights in our agency, we can let go of unhealthy relational and emotional limitations, and chart new courses for our lives.

In an open and relational system, our lives are intended to be expansive in nature, pushing beyond the impact of past experiences, negative as well as positive, toward new horizons of personal and relational growth. God confronts dysfunctional behaviors and relationships and seeks to eliminate anything that blocks our full humanity in partnership with our Creator and our fellow creatures.

We know that one's age or life stage does not determine spiritual, intellectual, emotional, or relational growth. One of my favorite scriptures describes Jesus' spiritual and relational growth: "Jesus grew in wisdom and stature and favor with God and humankind." (Luke 2:52) Being older doesn't necessarily make us wiser, and a child or teen can lead us to imagine a different way of life. Think of Anne Frank or Greta Thunberg, or the surprising wisdom beyond the years of our own children and grandchildren.

As pastoral caregivers, psychotherapists, and spiritual directors realize, "stature" (Luke 2:52) is more than "years." Despite being at an older age, and whether they are the head of a family or a nation, if they show no significant personal, emotional, or relational growth, then families and nations suffer from their leaders' stifled and cramped emotional lives.

In the Luke passage, Jesus differentiates himself from his parents. He recognizes that he has choices and must take responsibility for his own spiritual growth in the context of responsibilities to his parents. In so doing, Jesus explores new possibilities, and begins charting and claiming his future vocation. Though he doesn't abandon his commitment to his parents and siblings and accepts his role as a carpenter contributing to his family's economic wellbeing, Jesus is growing into a newer, larger self that will embrace and transcend the familial, religious, and social structures of his time. Though his external behavior reflects social norms of his family-focused social structure in which individual self-expression is subordinate to family identity, his inner life is dramatically changing and will eventually draw him away from the carpenter shop to his spiritual vocation and mission to all creation.

In its quest for theological, relational, and psychological stature, open and relational theology affirms the sentiment of process-relational theologian Bernard Loomer:

> By size I mean the stature of a person's soul, the range and depth of his love, his capacity for relationships. I mean the volume of life you can take into your being and still maintain your integrity and individuality, the intensity and variety of outlook you can entertain in the unity of your being without feeling defensive or insecure. I mean the strength of your spirit to encourage others to become freer in the development of their diversity and uniqueness.

The open and relational God wants big-spirited persons, mahatmas, and "fat souls," to use the imagery of theologian Patricia Adams Farmer, who become agents of their personal destinies and positively shape the world around them by identifying their growth with the growth of their communities, nation, and the planet. The open and relational God desires open and relational people and communities.

Wholeness involves expansiveness of spirit, relating to the past, present, and future, as well as one's environment and relationships. The goals of spiritual direction, pastoral care, and psychotherapy, involve, among other things, embracing as much of your life as possible and recognizing the dreams of youth, the roads not taken, choices made and rejected, and tragic realities as well as unexpected successes that have shaped your life. Denial saps us of emotional and relational energy, whether it involves denial of emotional issues, fractured relationships, or a nation's history of injustice. Failure to embrace our failures, grief, trauma, and the impact of our decisions and the decisions of others on our lives constricts our experience and stands in the way of new and adventurous possibilities. We remain prisoners of conscious or unconscious past experiences.

In contrast to the path of denial, which is ultimately a pathway of hopelessness and passivity, the goal of pastoral care, spiritual direction, and psychotherapy from an open and relational perspective is to invite people to listen to their whole lives, to experience in mind, body, and spirit, as much of their personal history as possible and lift into consciousness undiscovered aspects of their lives, as the prelude to letting their lives speak in creative relationships and activities. In the embracing of our whole lives, we grow in wisdom and stature and become self-aware, mindful people who are agents of our own destiny. In embracing the fullness of our lives, we encounter a loving God moving within our lives, calling us to deeper encounters with the holy in our finite, flesh and blood experiences and relationships.

The Hebraic patriarch Jacob dreams of a ladder of angels joining earth and heaven, body and spirit, and unconscious and conscious, and awakens to realize that the ladder is the gateway to God, and that divine messengers are found in his conflict-ridden life. "God was in this place"—my life and relationships—"and I did not know it," stammers Jacob. Growth in stature involves wrestling with dazzling darkness of divinity and our deepest selves, as Jacob later discovers in his nocturnal encounter at the stream of Jabbok. (Genesis 28:10-19 and 32:22-32)

The graceful open relationality, necessary for the synergetic growth of the pastoral caregiver/psychotherapist/spiritual director and their client/congregant/spiritual directee is captured in the words of Frederick Buechner.

Listen to your life. See it for the fathomless mystery it is. In the boredom and pain of it, no less than in the excitement and gladness: touch, taste, smell your way to the holy and hidden heart of it, because in the last analysis all moments are key moments, and life itself is grace.

Open and relational theology undergirds growth-oriented counseling, pastoral care, and psychotherapy. When we grow, we join in spirit and agency with an open-spirited God who wants us to grow and God grows along with us, a healing companion who aims at wholeness and beauty, and who invites us to go from cramped self-interest to cosmopolitan openness to our own lives and the moral and spiritual arcs that flow through us. The future is open, and God wants us in our journeys of wholeness to choose our own adventures. An open and relational God says to care giver and client alike, "Surprise me! Create something that I haven't fully imagined! Bring forth a new creation, first in your wondrous self-discovery and then in your dynamic agency! Help me fashion a healing and healthy future for yourself and others!"

In listening to our lives, we find the courage and direction to let our lives speak and discover untapped resources for healing and agency. This may mean leaving an abusive relationship, exploring new professional possibilities, or protesting injustice in your community. In the words of Frederick Buechner, we find our voice and vocation, "the place God calls you to is the place where your deep gladness and the world's deep hunger meet."

In over forty years of pastoral care and spiritual direction as well as academic and professional mentoring, I have been guided by the spirit of process and open and relational theologies. My image of God has inspired my practice of pastoral care and mentoring. When I meet with someone seeking to live more deeply, passionately, and abundantly, someone in search of their vocation or struggling to find healing, I am guided by the following theological affirmations:

- God aims at abundant life, even if this means making significant changes in our personal life and relationships.

- God leaves our future open, does not demand a particular outcome.

- God welcomes creative transformation and personal agency.

- God is more interested in growth and process than a predetermined outcome. Accordingly, there are many positive outcomes we can pursue in our personal and relational growth, and what we perceive as failure may open to new possibilities for adventure and creativity.

- God rejoices in our agency, even if it means abandoning past limitations and relational patterns, to embrace our current vocation.

- God's uncontrolling love accepts us as we are and lures us toward new dimensions of ourselves.

- God's love undergirds us regardless of our success or failure in realizing our personal, relational, or vocational goals.

- God is present, inspiring pastoral caregiver and client alike. As a caregiver, I am part of the process and am invited to grow in compassion and creativity in the context of putting my client's/congregant's/spiritual directee's needs first in our pastoral care relationship.

A God of sufficient stature, leaning toward an open future, can embrace diversity, contrast, change, and conflict, in ways that inspire the quest for stature and wholeness in caregiver and client alike. This is the healing gift of open and relational theology for the interdependent practices of pastoral care, spiritual direction, and psychotherapy.

Bruce Epperly has served as a university chaplain, seminary professor and administrator, and congregational pastor for over forty years. Ordained in the United Church of Christ and Christian Church (Disciples of Christ), he is the author of over seventy books, including Process Theology and Pastoral Care, Process and Ministry, The Elephant is Running: Process and Open and Relational Theologies and Religious Pluralism, *and* Prophetic Healing: Howard Thurman's Vision of Contemplative Activism.

32

KILLING GOD, FINDING GOD

BRAD D. STRAWN

Those who believe in a controlling God will have a harder time coping with tragedy, as it makes it difficult for them to bring their anger to God.

After a period of complaining angrily and deeply grieving, my patient said to me, "Maybe God is not who I thought [he] was." My patient had finally *killed* God and now was in the position to begin to *know* God in new and different ways.

D. W. Winnicott, the British pediatrician-turned-psychoanalyst, was an important figure in contemporary psychodynamic psychotherapy. Winnicott believed that children initially come into the world utterly dependent on their caregivers and in some ways undifferentiated from them. For the infant, there is no "mommy and me" there is just "me." If the infant has a vague discomfort (e.g., hunger) she becomes upset and *presto* something arrives (e.g., food) to ease the pain. From the infant's perspective it feels like they were responsible. If the infant could speak, she might say, "Look what I created!"

Winnicott described this first stage in an infant's life as a period of *omnipotence* in which the child experiences the world as pure projection. "Look, I created this!" Over time through a normative series of non-traumatic disillusionments the child learns to give up her omnipotence and by doing so comes to recognize the real and objective other (e.g., mommy).

Over time, children learn that they don't entirely *create* the world; they also *discover* the world. But this is not an easy transition and Winnicott warns us that it usually involves much protest on the part of the infant—what he calls "destruction." The child "destroys" the parent (in fantasy) through aggression (complaining, protesting, saying "no," etc.) and if the parent survives (i.e., does not retaliate or abandon the child) the child learns that they are not omnipotent, cannot control others and will begin to experience the parent as a real other, not simply a product of their projections.

However, if a parent is not able to withstand these "destructions" (e.g., crying, tantrums, saying "no," etc.) without retaliation or abandonment, the child learns that her feelings are not allowed and are overwhelming to the parent. This last point is important because if a child feels that her feelings are overwhelming to the parent she may stay locked into an overvaluation of her impact on the world. In Winnicott's language the child stays locked in a world of their own projections. They have a terrible and overwhelming sense that they can control others and that they themselves are dangerous.

The Old Testament theologian and scholar, Walter Brueggemann, actually uses the work of Winnicott in his article, "The Costly Loss of Lament." In that paper Brueggemann argues that if we can't raise our voice in protest to God, we create false selves (another Winnicott term) that can only sing praises to God. And we also create a false God that can only hear praise. God is a controlling dictator, possibly narcissistic, who doesn't change and doesn't want to hear from us. Lucky for us, Brueggemann points out that there are numerous examples in scripture in which the Israelites cry out to God, protest to the Holy One, and even demand that God give an account. These go back as far as the Israelites' groans under the slavery of Egypt and include the numerous psalms that are categorized as laments. When persons are able to engage in this kind of address toward God it is a reestablishment of the covenantal relationship in which *both* parties have a voice. Both parties are free, if you will, and cannot be controlled by the other. Humans can speak, God will hear, and both parties can respond.

But if there is no lament, there is no voice, and we end up with this false self of compliance and a false God tyrant who must be responsible for our pain. Not only does this mean that humans live by means of "coercive obedience" but that questions of theodicy must not be voiced. If God can't take our complaint (i.e., our aggression) then how do we go to the throne demanding that something needs to change?

I want to suggest that there is a corollary here for some Christians when they go through a period of pain, trauma or heartache in their lives and subsequently can't square their experience with their understanding of God. Some individuals give up God altogether, because they can't reconcile their previous idea of God (what psychologists commonly call God *representation*) with what they have gone through. Others cling to their original image of God and reframe their understanding of their pain. They may say things like, "God is using this to teach me something," "I have brought this on myself", or "If I just have more faith and patience surely God will deliver me." These individuals can't be angry with God—they can't destroy or kill God and subsequently they stay locked in a world of their own projections. They stay stuck in the image of God that they have created (with the help of parents, faith tradition, etc.) unable to see their way clear to a new, possibly more accurate image of God. They develop a false self (i.e., one that can only praise) in relationship with a false God (controlling).

But some lucky believers may find a community (or therapy) that can come alongside them and support their grief and even anger at God (destruction). If these individuals are assisted in finding and giving voice to their pain and sorrow they may be able to go through a similar process to the young infant described above. They need permission to angrily complain to God, to call God to give an account, to "kill God" and see if God can survive. Of course what these individuals are killing is their projection of God. They are destroying the image of a controlling God that they have created from the fragments of their history. On the other side of this process, they just may find the more open God of uncontrolling love.

My client arrived at the conclusion that perhaps God was not who she had always thought God was *only after* a period in which we created space for her to destroy or kill God... with her complaints, groans, and protests. And believe me, she had lots of legitimate reasons to be angry! When God didn't strike her dead, or abandon her, and when I didn't leave or shame her (beliefs she had internalized from her faith community and her interactions with parents), there was space for her to begin to "find" God in new and different ways. Maybe God had not rescued her from a life of trauma, maybe God had not delivered her from the consequences of that evil, but maybe—just maybe—God was still at work. Perhaps she could get to know this new, more open, uncontrolling God without throwing him away, living with a false self, or living with a false God.

Brad D. Strawn *is the Evelyn and Frank Freed Chief of Spiritual Formation and Integration, Dean of the Chapel and Chair of the Integration of Psychology & Theology at Fuller Seminary. He is co-author of Enhancing Christian Life: How Extended Cognition Augments Religious Community and other books. He has a private practice and is an ordained elder and part-time pastor in the Church of the Nazarene (https://www.fuller.edu/faculty/brad-d-strawn/).*

– 33 –

GOD'S THERAPEUTIC APPROACH

JENIFER R. BUTLER

When things do not go in a positive direction, and they will,
God's love will find us.

The book of Isaiah 55: 8-9 notes that God's ways are not our ways, nor are God's thoughts our thoughts. In this way, God's love is oxymoronic. While God has the power to control God chooses to give freedom and individual autonomy. The control God uses is to not be controlling. God's love is therapeutic. God urges, rather than forces. God's love guides, rather than controls.

A controlling person is fearful that if they do not control a person or a circumstance, something will go array. But God does not control in this way. God has made provision, even before the foundation of the world. Therefore, when things do not go in a positive direction, and they will, God's love will find us. God created humankind with original goodness while fully understanding the consequences of original sin. Yet, God declares that humankind is good, in fact, "very good." God's uncontrolled love meets us where we are. This does not excuse the evil of the world. But reveals the nature of God.

God could exert control over an individual's rights, autonomy, and free will, but that would be a form of abuse. According to the National Domestic Violence Hotline, abuse is a behavior that a person, or deity in this case, uses to maintain power over another individual. God does not need to be controlling because God has ultimate power and as Paul writes in the book of Romans, brings all things together for our human good.

Further, the scientific definition of "control" notes that the control group or individual must be in competition with an opposing force, an individual variable, amid extraneous variables. While there are negative forces present, there are positive forces that appear in the form of unconditional positive regard.

The hymnologist Thomas Obadiah Chisholm writes, "In times of distress, my soul has often found relief, Great is Thy faithfulness, Lord, unto me." What joy fills the soul, with the understanding that God's love finds us in distress tolerance. The United States Chaplain Dr. Barry Black in his book The Blessing in Adversity writes, "after gaining perspective on your troubles, meet the challenges of dark days by relinquishing control." God's love is made known, in the quiet stillness and God does not have to control us nor opposing forces. God's love comforts the brokenhearted.

One of the first things I learned in the therapeutic room was that God was the God of my understanding! Yes, God was still the God of my ancestors, still a God that leans towards justice, love, and hope. God practices love, through a person-centered approach. God gives trauma-informed care to those who recognize the world is dialectical in nature, a combination of good and evil. In this person-centered, an individualistic God could understand my personal groanings. Through the form of love, God would make sense of trauma. Victory occurs when God reveals God's self as an uncontrolling lover the soul.

God's love always reaches towards compassion. The word compassion, in its root form means to suffer with. God may not remove the obstacle, but God finds the oppressed. Clients who have experienced trauma, seek to understand the why? While that question may never be answered, the role of the therapist is to help the client understand what they can do and how they can do it.

1 John 4:8 notes that God is love, while the apostle Paul posits in 1 Corinthians 13:4-8a that "Love is patient and kind; love does not envy or boost, it is not arrogant or rude. It does not insist on its own way, it is not irritable or resentful; it does not rejoice at wrongdoing but rejoices with the truth." The truth is "love does conquer all." God's love reaches to the highest mountain and flows to the deepest valley. While in opposition, God's love meets people where they are in their own language of understanding. Though the seasons of life may change, God's love remains constant, uncontrolled by the actions of other influences. God's love is uncontrolled by the law of human man, it is controlled by the notion that all may come to know the God of their understanding, through this evidence of uncontrolled love.

So why then, does God not intervene when tragedy strikes? When contemplating this notion, I think of Job. An individual who was morally righteous.

Yet, Job found himself grieving the death of his children, his possessions, and his health. However, amid his devastating losses, Job demonstrates distress tolerance. Job did not renounce his belief in God, nor accuse God of being an uncaring by-stander. Job simply notes that even during tragedy, God was still good. Job was not restored to his original position. His children could not have been replaced. Job was given a better gift, the reasoning that although terrible things happen to good people, God can be trusted to show love, by being present amid afflictions.

While God and people have individual agency. God's agency is demonstrated by love, people's agency can be demonstrated through other means. Nonetheless, God's love makes provision. Prevenient love finds the dark places of our lives and calls the individual to seek peace. Considering all the extraneous factors that might affect the results; God loves speaking. While in the Lion's den Daniel, experienced God. While in the fiery furnace, the three Hebrews boys saw God in the fire with them. While imprisoned, Paul declared God's love. While being crucified, Jesus called on God.

Cognitive Behavioral Therapy vs. Dialectical Behavioral Therapy

Two common therapies frequently used are Cognitive Behavior Therapy (CBT) and Dialectical Behavior Therapy (DBT). These two treatment modalities do not seek to erase the presence of trauma but seek to change the individual's viewpoint of the trauma through various skillsets.

Cognitive Behavior Therapy (CBT) is a therapeutic modality that explores how thoughts influence behavior and seeks to reframe negative cognitive distortions in a positive manner. The theory is centralized in the notion that human nature contains the capacity to control their thoughts, feelings, and regulate their actions. With individuality and autonomy, at its core, CBT seeks to explore thoughts and feelings as separate from personhood. The role of the therapist is to actively listen for faulty assumptions and help the client reframe their initial thoughts and feelings in any given situation.

Dialectical Behavioral Therapy (DBT) is another form of cognitive behavioral therapy which seeks to assist the client in not only identifying faulty assumptions, but also learning to tolerate distress and demonstrate emotional regulation with mindfulness. The word dialectic is defined as the synthesis of opposing forces. The universe is filled with opposing forces. Atoms contain both positive and negative particles. Likewise, good and evil can coexist given proper perspective. The role of the therapist is to help the client to recognize the activating event, and exert control of their personhood, rather than the event.

From An African American Perspective

In African American faith-based communities, the phrase "God is in control" is often used to bring a sense of comfort. The world is filled with systematic justices that are immoral and oppressive. "God is in control" is an idiom which expresses the person's need for God to show power through love. God has power, simply put to show the way, rather than control the event! In the by and by, God's love prevails. This does not remove other powers. It does not affect the power to make one's own decisions, nor the power of immorality. Rather, God's control is rooted in the notion that whatever the challenge, circumstance or dilemma God has the power to demonstrate unconditional providence. The phrase "God is in control" does not excuse the recognition that there are other forces at work in the universe. God's love simply specializes in the care of the individual.

Jenifer R. Butler is a Licensed Graduate Professional Counselor in the State of Maryland. She earned a Master of Arts Degree in Counseling Psychology from Bowie State University and Master of Arts Degree in Ministry and Leadership from Lancaster Theological Seminary in Lancaster, Pennsylvania. Jenifer is seeking ordination as a Deacon in the United Methodist Church. She is married and has four children.

34

UNCONTROLLING LOVE, FREE WILL, AND RESPONSIBILITY

NOEL COOPER

God created us with free will, which comes with responsibility.
Therapists can help people face the anxiety of that and take
responsibility for their lives.

*T*he necessary corollary to God's uncontrolling love is human free will. God's creative plan for us necessitates that we are free to act, to choose our path and create our world. A sometimes-overlooked aspect of free will is the importance of individual responsibility. If God does not force us or compel us to go in a particular way, then we must then decide for ourselves which path to take. To freely choose is a freedom that comes with its own weight. To have the responsibility for one's decisions also means accepting the consequences of those decisions, a heavy burden indeed, and one that can inspire a great deal of anxiety in the face of life's big choices. Every choice involves uncertainty because the future is unknown and unpredictable, but humans have a strong preference for certainty and become distressed when it is not available to them.

Existential and Gestalt psychologists have made human responsibility central to their theories. They encourage clients to take responsibility for their actions and choices and embrace the uncertainty of life. Existential therapy particularly emphasizes confronting the anxiety entailed in responsibility. Humans try to avoid, deny, or deflect their anxiety, but this evasion only exacerbates the anxiety and prevents people from living whole and authentic lives.

Sometimes clients are truly unable to see that they have a choice, or they have any agency or free will in a situation. They feel swept along by forces outside of their control. And it is important to acknowledge that there are plenty of circumstances in life that are outside of our control. Structural racism, economic inequality, disparities of all kinds—these are all outside the control of any one person. And many tragedies and hardships, that we are not responsible for, come to us. But in the face of all these situations, we always have a choice in how we respond, both internally and externally.

Christians are sometimes eager to relinquish some of this responsibility of free will to God: "If it's God's will, God will make it happen. God is in control, so I'll just wait on God and see what happens." While their faith is genuine, their abdication of responsibility for deciding and choosing a course of action allows them to avoid the anxiety that is entailed. God then becomes a kind of scapegoat for things not working— "I guess it just wasn't God's will." This kind of thinking is not consistent with the theology of a God who is self-limited by love.

Moreover, most people do not implement this kind of thinking where God is given full control consistently. They are perfectly happy to make smaller, less anxiety-provoking, decisions on their own, e.g., what to wear, what to eat, which show to binge watch next. These decisions have fairly minor consequences, so individuals feel competent to exercise independence and free will. But when faced with more important decisions, like what career to pursue, who to marry, or whether or not to make a particular life change, God becomes their fallback. Anxiety for the unknown can make them hesitant to act in their God-given free will.

Therapy clients might try to avoid their responsibility by sharing it out with the therapist: "What do you think I should do? Can you give me any advice?" And if not from their therapist, they are often asking others in their life for the same advice, as if getting input from others lessens their own sense of responsibility and subsequent guilt if things don't go right. An overly submissive stance to authority also allows clients to bypass accountability— "I was just doing what I was told." All of these attempts to evade anxiety only worsen the problem.

The role of the therapist then is two-fold: to help clients see their options where they feel like they have none, and to help clients face the anxiety of making a choice that is wholly their own responsibility. In the first part, the therapist helps the client imagine different possibilities for themselves than the ones they thought to be constrained by. There is a creativity required to help expand their way of seeing the world and their way of seeing themselves. The therapist's questions seek to draw aside the veil that has been obscuring their vision: "Does it have to be that way? Is there another choice you could make in that situation? What might you be able to do differently?" Clients are often surprised to find that there are more possibilities than they thought when they really stop to look. For some clients it is a relief to be able to make their way out of where they were stuck. But often there is an anxiety and dread that may accompany that relief, because now it is indeed their own choices that will direct their path. There is a felt safety in being carried along by outside forces, even if they are unpleasant.

And thus comes the second role of the therapist, to help clients face the existential dread and anxiety that are the natural consequences of free will. First, we help clients name and identify what they are feeling. They might not recognize that they are procrastinating a decision, continually seeking advice, or just generally avoiding change because of anxiety due to the responsibility of free will and the uncertainty of the future. Once they can recognize that, we can normalize it for them. This existential anxiety is part of the human condition. This was recognized by the existential philosophers—to be human is to be free, and this freedom is anxiety-inducing because we cannot know with certainty the outcome of our choices.

Nothing will completely remove this anxiety. But we can come to accept it, embrace it, and stand firm despite it. When we stop avoiding anxiety, it loses some of its power over us. We can face the unknown and dare to move forward anyway, living courageously. God created us to be free and to exercise free will, so when we do so we are living in the fullness of God's creative intentions. Therapists will stand together with their clients at the edge of the abyss of the unknown and let them know that it is okay to not know, because no one can know, but they can still make a decision. Therapists will be with their client in a stance of empathy, acceptance, and unconditional positive regard. These "core conditions" of therapy mirror the love God has for us, that therapists can reflect to their clients.

And it is ultimately in the love of God that the courage to face the anxiety is rooted. We are not alone. God will not control us, compel us, or coerce us, God may not even give us a definitive answer about which direction to take. But God will always be with us, and the love of God is unconditional. "The steadfast love of the Lord never ceases, and his mercies never come to an end." Regardless of the consequences of our decisions, God's love for us will not change. In the midst of so much that is uncertain and unknown, God's faithfulness remains. No matter what existential dread comes our way, we can count on God's faithful presence in the midst of anxiety.

Noel Cooper *is a professor, therapist, and clinical supervisor in Riverside, CA. She earned her Psy.D. in clinical psychology and her M.A. in theology at Fuller Theological Seminary. Noel is passionate about helping clients understand themselves better. She is married with three children.*

35

WORKING WITH GOD

ANNIE L. DEROLF

*A theology of occupation could be God's (uncontrolling)
love language.*

*D*uring the first World War, *shell shock* (or *post-traumatic stress*) impacted soldiers' abilities to think, talk, and move functionally, which greatly limited their participation in daily life. For human creatures, the cost of such a limitation is as devastating as it is harmful. Herbert Hall, a physician during the late 18th and early 19th centuries and one of the founders of occupational therapy, believed that "idleness too long continued is as deadening to the spirit as it is disabling to the body…it too often means degeneration, and in the end, increased suffering." It stands to reason that viewing God as idle and self-limiting in the face of tragedy can be just as deadening to the spirit, and it can certainly lead to increased suffering.

In 1917, the United States Department of War relied on *reconstruction aides,* or civilian women serving in military hospitals, to help *reconstruct* the lives of disabled soldiers. These aides—working alongside nurses and working against militant sexism—uniquely taught soldiers creative and vocational skills, "energizing their mind and will to influence the state of their own health" (to quote the words of the influential Mary Reilly).

These "unconventional" treatments provided by reconstruction aides during World War I—arts, crafts, and other functional activities like using tools or making one's bed—were used to redirect the mind, increase physical activity, and improve motivation. These principles were among the first seeds planted in the field of *occupational therapy*: a unique and holistic profession which meaningfully and therapeutically uses *occupations* (the life activities we all do to *occupy* our time) to influence the state of one's health and wellbeing. Ultimately, what was reaped from this field was life itself, and what was true then is true now: there is something curiously sacred about *doing*. When people have autonomy, choice, and consistent access to doing the things they find personally meaningful and/ or necessary, they flourish. Thinking of Saint Paul the Apostle, perhaps we must "work out [our] own [life] with fear and trembling; for it is God who is at work in you enabling you both to will and work for God's good pleasure" (Phil. 2:12-13). Using the most common understanding of *occupation* to my advantage, humans being occupational in nature may be spiritually akin to being employed to work with God.

During the 20th century, physicians caught on to occupational therapy's unique value in mental and physical rehabilitation, and in 1921 prominent psychiatrist Adolf Meyer articulated its first philosophy. Rather than diagnosing an illness and following a given treatment plan (medications, institutionalization, or even a 'rest-cure'), Meyer argued for an understanding of "illness" as a "problem of adaptation" and "work" as a "sovereign help." In his own words:

> A pleasure in achievement, a real pleasure in the use and activity of one's hands and muscles and a happy appreciation of time began to be used as incentives in the management of our patients, instead of abstract exhortations to cheer up and to behave according to abstract or repressive rules.

In other words, it was neither platitudes nor repressive rules that brought about healing and flourishing. It was the *work*, the *doing*, the *adapting*, the "use and activity of one's hands and muscles and a happy appreciation of time," that brought about change. Living out our purpose gives us a productive means to work out the tension between God's agency and our own. By participating in everyday life we generate our own power to participate with God.

We now understand that humans are ready-made to be occupational. We are primed for doing and possess an innate drive to shape, influence, and adapt to our personal contexts. Thomas Jay Oord expressed in *God Can't* that "God's loving nature determines, shapes, or governs what God can do." Similarly, our occupational nature shapes what we do and provides us with a sense of self-regulation, life purpose, and identity. Conspiring with God's own nature, we are empowered to enact our personal responsibility and social accountability. We can think of ourselves as *working with* God.

For both Meyer and a God of uncontrolling love, time plays an important role. It surrounds us, and as long as we are alive it will continue to present us with opportunities to use it. The awareness of this truth is what Meyer deemed "a religious conscience of time" which allows us to "find a world of ever new opportunity and achievement in healthy harmony with human nature." Human creatures actualize themselves through the things they do; in Meyer's words, "it is the use that we make of ourselves that gives the ultimate stamp to our every organ."

Can God be actualized through these same means? "In the beginning when God created the heavens and the earth, the earth was a formless void" (Gen 1:1-2), and through this opportunity God *created, spoke, "finished the work"* (Gen 2:2), and *rested*. In Meyer's words but in God's image, human creatures organize time in terms of doing: work, play, rest, sleep, and other activities such as prayer or worship. Through these seemingly mundane, everyday tasks, we participate in and influence the world, relating to both ourselves and others.

Our ability as human creatures to *do* and *respond* is the "sovereign help" of which we have been waiting but instead projected onto the version of God who is in complete control. Indeed, there are things that an uncontrolling God of love *cannot* do, but as occupational creatures we are able to *work with* God, and in so doing we are able to *love* God.

In *God Can't*, Oord states that "to love is to act intentionally, in response to God and others, to promote overall well-being." Just as the reconstruction aides of World War I helped to reconstruct the lives of injured soldiers, we, too, can reconstruct our lives and the world around us in our response to God. Perhaps you cooperatively (not coercively or codependently) work with the newcomer at the same Alcoholics Anonymous meeting who asked if you'd be their sponsor; maybe you provide a child with rich opportunities for *play*, or you practice the use of your client's neo-pronouns before your session... Such examples reflect everyday actions that can be viewed as intentional, loving responses to an uncontrolling God: one who, in their own image, encourages us to provide others with opportunities to occupy the sacred space of their lives. After all, "the gospel and salvation of the day" is that the fountain of time sustains us in living our faith, living with purpose, and reconstructing the world around us.

Annie DeRolf, OTD, OTR is an occupational therapist with expertise in LGBTQIA+ affirming care and currently working as a Clinical Assistant Professor and Doctoral Capstone Coordinator in the Department of Occupational Therapy at Indiana University in Indianapolis. She is a current MA in Religion and Theology student exploring the intersections of theology, philosophy, and occupational therapy.

36

NON-POSSESSIVE DELIGHT

KENNETH E. KOVACS

*Love is the non-possessive delight in the particularity
of the other.*

"*L*ove is the non-possessive delight in the particularity of the other." This is how James E. Loder (1931-2001) characterized the nature, movement, and purpose of love. This definition is one of the best I know.

Loder's life was shaped by two life-changing religious experiences where he encountered the transforming love of God. He went on to develop a way to talk about the life of faith as the intimate relationality of the human spirit and the Holy Spirit. As a professor of practical theology at Princeton Theological Seminary for decades, Loder, who had a background in theology and psychology, wrote much about what it means to be human and fully alive.

A gifted counselor, Loder often made time for students, including me. Looking back on our weekly sessions, I am unsure how to describe them. They were a combination of deep listening, psychotherapy, serious dream work, and spiritual direction. Jim embodied his definition of love and invited me to step boldly into my life.

Thirty years later, in addition to being a parish minister, I am also a Jungian analyst-in-training. In my work, both as a pastor and now working with clients, I often return to Loder's definition of love. His vision informs how I relate to both parishioners and clients. I believe Jim's understanding of love has much to offer those who struggle with the meaning and nature of the Christian life.

What does it mean to say that love is *non-possessive*?

Loder believes this is describing the unique stance of the one who loves another. There is no desire to possess or "own" the other, whomever the other might be. Loving this way means never seeking to control, manage, or deny the otherness of the other. "Where love reigns," C.G. Jung (1875-1961) wisely said, "there is no will to power; and where the will to power is paramount love is lacking."

Love has nothing to do with coercive power. Instead, love empowers the other to be other. One sees the other as *other* and does not try to pull the other into one's orbit or "use" the other for self-interest. It is a love that consciously and intentionally strives to preserve the otherness of the other because the other is not an extension of one's ego, selfish desires, fears, or anxieties.

When power games are set aside, love takes delight and joy in the full *particularity* of the other. Love rejoices in the uniqueness of the one who stands before you in all their glory and goodness, beauty, oddness, pain, brokenness, and fears—all that makes them who they are, the totality of their being, their past, present, all that you know and all that you don't know about the other.

Delight paves the way for radical acceptance. Delighting in one's particularity requires genuinely *seeing* the other. It requires *attention*. And love requires *intention*, which means we must bring something of ourselves into the exchange. You bring yourself fully to the moment, to the person before you, and you strive to really see the other. Poet Kathleen Raine (1908-2003) once said, "Unless you see a thing in the light of love, you do not see a thing at all." There's so much truth contained in that statement.

Love is the light that illuminates the darkness. It is what allows us to see. Without love, our vision is distorted. We might think we see or know someone, but unless our gaze is mediated through love, then s/he remains invisible to us. Without intentional love, we only see what we project onto people, what we fantasize them to be, and what we want them to be. Or we project our fears, even our hate, upon them and prevent them from being who they are authentically. Through love, an individual comes into focus and becomes visible before our eyes—and this kind of love, directed toward God, brings God into focus, as it were, shaping one's image of God.

A radical shift occurred in my heart when it struck me that Loder's definition of love can also inform how I imagine God's love for me. What if God relates to me with a non-possessive delight in my particularity? While God's love is a "love that will not let me go," as the old hymn says, it is a love that holds me loosely, non-possessively, a love that grants me freedom to be *other* before God, free to be who I am in all my particularity. Such a love liberates me and invites me to discover who I am, taking delight in how I grow and mature. This love creates a space for me to develop and thrive but also fail, again and again, still in the wide embrace of God's presence. This kind of love empowers and enables me to enter my life, embrace my full humanity and become more authentically human more fully. Irenaeus (b. 130) was correct: "The glory of God is the human being [or becoming] fully alive."

The Christian life is inherently relational, sustained, and empowered by a love that fosters human growth and transformation that summons one to life. The therapeutic dimensions of such a perspective are considerable. I have found that such a view is almost always received with amazement and disbelief—"You mean I am free to be myself?"—followed by extraordinary gratitude. Sadly, too many Christians and non-Christians believe that to be a person of faith, one must become someone other than the person one knows oneself to be.

Instead, God's love moves in a still more excellent way (1 Cor. 12:31). "The grace of God," Walter Brueggemann said, "is that the creature whom [God] has caused to be, [God] now lets be." God creates by "letting-be." And in "letting be," we are free to make, form, and create in our own way. We are free to grow, flourish, and bear fruit. In "letting-be," God forms and then lets us go in order for the creation to fulfill its purpose, to evolve and change, blossom and grow, yield and bear fruit—as well as make terrible, tragic mistakes. Without controlling or micromanaging us, God gives us space to grow. God risks freedom and trusts us to grow, watching and patiently waiting for the unfolding of our lives.

As a therapist, I strive to work with all this in mind. The therapeutic relationship creates a "container" or space for something new to emerge in the client's life. I'm concerned less with the presenting pathology (although I listen for it) than I am with what is trying to come to life in an individual.

In love, I endeavor to create a non-possessive, non-controlling "frame" or space and work hard not to fill it with my projections. Instead, I "hold" the space and then step back, as it were. I consciously invite the client to step in, to show up, and, by grace, step more fully into their own life in all its particularity. With radical respect for them, I trust the process and wait for something new to unfold.

I believe God does not wish to be God without us. I've come to believe that God has radical respect for us and values us, and therefore God wants us to grow into our humanity, step into our lives, listen to our hearts, and participate more fully in the world as individuals. And I have come to believe that one way God gets us to grow is by intentionally stepping back and inviting us to step in. This is a notion found in Jewish mysticism, in the Kabbalah, and I have come to see its value, wisdom, and truth. It's known as *zimzum*, meaning "contraction." It's most associated with Rabbi Isaac Luria (1534-1572), who said God created the universe by "contracting" or "withdrawing" a part of God's self to create a space, a void, to make room for the creation of the world. Creation, humanity, truth, reality, and freedom emerge when, in love, God withdraws, contracts, and pulls back, inviting something new to emerge within that space. I have a hunch that God continues to create this way.

God's desire to be in relationship with humanity entails contraction and stepping back, and in the vacated space something new is invited to step, to come into being, something other than Godself, in whom God takes great delight. Remarkably, God doesn't seek to control creation but trusts the goodness of creation and frees it to evolve and emerge. God gives creation—*gives us*—the freedom to be, to flourish, yes, to fail, but ultimately to grow. All of it is given in love.

Kenneth E. Kovacs, Ph.D., *is pastor of the Catonsville Presbyterian Church, Catonsville, MD, and an analyst-in-training at the C.G. Jung Institute-Küsnacht, Switzerland. A graduate of Rutgers University and Princeton Theological Seminary, he received his doctorate in practical theology from the University of St. Andrews, St. Andrews, Scotland. Ken is the author of* The Relational Theology of James E. Loder: Encounter and Conviction *(New York/Bern: Peter Lang, 2009) and* Out of the Depths: Sermons and Essays *(Parson's Porch Press, 2016).*

37

WHY CONTROL FEELS SAFER THAN LOVE

MOLLY LACROIX

Parts of us that fear adversity take control of our internal family, pushing love aside.

$\mathcal{J}$ esus offers hurting people companionship, wisdom, and relief. "Come to me, all you who are weary and burdened, and I will give you rest. Take my yoke upon you and learn from me, for I am gentle and humble in heart, and you will find rest for your souls" (Matthew 11:28-29, NIV). In the presence of Love, troubled souls find peace and gain strength for their healing journey.

This offer is clear and compelling, yet—in response to suffering—people often turn instead to "God won't give you more than you can handle." The verse that underlies this twisted interpretation refers to temptation and reassures us God provides a way out of it (1 Corinthians 10:13).

How do you feel when you read the passage from Matthew compared to the statement, "God won't give you more than you can handle"? Do you notice the protective energy in the latter, as though the person saying it wants to distance themselves from your struggle?

When we are struggling, we feel vulnerable. We have an exposed wound that is tender and easily reinjured. We need compassion but instead we are often met with the message that God is in control of the situation. God's control is not offered as comfort but as a way to distance from—or minimize—distress.

Why is this such a common reaction to challenges? Because humans are vulnerable *and* afraid of vulnerability. Fear of vulnerability is a driving force that shapes our response to adversity.

Everyone experiences adversity. Sometimes, adverse experiences are traumatic. Whether or not your story contains trauma, you have experienced adversity.

The most common adverse experience is universal: You did not have primary caregivers who were always perfectly attuned to your needs. Sometimes you were tired, hungry, or sad, and the people responsible for your care did not meet your needs.

And no matter how hard you tried to please parents, teachers, or coaches, you sometimes failed and were shamed. Other adverse experiences—loss, racism, financial insecurity, moving frequently, and bullying—leave burdens of painful emotions and distorted negative beliefs.

Until we heal those wounds, they pose a risk to our well-being. Distressing emotions such as shame, grief, terror, and panic can resurface. The conviction that we are unlovable, abandoned, or not good enough can feel utterly true. We hold these burdens in our bodies as tension, anxiety, chronic illness, and pain.

How do we get through life with all of this going on? And how does our vulnerability impact our view of God?

Answers lie in a new way of understanding ourselves. As with every aspect of creation, from the Triune God to atoms to ecosystems, humans are best understood as a system. An innovative psychotherapy model provides insight into the human system.

Richard Schwartz, the developer of the Internal Family Systems (IFS) model, was not satisfied with patients' progress. Setting aside what theories told him to expect, he listened with open curiosity. He noticed people referring to "parts" of themselves, and he was surprised to discover familiar family dynamics occurring between these parts in clients' *internal* family systems.

Ideally, our internal family system functions harmoniously under the leadership of the "Self." From a Christian perspective, the Self bears God's image and is endowed with resources to support optimal functioning. A variety of inner family members contribute valuable qualities. Ideally, the Self leads the system—in harmony with the Spirit—with each member contributing their unique talents and abilities.

Unfortunately, adverse experiences throw off the harmonious balance of the system. Parts of the system become burdened with distressing emotions, beliefs, sensations, and images. This material threatens our well-being because we don't function very well when we are overwhelmed by it.

To adapt to this threat, some internal family members respond by exiling the vulnerable, burdened parts—called *exiles*. Think of exiles as family members locked in the basement of the family home. Their jailers are a team of *protectors*—inner family members forced by adversity into protective roles.

Protectors help us get through life but also block or constrain our God-given resources. They take over the leadership of the internal family, *opting for control over love*. Let's look at typical examples to see how adversity shapes the internal family.

Brian grew up in a home that appeared to offer all a child needs to thrive. In his mid-20s, he was confused by a lack of motivation and how often he felt "dead" inside. When Brian focused on one of his primary protective strategies—procrastination for fear of failing—the sensation and emotion he felt pulled him back to the many times his dad dismissed his offer to help with projects. Those memories contained grief, shame, and the belief he was not good enough to merit dad's time and attention. When Brian tried new things, these painful memories surfaced, and his protectors jumped in to numb the pain or talk him out of trying something new.

A successful professional married with three children, Amy reached a point where the many ways she had attempted to contain childhood trauma failed, and she was overwhelmed with panic and grief. She had relied heavily on a team of protectors, including an analyst who thought she could rationalize away the impact of trauma and a minimizer who dismissed or denied painful memories. These dedicated protectors attempted to control two exiles: a four-year-old molested by her dad and a ten-year-old who tried—but failed—to take care of all the household tasks so mom wouldn't rage at her.

Veronica couldn't stand her mother's affection. Part of her made sure she kept her distance, physically and emotionally. Throughout childhood, Mom was intrusive. She hovered over her, telling her how beautiful she was and sharing her deepest fear—that someone would kidnap her. Mom got angry if she was too playful or loud or was ever "unkind" to someone. Part of Veronica was enraged by how Mom tried to control her. Keeping her distance kept the rage from taking over. Underneath protective layers, Veronica's exiles felt their needs didn't matter, and they weren't safe.

In each of these cases—as is true for all of us—distressing beliefs and emotions held by exiles threatened the internal system—prompting protectors to attempt to control or contain the pain.

Some protectors proactively avoid situations that trigger pain. They use strategies such as distance, denial, minimizing, perfectionism, criticism, and blame.

However, pain inevitably surfaces, so other protectors reactively use distractions or numbing to soothe or contain it. Protectors are all well-intentioned, and they believe their strategy is vital for maintaining safety.

But when either proactive or reactive protectors dominate our internal family, the Self—the leader who bears God's image—is pushed to the side. Our God-given resources are blocked or constrained. We lose access to healing qualities such as compassion, curiosity, calm, clarity, and creativity.

Protectors who are driven by *fear* block the Self who is motivated by *love*. They seek power over powerlessness through control. Their warped perspective—that control is stronger than love—informs their view of God. They don't trust the Self to lead the system, and they don't trust God. When they lead the internal family, their perspective informs a person's view of God. They trust the safety of control over love.

How do we return to the ideal situation where the Self leads the internal family—in harmony with the Spirit—where love in myriad forms flows to all inner family members, healing exiles' wounds and freeing protectors from fear? How do we trust love over control?

We restore relationships between the Self and various family members—exiles and protectors.

Because protectors took over leadership, opting for control over love, the first step is to regain their trust. Connecting with them builds hope in the Self as a leader who can bring healing resources to the vulnerable exiles. It gives them access to the power of God's love to transform pain.

We connect with protectors by welcoming them just as they are. The presence of loving curiosity builds trust in the resources the Self offers the system. Ultimately protectors share what they fear will happen if they stop trying to control the internal family: they reveal vulnerable exiles. With newfound trust, they are ready to move aside so Self and Spirit can bring the fullness of God's love where it is needed most. In the loving presence of Self and Spirit, the most vulnerable members of the internal family share their story—all of the beliefs, images, sensations, emotions, and impulses they have held since they were wounded. The story unfolds in a sacred space where their needs are honored.

Protectors are watching. They experience the power of love that welcomes vulnerability—"the most excellent way"—the way of love (1 Cor. 12:31). As they trust the power of love, they release control and trust the Self and Spirit to lead.

Through a spiritual practice of welcoming all internal family members just as they are, Self and Spirit meet the internal family's needs with the most powerful resource of all: love.

Molly *is a licensed marriage and family therapist specializing in treating the impact of trauma and adversity. She earned her MAMFT from Bethel Seminary San Diego, where she returned as adjunct professor. Her book* Restoring Relationship: Transforming Fear into Love Through Connection, *helps readers identify and resolve barriers to loving themselves, others, and God. Learn more about Molly at https://mollylacroix.com/.*

38

Ways a Love-Based Psychotherapy Resonates with Oord's View of a Loving God

Dave Tenney

A love-based psychotherapy applies love in ways that affirms within a psychological context what Thomas Oord promotes in his theological one.

*G*reetings beloved reader. I am intentionally welcoming you in this manner as I want to relate to you in a personally loving way in my role as the writer of this essay on these matters of love. I intend to share a lot of interesting information about love and psychotherapy in ways I hope will be both enjoyable and beneficial for you. I suggest a loving God would want those acting in the role of a pastoral counselor, psychotherapist, or other similar counseling roles, to also relate with the person intentionally in therapy in a loving way within those contexts.

So, you might ask what does it mean to intentionally act lovingly toward another, including in a therapeutic context? The Christian theologian Thomas Jay Oord, in his writings that emphasize a theology of love, makes the point that Jesus masterfully provided a clear example of what it means to lovingly act through the loving way he lived his own life. Both his living example and his teachings greatly inform Oord's definition of love for his own field of theology: "To love is to act intentionally, in relational response to God and others, to promote overall well-being." Oord also provides a more concise, simple, and generally serviceable meaning for love as "aiming to do good." He writes that the inherently loving nature of God is unchanging and yet how it is manifested in relation to all of creation is "pluriform," that it can take many forms depending on any given context. Pastoral counseling, psychotherapy, and related counseling fields likewise have a plurality of forms and approaches for facilitating greater self-acceptance, personal growth, fulfillment, positive change, capacity to love oneself and others, and well-being, etc.

Some therapists may fully embrace Oord's initial definition, whereas others such as those serving people in a strictly secular setting or those therapists having a non-theistic personal orientation may only partially concur. I'll assert that Oord's more concise meaning of love as "aiming to do good" would resonate with nearly every therapist in a way that would enable them to "act lovingly" in their particular professional context.

The question now is: What might psychotherapy look like if informed by love of the un-controlling type that Oord describes God as having?

I'll begin to share my view by providing a serviceable definition of a "love-based psychotherapy" derived from an extensive literature review of several philosophical, religious, and psychological perspectives of love. Love-based psychotherapy is an approach that can be defined as a *process predominantly guided by* the *principle, power, and presence* of a *compassionate and benevolent intention to foster the client's fullest well-being, and that involves the cultivation of that intention in both the psychotherapist and the client.* In other words, a love-based psychotherapist can set the intention to ground his or her interventions through the principle of love, use the power of love to facilitate positive changes, and or share the presence of love with the client in a manner allowing love to inform and co-create the entire process of psychotherapy. I believe the meaning I am conveying by using the phrases "compassionate beneficial intention," and "fullest well-being" are quite resonant with Oord's "aiming to do good," and his phrase "overall wellbeing." I would like to clarify that "fullest well-being" encompasses the optimal "flourishing" of the individual interrelatedly with all others and life as a whole,—a holistic view consistent with Oord's own.

A love-based approach can be characterized as a co-creative relational process, compassionately responsive to both the person and to the guidance experienced when engaging the principle, power, or presence of love (or of "God's love," if you prefer). I wish to be inclusive for the general reader so I offer both understandings as viable meanings in therapy, given that either way the intent to respond to love's guidance is essentially the same in spirit.

The nature of a love-based approach is "pluriform" in application, involves unconditional loving, encourages the person's free will unfolding of an open future, is inclusive of nurturing love for oneself as well as others, and fosters a wholly integrated form of well-being.

I'll share some interesting ways that various therapists address these concerns that relate to Oord's theological view of an un-controlling God of love. First, however, I want to briefly clarify what kind of "love" is meant (and what is not) within a psychotherapeutic context.

Ellen Berscheid's taxonomy of love has relevance for clarifying the type of love most appropriate for a love-based psychotherapy. She identified "four varieties of love" (attachment, compassionate, companionate, and romantic) with compassionate love involving "concern for another's welfare and taking actions to promote it, regardless of whether those actions are perceived to result in future benefits to the self." That seems wholly fitting for a psychotherapeutic context, and it's also consonant with Oord's emphasis on promoting wellbeing. The fourth type, "romantic love," given its association with sexual desire, is generally understood in the field of psychotherapy as unhelpful, inappropriate, and ethically unacceptable.

In the history of psychology, there have been numerous psychotherapists of various theoretical perspectives who considered some form of love to be a key factor in psychotherapy. I'll now review a few of the views and methods of therapists who I would consider essentially love-based that speak to the key points related to Oord's view of an un-controlling God of love.

First, I'll say that love is the base upon which the rest of the therapy rests, just as it's the base of Oord's theology. Joseph Natterson, a Neo-Freudian therapist, asserted that "love is a fundamental element of the therapeutic process itself," and that "the therapeutic relationship becomes a loving relationship, and the therapeutic dialogue is basically about love and the expansion of its role in a person's life." Erich Fromm combined both Freudian and Jungian perspectives and similarly viewed the therapeutic process as "essentially an attempt to help the patient gain or regain his capacity for love."

The intention to love is the essence of a love-based approach, but the forms through which it can be applied are many, as Oord similarly says about God's love being changeless in essence yet "pluriform" in expression. A "love-based therapist" brings whatever forms of therapeutic training, orientation, or skills they might have to the love-based process of therapy.

Oord emphasizes in his writings that God is "un-controlling," and thus cannot predetermine mortal creatures' lives, interfere with free will, or act "single-handedly" to prevent unloving behaviors by others. However, Oord also believes that as a universal spirit, God does rely on us to act locally as living agents of love on God's behalf.

Rollo May, a leading voice of Existential and Humanistic Psychology, valued an open-ended therapeutic process and wrote that "the reuniting of will and love" is an important therapeutic task and saw it as rooted in intentionality. He sought to unify three parts of a client's conscious process: wish, will, and decision. The therapist helps persons identify their deepest unconscious yearning, (or what love is calling forth from within), so the person can consciously nurture its manifestation in unity with his or her will, decision-making, and behavior, as a whole integrated being. May's open-ended exploration is an example of nurturing free will vs. being directive or having a predetermined outcome simply based on adjusting to social norms.

Carl Rogers, a pivotal figure in humanistic psychotherapy, developed Person Centered Psychotherapy and emphasized the inherent capacity of the person to discover the best way toward healthy functioning. He valued the therapist-client relationship and directly experiencing people just as they are. "Unconditional positive regard" was a core principle that emphasized the therapist providing a caring, empathic response regardless of the client's attitude or behavior. I see Rogers' unconditional positive regard in a therapy context as roughly equivalent to the unconditional love taught by Jesus, and to Oord's unconditionally loving God.

There are numerous therapists including Assagioli, Wellwood, and Vaughn, who could be considered love-based in what is known as Transpersonal Psychology, wherein the mostly secular field of psychotherapy meets the spiritual to lovingly foster well-being. The transpersonal dimension is "a spiritual reality intrinsic to all that is," and "transpersonal psychotherapy views all psychological processes against the backdrop of spiritual unfolding" (Cortright). This perspective often involves ways of being present with love's presence so it has particular relevance for love-based psychotherapy in relation to a God of love. It opens the therapy door to what author and psychologist Jean Houston calls "sacred psychology," in which the therapist can serve as a "mediator of love" or living "instrument of grace" to "transmit the light of love to another," an example of what Oord refers to as being an active "agent" of love.

It may interest you to know there are many love-based therapists that incorporate various practical methods and techniques before, during, or between sessions that can actually cultivate greater love and well-being in one or both persons of the therapy relationship. A few examples are two evidence-based ones "Lovingkindness Meditation" (Frederickson) and Self-Compassion Meditation

(Neff), as well as heart centered creative visualizations (Ladner, Roland), "Loving Presence" (Kurtz), and "Love Centered Meditation" (Tenney). Love-based therapists and the persons in therapy can also regularly practice asking themselves "how can I be most loving" or prayerfully seek the same within. This could cultivate greater synchrony between the prefrontal lobes and other parts of the brain associated with higher values, the "heart, love, compassion, empathy, and understanding" (Pearce), and one's higher or "superconscious" mind involved with much of the same (Assagioli).

There is also a growing body of research showing that one person can favorably influence, through their own psychological and physiological well-being, another person's psychological and physiological well-being and their capacity to experience love! A few examples include via: "limbic resonance" and "limbic revision," (Lewis, et.al) "empathic resonance" (Goleman), and by increasing synchrony of brain wave activity and heart EKG rhythms with heartfelt thoughts (McCraty, et. al). Many love-based therapists are informed by this relevant research that is also pertinent to Oord's views and love-based living in general.

A love-based psychotherapy applies love in ways that make Oord's type of loving God's love come alive in its relational interaction. I've described numerous ways that such a therapy approach resonates with and affirms within a psychological context what Oord promotes in his theological one. It asserts the primacy of love, is "pluriform" in application, involves unconditional loving, encourages persons' free will unfolding of an open future, is inclusive of nurturing love for oneself as well as others, lets the therapist act as an agent of love, fosters an optimal wholly integrated form of well-being, and cultivates greater love-based living.

David S. Tenney, Ph.D., is a retired clinical psychotherapist having over forty years of experience practicing in New Hampshire. Dave completed his doctoral dissertation in 2013 at Saybrook University on "The Theoretical Parameters and Practical Value of a Love-Based Psychotherapy." It informs both his own approach to psychotherapy and this essay. Dave enjoys being in nature and learning to love.

39

The Drama Triangle, Relational Dysfunction, and Uncontrolling Love

Shane Moe

The drama triangle's dysfunctional Persecutor, Victim, and Rescuer roles create systemically self-perpetuating psychosocial problems that uncontrolling love avoids and helps heal.

After one of my clients, who struggled with overwhelming levels of chronic shame and anxiety, tearfully described the highly critical, controlling, and rigidly conservative Christian family in which he was raised, I remember saying to him, "Yeah, your family wasn't a *support* system—it was a *suppression* system." He nodded in agreement, with a softened facial expression and attending exhale that conveyed a sense of feeling seen and validated.

On another occasion, when I was seeing a couple for marital therapy, they began locking horns in a bitter disagreement during one of our early sessions. Each was trying to forcefully change the other's perceptions through verbal jousting and volume. I interrupted them and asked, "What's more important to you right now— the *relationship* or being *right*?" They both sat quietly, reflecting on how they had been going about the interaction, and eventually resumed their exchange with less defensiveness and emotional charge.

On yet another occasion, one of my clients, who was struggling with complex trauma born out of years of spousal abuse, told me she had thought of her previous therapist as the "captain" of her proverbial ship and that she was hoping I could be the same. I responded by saying, "Actually, I don't *want* to be your captain. I want to support *you* being the captain of your ship." She sat silently, maintaining steady eye contact and appearing perplexed, but also intrigued to hear more.

These brief anecdotes highlight some of the relational dynamics that therapists routinely hear about and encounter in our work with our clients. In what follows, I'm going to use one particularly helpful and more systemic framework to describe some of the ways in which relationships (and families, churches, or other social/relational systems) characterized by interpersonal *control* become significantly problematic. At the same time, I'm going to note how these dynamics and their destructive consequences contrast with those of uncontrolling love.

Psychiatry professor and clinician Stephen Karpman's famous *drama triangle* is a tool therapists sometimes use to discuss the problematic roles and relational positions people often take in unhealthy relationships or social systems characterized by destructive relational dynamics (whether families, churches, schools, companies, governments, societies, or otherwise). Persecutors irresponsibly attack, blame, control, and otherwise oppress or abuse others—whether verbally, psychologically, spiritually, emotionally, financially, physically, sexually, or otherwise. Victims irresponsibly "play the victim" to avoid having to take responsibility for themselves, typically by feigning helplessness, complaining about how unfair everything is, or expecting others (and frequently guilting them) to rescue them from the consequences of their actions or inactions. They invoke an irresponsible victim *mentality*, which we need to distinguish from the *reality* of being a victim or of having been victimized by a Persecutor, an injustice for which the victim is *not* responsible and about which they may have to critically speak up or speak out in order to effectively address (rather than reinforce and systemically help perpetuate) the injustice.

Rescuers then—often as a result of thin emotional boundaries, a desire to make themselves feel better, a grandiose sense of superiority, or to avoid taking responsibility for their own issues—over-responsibly seek to shelter, take over for, or otherwise rescue a perceived Victim, ultimately serving to enable and reinforce the latter's irresponsibility/under-responsibility and maintain that person's unhealthy dependence upon them (along with any enmeshment and codependency in the relationship). And while such rescuing often looks a lot like love and gets easily mistaken for it—to say nothing of often awarded hero or martyr status—it does not actually operate in the beloved's best interests and is, instead, born out of the Rescuer's own psychosocial deficits and discomfort.

The nature of the drama triangle (sometimes called the "VPR Triangle") is such that those who are caught up in its toxic "dance" tend to just rotate amongst the triangle's problematic roles or positions, ultimately serving to circulate, sustain, and amplify the system's dysfunction (be it a family, church, company, or otherwise). Persecutors, for example, often rotate to playing the Victim when being held accountable for or suffering from the negative consequences of their persecutory behaviors, or to the role of Rescuer when wanting to distract from or make up for those irresponsible behaviors. Rescuers often rotate to the position of Persecutor in their impulsive attempts to rescue others, or into the role of Victim themselves when their attempts to rescue someone fail or are not sufficiently appreciated. And those playing the Victim role often rotate to the position of Persecutor through a responsibility-avoiding litany of harsh complaints about others, if not to the role of someone's Rescuer to feel a compensatory sense of power, relief, or self-worth.

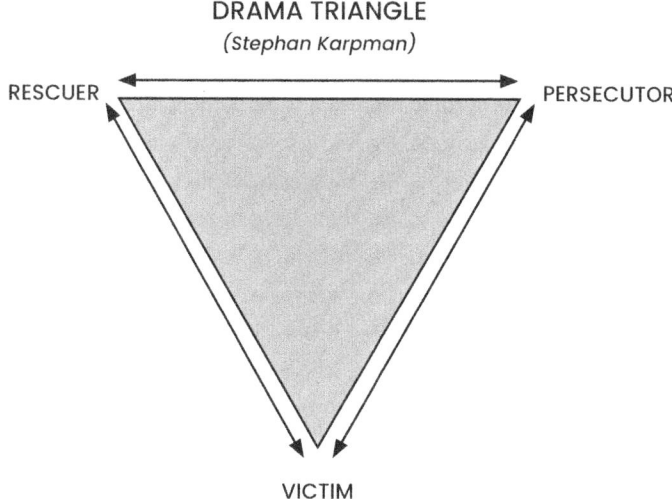

DRAMA TRIANGLE
(Stephan Karpman)

RESCUER   PERSECUTOR

VICTIM

When we examine them more closely, we find that, contrary to the characteristics of uncontrolling love delineated in 1 Corinthians 13:4-7 (as well as the fruit of the Spirit in Galatians 5:22-23 and characteristics of divine wisdom in James 3:13-18), the drama triangle's problematic roles and relational dynamics routinely traffic in both overt and covert patterns of interpersonal control that lead to significantly problematic natural consequences which then feed back into the relational system and serve to further perpetuate those corrosive control-based dynamics. For example, where loving someone in an uncontrolling way is more likely to promote feelings of self-acceptance or self-worth, of calm or safety, and of a sense of healthy agency or empowerment in others, the drama triangle's

dynamics of interpersonal control, even when engaged in by seemingly well-intentioned Rescuers, routinely contribute to significant levels of shame, anxiety, and
anger in the parties involved. Reciprocally, then, these distressing feelings often
serve to fuel people's compulsion to control and further engage in the triangle's
various roles. In cases of a Perpetrator's more severe or chronic abuses, of course,
their entitlement-driven efforts to exert power and control over others often contribute to full-blown post-traumatic stress or complex trauma in their victims, or
in some cases even to their own moral injury (i.e., severe psychological torment
over how one has harmed others), all of which contribute to both them and their
victims being more vulnerable to further engagement in the triangle's problematic
roles. Uncontrolling love, on the other hand, is neither driven by fear and anxiety
nor abuses and traumatizes the beloved. In fact, it helps people better manage all
of these difficult emotions and heal from the interpersonal abuse and trauma that
have so often contributed to them.

In addition, whereas uncontrolling love evidences a healthy humility and
non-defensiveness, the drama triangle's roles and control-based dynamics are
routinely born out of—as well as serve to fuel, reinforce, and increasingly rigid-
ify—people's pride and related psychosocial defenses (e.g., denial, suppression,
rationalization, projection, displacement, compensation, idealization, and so on).
Defense mechanisms, sometimes called *ego defenses,* are generally psychological
processes (typically born out of fear and shame) that conveniently serve to insulate
someone from having to face, feel, and deal with their own vulnerable emotions or
problematic behaviors. And of course, where you find unhealthy pride, psychosocial
defense mechanisms, and strong (often blinding) emotions—you commonly find
intellectual rigidity and a lack of, or significant deficits in, self-awareness. By contrast, the humble, non-defensive, and flexible nature of uncontrolling love is more
conducive to healthy self-awareness and psychological (both intellectual and emotional) flexibility which, in turn, further helps one love others in uncontrolling ways.

Along with the emotional fallout, unhealthy pride, and problematic psycho-
social/ego defenses just mentioned, the drama triangle's roles and control-laden
relational dynamics commonly contribute to patterns of unhealthy relational dependence (e.g., codependency) and to an increasing psychological dependence
upon engaging in those roles, with people becoming increasingly emotionally dependent upon persecuting, rescuing, or being rescued. All of which then feeds back
into and further perpetuates those systemic dynamics of interpersonal control.

Uncontrolling love, on the other hand, helps free people from unhealthy psychological and relational dependence, helps enhance a healthy sense of personal

agency and self-efficacy, and helps empower others in healthy ways that actually serve their best interests. By contrast, the roles and relational dynamics of the drama triangle—even those of the purportedly magnanimous Rescuer—generally serve to keep people captive in unhealthy psychological and relational dependence, erode any healthy sense of agency or self-efficacy, and in the end serve to disempower rather than healthily empower. All of which fails to really serve anyone's best interests. In fact, these dynamics can render people increasingly psychologically dependent upon having or exerting power over others—with power effectively becoming one's "drug of choice." Uncontrolling love, on the other hand, doesn't share this corrosive and corrupting emotional attachment to power. Rather than controlling others through the exercise of *power over,* uncontrolling love exercises *power under* (as theologian Greg Boyd famously called it), lovingly empowering others in ways that recognize, honor, and invest in their personal agency on behalf of their best interests.

Finally, and intimately connected with each and all of its problematic natural consequences (and reciprocally contributing factors) outlined above, the drama triangle's control-laden roles and rotations militate against the development or maintenance of healthy psychosocial boundaries and a well-differentiated sense of self. When people lack healthy emotional or interpersonal boundaries, they fail to appropriately differentiate between self and other, to know and respect where one stops and the other starts, and to know what belongs to oneself as properly one's own responsibility (such as one's own body, thoughts, feelings, and choices or agency) and what belongs to someone else as properly theirs. Which, of course, makes them ripe for controlling or being controlled. They're more likely to exhibit what the brilliant family therapists and addiction specialists Claudia Bepko and JoAnn Krestan, in their incisive book *The Responsibility Trap,* call *under-responsibility* (a failure to appropriately take responsibility *for* self and be responsible *to* others) and *over-responsibility* (problematically taking responsibility *for others* and their responsibilities, which typically renders one under-responsible for oneself in certain ways by default). And in keeping with the title of Bepko and Krestan's book, people often wind up trapped in interlocking, mutually reinforcing, systemically self-perpetuating patterns of *both* under-responsibility and over-responsibility in their relationships with others (and even in their relationship with themselves). Each role in the triangle is largely characterized by under-responsibility, over-responsibility, or some combination of both, and these problematic distortions of healthy responsibility, like the roles of the triangle that traffic in them, routinely manifest in the destructive dynamics of interpersonal control.

When people lack healthy psychosocial boundaries, or what family therapists sometimes call *self-differentiation*—namely, the ability to maintain an "I" in the midst of the "We," to separate one's thoughts and feelings from those of others, and to hold on to self in the midst of the often psychologically fusing and assimilative forces of togetherness in relationships—they're more likely to feel the need to control others (or if they can't control them, then relationally cut off) in order to regulate their own anxiety or other emotions. As one of my colleagues profoundly put it, "We tend to be more selfish *in* relationships when we don't bring a self *to* the relationship." And where uncontrolling love is *self-controlled* and promotes self-differentiation by honoring the other's "otherness," personal boundaries, and self, the roles and relational dynamics of the drama triangle are so often *other-controlling*, ultimately serving to dismiss, override, assimilate, or in some other way try to eliminate the other's otherness, boundaries, or self (engaging in forms of what theologian Miroslav Volf has called *exclusion,* as opposed to the Christlike *embrace* that welcomes, accepts, and includes the other in their otherness). Where the triangle's roles and controlling dynamics (including the often *controlling love* of the triangle's Rescuer) serve to prevent self-differentiation, uncontrolling love serves to foster it.

Ultimately, self-differentiation reflects an *interpersonal* relational ability that is itself intimately related to one's *intrapersonal* ability (in one's relationship with self) to adaptively balance or differentiate between one's emotional and logical processes, which allows one to effectively manage one's anxiety in the naturally anxiety-conducive realm of interpersonal relationships, intimacy, and difference.

The majority of my work as a therapist involves helping my clients improve their intrapersonal and interpersonal relational processes, boundaries, and health—and consequently their level of self-differentiation. Their increasing self-differentiation, then, helps them escape from or avoid getting sucked into the destructive roles and rotations of the dreaded drama triangle. When my clients are suffering emotional distress as a consequence of someone else's engagement in the triangle's problematic roles, I help them attend to and work through it both intrapersonally and interpersonally. And when my clients themselves are engaging in the poorly self-differentiated patterns of the triangle's Persecutor, Victim, or Rescuer roles, or any combination thereof, I help them more clearly see what's happening, help them better understand how it is working against their mental health and relationships, and help them increase their level of self-differentiation, all the while being careful to avoid falling into the triangle's presumptuous and poorly self-differentiated Rescuer role myself.

How do I do this? Largely by letting uncontrolling love inform and shape my therapeutic relationship and work with my clients. Psychotherapy that is informed and shaped by uncontrolling love not only helps people avoid engaging in or colluding with the drama triangle's problematic roles and rotations, it also helps them experience healing and freedom from its enslaving and destructive natural consequences. It helps them heal and gain freedom from the shame, anxiety, and anger; from the pride, defensiveness, and rigidity; from the unhealthy relational dependence, disempowerment, and lack of self-efficacy; and from those deficits in one's psychosocial boundaries and self-differentiation. As noted above, these destructive consequences both result from *and* systemically feed back into the drama triangle's problematic, poorly boundaried, and control-saturated relational dynamics, ultimately serving to perpetuate them and sustain so much of what is broken and in need of healing in the human condition.

Uncontrolling love is key to this healing. Where the drama triangle ultimately burdens and enslaves—as they say, in the drama triangle everyone winds up a victim—psychotherapy informed and characterized by uncontrolling love helps unburden and liberate, as well as helps people increasingly exercise uncontrolling love themselves.

Shane Moe is a licensed marriage and family therapist and trauma treatment specialist in private practice in the Twin Cities south metro. He is a certified EMDR clinician with additional specializations in the DBT and IFS models of psychotherapy. He earned a Master of Divinity degree in 2008 and a Master of Arts in Marriage and Family Therapy degree in 2011, both from Bethel University.

40

DIFFICULT PEOPLE AND GOD'S UNCONTROLLING LOVE

STEVEN A. LUFF

Modeling our understanding of God's uncontrolling love may be easy in mutually rewarding relationships, but what about with difficult people?

*M*any of us want to model what we believe to be God's uncontrolling love. We want to accept people where they are and allow them the space to explore, make mistakes, learn, and grow. This process is easier with some people in our lives than others. The parent, sibling, partner, or friend who has demonstrated patterns of facing life's challenges with curiosity, resolve, support, and ownership are much easier not to control and by virtue of that, to love. Demonstrating our understanding of God's uncontrolling love in those cases often makes us feel good about ourselves. We were there for someone in need. We accepted them unconditionally. We brought wisdom.

But not all of the people in our lives are like this. Some of the people in our lives are unmotivated, isolated, and blaming, often blaming us. They are rude, entitled, and sometimes emotionally and physically abusive. What does it mean to demonstrate God's uncontrolling love in those situations?

The short answer to this question is whether your own choices in dealing with difficult people in your life are motivated by a true desire to help the other person grow or to hurt them directly or indirectly. So really, when we are discussing modeling God's uncontrolling love in our response to difficult people, we are talking about detaching from the experience, seeing the people in our lives from a bird's eye view, and understanding them in developmentally appropriate contexts. Once we can see them in this way, we can have and hold boundaries that are not controlling, but instead allow these people the opportunity to mature and grow.

For many of us, knowing to set and hold a boundary with a protesting six-year old when they want more than their allotted share of cookies is a much clearer direction than say, setting and holding a boundary with a sixteen year-old who continues to abuse drugs and alcohol while telling you "everyone else is doing it," or setting and holding a boundary with your partner who continues to spend your savings on gambling while explaining "it's normal to lose some before you hit the big winnings."

Many of us are faced with circumstances like these and circumstances far graver like an adult child who continues to abuse you verbally or physically in your own home. Even when you know for sure this is not developmentally appropriate behavior, and that it may not be in their best interest to continue to be living with you, you may think to yourself, "Where would they live? I can't have them live on the streets. God wouldn't turn them out, how can I?"

If there is one thing we know about the nature of the world in which we live (the nature of *God*?) it is that when any organism is faced with resistance, it adapts to that resistance, which means it grows stronger. Stronger is better. Stronger means that the organism can survive on its own and can thrive. In what ways, when we do not hold developmentally appropriate boundaries with difficult people in our lives, are we preventing these people from experiencing opportunities to strengthen and grow, to improve and mature, to *thrive*?

Of course, there are times when organisms are faced with *too* much resistance when they are not strong enough yet and that resistance kills the organism, but that is some of the discernment I am talking about here. What boundaries are developmentally appropriate for the people in our lives? When are we crushing them with our boundaries and when are we giving them opportunities?

A child will not starve to death if they do not get the extra cookie and might just gain some skills in delaying gratification, the greatest predictor of future success. An adolescent sent to a recovery program when they are abusing drugs and alcohol will not experience irreversible psychological damage; instead, they might just have the opposite occur in learning how to manage emotions through healthy relationships instead of substances. A partner who no longer has access to your financial assets will still have their next meal and a roof over their head but may need to learn how to manage their money better if they want more from life. And the abusive adult child who has been evicted from your home most likely will not die on the streets, will most likely find a new place to live, and may just learn the lesson that it is a privilege to have access to a home for which they are not paying.

Setting and holding boundaries like these is not easy to recognize as godly, uncontrollingly loving, and perhaps the right thing to do. But instead of that difficulty being a sign that doing so is cruel and unloving it may be a sign of your own opportunity for growth. First, to know whether a boundary is uncontrollingly loving requires learning about what is and is not developmentally appropriate. Maybe we are not even holding ourselves to those standards. And second, what does it say about us and our own value and worth when we struggle with watching other people face life's challenges?

Learning what is and is not age appropriate requires resources, support, and education. It also requires a bit of distance from the difficult people in our lives to see that they are not special cases. They may be special to us, but they are not special cases. Just because they are our parents, siblings, children, partners, or friends does not make them exempt from what is expected from the rest of humankind. Also, accessing resources, support, and education takes time, and patience. And if there is one thing that will undoubtedly mature us, it is waiting. Remember the earlier comment regarding the greatest indicator of future success?

Once we can see these difficult people in our lives are just as much a part of humankind as the rest of us, and require the same level of developmentally appropriate boundaries, the next question for ourselves if we are still struggling with holding those boundaries is, why are we still struggling? Are we struggling because we have difficulty trusting our own wisdom? Are we struggling because we feel that our own past mistakes make us unworthy of being respected? Are we struggling because if we do hold boundaries, we believe we will ultimately be alone in life? Are we struggling because the consequences of holding those boundaries may broadcast to other people in our lives that we are heartless, unkind, and un*godly*?

Interestingly, when we do decide to dedicate our lives to modeling God's uncontrolling love through developmentally appropriate boundaries, we draw closer to God instead of alienating ourselves from God. Fundamentally, when we have and hold developmentally appropriate boundaries with others, we recognize a fundamental truth about existence: we can only control ourselves, not other people, which means that when we set and hold boundaries with difficult people in our lives, we are relinquishing these people into God's hands, into God's *love*. Can we really let them go, and trust that they are ultimately cared for? Talk about uncontrolling love!

Modeling God's uncontrolling love with difficult people in our lives may be the most difficult thing we will ever do. Humans are built for connection and through control we believe we can keep people connected to us. But keeping difficult people close regardless of how they treat us is not love. Rather it is subjecting ourselves to abuse. As you hold boundaries, and work your way toward understanding and building healthier relationships, you have the option of focusing on God's love. God's love for *you*!

To summarize, what is in our control when dealing with difficult people in our lives is educating ourselves about what boundaries are developmentally appropriate, having and holding those boundaries (sometimes through legal channels), and gaining support through support groups. Support groups may come through our religious communities, but if those communities are not helpful, or if you would like to keep your challenges confidential, you can always find them in 12-step programs such as Al-Anon (for friends and family of addicts) and CODA (Co-dependents Anonymous).

Remember, we do have control of letting go of control (ironically!). And letting go of control is trusting that God, the ultimate non-controlling and loving force in our lives, is working all of existence in a benevolent direction. Set and hold developmentally appropriate boundaries with the people in your life and trust the direction of life's flow. Trust in God's uncontrolling love.

Steven A. Luff is a licensed Marriage and Family Therapist in California. Through his Faith & Sex Center (www.faithandsexcenter.com) he works with clients to transform their understandings of God into frameworks that promote personal and communal well-being, especially as it relates to sex. He is the principal author of Pure Eyes: A Man's Guide to Sexual Integrity.

41

STICKS AND STONES

SYLVIA CORTEZ MASYUK

Words do have the power to affect and deeply wound us.

Sticks and stones may break our bones, but words can never hurt us. Many of us can recall a parent or friend using this phrase when we were young to combat verbal bullying. However, we all know that words do have the power to affect and deeply wound us. Ironically, the words we use can hurt those we are trying to comfort, particularly those experiencing trauma. Sadly, this often occurs in places least expected—communities of faith.

Chad was a handsome young teenager who loved surfing, skateboarding, and hanging out with friends at the beach until a horrible surf accident severely injured him. Chad was lucky to be alive but traumatized. Chad regularly relived his trauma, battled chronic pain, gained weight from medications, and became only a shadow of his earlier self. He could not shake the violence of what had happened and how it had changed him. Chad was surrounded by a loving Christian community who cared deeply for him and wanted him to improve. He met with therapists. But no one could help Chad transform his pain and suffering. Trauma had ruptured his life to such an extent that trauma recovery felt impossible, despite how much others wished that for him.

Sometimes, our attempts to comfort others with the good news of the gospel can be deafening to those enduring the long and challenging process of trauma recovery. Our words and even the violence of our silence or absence can result in unintended bullying when we attempt to rush trauma victims toward recovery. Proverbs 25:20 says,

Like vinegar on a wound
  is one who sings songs to a heavy heart.
Like a moth in clothing or a worm in wood,
  sorrow gnaws at the human heart.

Though surrounded by love, all family and faith community efforts were somehow insufficient. Chad committed suicide. The unresolved trauma in Chad's life and many others begs for a re-examination of our trauma responses. As Deborah van Deusen Hunsinger notes, "Believers who have survived trauma stake their very lives on the power of the gospel to heal." As the Body of Christ, we all eventually stake our lives on it.

Why was hope so elusive to Chad? Are there any words that would have helped Chad? Were the Christian doctrines he held helpful in any way? And what is the role of the church for those struggling with trauma?

Unfolding trauma studies have concluded that post-traumatic recovery can be a difficult and long journey, and many survivors never experience a full recovery (a concept not without complications). Churches proclaim freedom in Christ, transformation, and wholeness. So perhaps it seems counter-intuitive that our congregations include persons who cannot experience joy in these ways and struggle to navigate community even after they have *found salvation*. Churches are glad to welcome the broken-hearted but expect them to eventually be mended. What happens when people do not experience healing and recovery?

Trauma is a serious issue we are still learning to recognize in ourselves and others. Trauma almost always precedes questions of theodicy — if God is good, why does evil exist? So the church must learn to honor the experiences and questions trauma survivors bring as they move toward healing. But theodicy is not at the core of trauma recovery.

Research has concluded that trauma recovery requires safety, remembering, mourning, and reconnecting to the world. This process often proves to be challenging in many faith communities. Christian narratives that sound beautiful and inspiring to many may not compute for those wrestling with trauma. *On a bulletin board of a church Sunday School class were the words from the gospel of Luke, "With God, nothing is impossible." A couple of days later, an anonymous person secretly tacked this note underneath, "But not for me."* This is the silent cry of trauma survivors who often cannot reconcile hope and lived experiences. Trauma survivors may be in our midst, but that does not mean they are moving toward healing. So what can faith communities do? There are at least three things. We can watch our words, listen to their words, and accept the absence of words.

First, we can watch our words by determining whether our theology is trauma sensitive. Church language is rife with challenges for trauma survivors. The language of *wholeness* and *perfection* may seem impossible for survivors whose trauma makes them feel bodily irreparable. Concepts like forgiveness, providence, and hope can be minefields for those navigating violent, traumatic experiences. Carelessly using language to cover over pain and traditional narratives of redemption that have no meaning for trauma survivors, may re-traumatize people. We also destabilize their experience of church as a safe space that can understand or at least hold the dissonance they experience. Trauma is deeply destabilizing. These are a few ways particular doctrines do not work in their traditional form for persons experiencing trauma. Or perhaps they ask something of the trauma survivor they cannot give at the present point in their journey. And church communities will be ill-equipped to engage trauma victims if they are fixated on a skewed narrative of the gospel. Instead, we can reimagine doctrines that honor lived experiences and reflect embodied experiences in scripture, such as acknowledging that Jesus' resurrection included his wounds, a significant image for trauma survivors. To focus only on triumphalism, Shelly Rambo warns, often shuts the door to very ordinary experiences such as doubt, fear, anxiety, and sorrow, not to mention injustice or violence. The dissonance trauma survivors experience from this language may lead to isolation and, ultimately, disconnection from God, others, and often their own bodies. Incapable of connecting with others, they remove themselves from an essential element required for trauma recovery — community.

Furthermore, the church has a rich text filled with trauma, suffering, and longing that we can tap into and learn from. The church can highlight these traumas and resist softening or covering over realities that are difficult to tackle in the gospel narratives. Seeing trauma inherent in scripture is paramount for trauma survivors. The church can proclaim the Good News and engage in the wisdom work of holding space for trauma survivors.

Second, we can listen to their words should they be willing to share their story or ask questions. A negotiation occurs with memory as the survivor attempts to make sense of what happened to them. But they cannot do this work alone. A caring person must come alongside, to listen and be a witness to the story. Helping to bear the unbearable is vital and is an act of creation, as healing and remaking occur in that space. As Hunsinger notes, a person begins to move toward healing when they can weave together a meaningful narrative about the trauma they endured while remaining emotionally connected to themselves and the person serving as a witness.

Third, we can accept the absence of words by offering embodied practices. Because our bodies remember the trauma, we know that trauma recovery does not merely entail cognition or talk therapy. Trauma is first felt in the body, and if healing is to take place, it may first need to occur in the body and not the brain. For those in pastoral ministry, this means paying more careful attention to bodies and embodied practices in the church that are critical to trauma survivors. Theology alone will not transform the trauma survivor. *Sticks and stones may break our bones, but doctrines alone do not necessarily heal us.*

Serene Jones argues that the rituals of the church, such as the Eucharist, are infused with trauma. Many trauma survivors, who often initially have trouble finding the right words for their experience, may find more comfort in embodied spiritual practices that do not require direct interaction—recited prayers, singing in unison, and participating in the Eucharist, to name a few. The Eucharist, in particular, is rooted in a story of trauma. When we come to the table, participants become bodied believers *together* and are re-membered, an act of particular importance to trauma survivors. The eucharist is an embodied practice we *do* with our bodies *as the body* that shares the same hope for life and resurrection. Traumas rupture. But we can move toward healing through ritualized practices.

Tragedies many of us face affect us emotionally, spiritually, and physically. So, part of the church's task is to bodily address the deep pain and suffering of those we walk alongside. This work requires sustained practices that shape our language, thoughts, and behavior to help reframe lived experiences. Language is problematic for trauma survivors, and our words can never be Band-Aids we use to cover human experiences. Because trauma survivors are in our midst, we must learn to watch our words, listen to their words, and accept the absence of words. When this occurs, our theology and liturgies, formed alongside bodily practices, can help us address, engage with, and may even transform our wounds.

Rev. Sylvia Cortez Masyuk *is currently enrolled in the NTS Doctor of Ministry in Spiritual Formation program and lives and ministers in Kyiv, Ukraine with her husband, Volodymyr.*

– 42 –

I'M LOSING CONTROL OF MY CHILD!

ANNIE ABERNETHY

If your parenting aim is well-behaved kids, you might be doing it wrong.

Over the years, I've heard variations of this statement from dozens of parents in my counseling practice. Usually, these parents show up accompanied by their grumpy, sometimes threatening, teenager. I often wonder if it's safe to shut the door to my office, trapping us all in this tiny space. Under other circumstances, I would cross the street to avoid these unpleasant humans. Nonetheless, here they sit, the pair of them, glaring at me.

What is a therapist to do? Thankfully, this is my jam. I'm all in, because I think I know what the problem is. It's all right there in the wild-eyed parent's high-pitched whine: "I'm losing control of my child!" Shall we unpack it together?

This dreadful sentence starts with the word "I'm."

For many parents, there is an inescapable pressure that starts at the arrival of their first child, and it only intensifies through the years. The sense that "I'm" ultimately responsible for everything that happens to this child; responsible for everything this child learns; responsible for every friendship they make; responsible for keeping sons out of jail and daughters from getting pregnant.

If you're chuckling at the absurdity, you may not be a parent yet. We parents…group sigh…we feel this pressure daily; moment by moment; sometimes in the middle of the very darkest parts of the night when we're supposed to be sleeping. And it's terrifyingly real.

But we should ask ourselves: where does this pressure come from, to turn out perfect, functioning, successful, mature human adults?

For those of us in the Christian tradition, we've inherited an expectation of well-behaved, pew-sitting, shiny-faced, obedient little charming treasures that proudly represent a good Christian family. Some of this came through programs promoted by churches that taught us there was a way to parent that was "God's way." This "way," however, turned out to be less about love and more about control; or at least it wedded love and control inseparably. More about that later.

But back to the "I'm." Even if we change it to "We," the implication is that it is a purely human endeavor to parent these children. We've completely overlooked the tender attention of the Creator, the Eternal Parent represented in Psalm 139; the Dad who doesn't sleep because He's counting hairs and pursuing us into the darkness into which we flee. Does He not have an obligation to tend to His Children? Is it possible He has at least as much of an interest in our children as we do?

Of course, we all know God loves our kids. "But what is He doing about it?" we yell into the dark of night. If we're really honest, our prayers for our children can be reduced to, "If I can't control them, why won't You do it?" Trusting our Father with our kids is not easy, but it's the only way to stay sane, even if we don't understand it. And if we listen for His answer to our black-of-night cries, we'll find constant affirmations of His Presence with us and our children.

"Losing." This is a depressing word, no matter how you read it. And for every parent, it can be a continuous, desperate sensation. Kind of like a film in slow-motion of a tornado or tidal wave, ripping a child from the safety of mama's arms. But it's a very short-sighted and limiting emotion. Most of us aren't actually losing anything. There are so many other verbs to experience with our kids. Connecting. Relating. Delighting in. Discovering.

Step into the Scriptures with me and into the life of Jesus. Imagine Mary and Joseph, traveling home from a lovely, if chaotic, trip to Jerusalem. Their 12-year-old first born son is lost. They have *literally* lost control of their child. When they find him, what is he doing? He's in the temple, "being about his Father's business." We know that Jesus' earthly father was not a rabbi or priest, but a carpenter or stonemason. So what does this mean?

Aside from the fact that Jesus was identifying with his own Heavenly Father (which is a whole other discussion), there is something useful for us parents to digest in this story. Jesus' desire to be in the temple was a clue to his parents about his character and personality and interests, and that is *super* important. This story can help us as parents reject temptations to control our children.

Listen carefully. What your children love are the avenues through which God has access to their souls. Certainly, that was true about Jesus. But here's what's really exciting. This means it can be the avenue for your connection with them, too.

It bears repeating. What our children love and are passionate about are the God-created invitations for relationship, both for God and for us. We dare not ignore that. Some of us do great damage by condemning our children's interests. And to what end? Ah…*that's* "losing!"

So what we end up *gaining* by being attentive to our kids' passions is much greater than what we *lose* by giving up control. Again…connection, real knowing of our kids, and a lifetime of discovery, alongside them, as their beautiful paths unfold.

Dare we address "control?" The first two words of the parent's statement above make me sad, honestly. But this word? Control? It makes me laugh. Because it's an absolute illusion. Where did we get the idea that control was something humanly possible? Some of us may even argue it's not divinely possible!

If we look again at Psalm 139, we notice that our Good Father is not controlling where we stand or sit, when we run away, or even how many hairs we have on our head. He is lovingly observing. Whoa. Imagine a Father being curiously observant instead of controlling?

What's more, Psalm 139 communicates that our Father is eternally pursuing relationship with His children. Sounds like a parenting plan, doesn't it? Maybe we can even say it's parenting God's way! My experience of attempting to control my children, for the most part, made me feel abusive. The Parent in Psalm 139 does not come close to abuse; rather His attention and protection and tender care inspire the psalmist's desire for relationship. The child wants to lean into the arms of that Father, thanking Him for his love and trusting Him with his life.

Let's turn our focus to the words "my child!" in the sentence above. In fact, this is where we find so much of the emotional energy of this statement. This child is *mine*. It's similar to the "I'm," but I'd argue there's a significant difference. Truly, none of us wants to admit the obvious truth: "My child's behavior and position in life reflect on me; and she'd better not embarrass me!"

I've heard versions of this statement from parents too many times to count: "While *my* child is under *my* roof they will obey *my* rules!" This expression of possessiveness and demanded obedience is toxic to kids. In fact, children are allergic to it. It either produces rebellion that leads to disconnection from you, or submission that leads to your child's loss of their own identity. I've seen it on my office couch played out innumerable times. For children reared in this environment, it's hard work to reestablish a sense of agency and belief in self. Trust me: for parent and child, it's a lose-lose.

"My child" thinking can also result in something more nefarious than your child withdrawing from you. It can lead to you as a parent turning away from your child. If we raise our children under this "my child" mentality, it can lead to statements like, "Well, that's not how I raised you." It can end in a forced separation that destroys your child's heart and may harden yours beyond repair. What child wants to come back to a relationship where these types of things have been said? My guess is the prodigal son heard no such things from his father. Meditate on that, parents of prodigals.

Essentially, a parent who rejects "my child" thinking simply refuses to lose their children. In fact, if you truly love your children, you give them the right to hurt you without the threat of losing you. That's right. They will never experience doubt about your presence and love. Sounds like Psalm 139 dad, doesn't it?

In summation, parents, since I'm the therapist to whom you bring your surly teens, allow me to review what we've been discussing.

It's not all on you. God is present. He is working and loving you and your children. You are never alone, and neither are your kids. And your loving presence is just as essential as God's in their lives.

That sensation of loss might just be a lie; especially if you are committed to supporting them, no matter what. Your child is *becoming* before your very eyes. You gain the opportunity to watch the unfolding of God's design for your child. And you get to discover with them the beautiful passions that result in connection with God and others.

Control is an illusion. It probably shouldn't even be in the same sentence with the word "love." Until loving your child is more important than controlling your child, you will never find peace.

Your job as a parent is not judged by how your child turns out. Remember, God looks at the heart, both yours and your child's. And you are responsible for the effort, not the outcome. This is not about your value or worth or your ego or ability. Do not pressure your child with "my child" demands.

My hope for parents and teens when they leave my couch is simply this: that the parents' statement would change from "I'm losing control of my child!" to "I'm more curious than critical, more trusting in God than myself, and I'm here for all of it!"

Annie Abernethy *is a licensed professional counselor in private practice. She is a graduate of Regent University's counseling program and is currently working toward an MA in Theology and Culture from St. Stephen's University. When not meeting with clients, Annie can be found reading on her front porch, playing or officiating volleyball, and hanging out with her hubby and three adult sons.*

– 43 –

GOD CAN EITHER LOVE US OR TRY TO CONTROL US— BUT HE CAN'T DO BOTH

ALAN R. ALLARD

What attracts people to a certain faith community often ends up being what drives them away.

Thirty years ago I was a therapist in private practice in the Chicago western sub-urbs—and a member of a large and growing high-control church organization. I witnessed first-hand how toxic theology damages and sometimes ruins people's happiness, confidence, sense of self-worth, and relationships. Especially their re-lationship with God. It also became clear to me that the same toxic theology that attracts people to a faith community often ends up driving them away.

My former client "Jim" illustrates what I'm talking about. He came to me because he was feeling "depressed and anxious." A few sessions into our work together, Jim said, I know this is therapy but can we talk about God? I just can't seem to live up to his expectations. I don't read my Bible enough or pray enough. What's wrong with me?"

Feeling something is wrong with you is a horrible feeling. I've been there. And if you know what it's like to feel that way, you know how destructive it is. It turned out that there was nothing wrong with Jim. Yet, his beliefs about what God was like made him feel like a spiritual failure and that stoked the fire of his depression and anxiety.

After a bit of listening to Jim, I said, "You're paying out of your own pocket to talk about God. Maybe you love God more than you give yourself credit for."

I'll never forget what he said. "I don't deserve any credit. You don't get it. This isn't me loving God. It's me being self-focused when I should be thinking of others first."

Wow!

This is some of the toxic theology Jim had learned and what he believed:

- He isn't important—but everyone else is.

- He could never please God.

- Even when he did something right, his motivation for doing it was suspect—or worse.

- His problems in life were due to not living as God told him to live—if he wanted his life to go better he had to do better.

- He could never feel good about himself because the goal was to become less and less like "self" and more and more like Christ.

I wasn't surprised then that Jim was suffering. The theology he learned was perfect for suffering.

What do we do with theology that creates suffering? That leaves us feeling unimportant, guilty, and ashamed. What do we do when we are told we are sinners far more than we are reminded that we are made in God's image? What do we say to people that are hurting and believe it's all their fault? That something is wrong with them?

Here's the essence of what I shared with Jim. "What if God just wants you to be happy with yourself and your life?" What if God doesn't have expectations of you the way you were taught? What if God isn't threatening us with awful consequences if we don't live up to his demands? What if we believed God is our partner in creating a wonderful world to live in right now and enabling us to fully be who we want to be? After all, isn't that what parents want for their children?"

Back then, my office was filled with people who came to me for many reasons: depression, anxiety, marriage problems, addictions, eating disorders, and more. In one way or another, they were hurting and confused—and they were seeking help.

I'm not blaming all that on toxic theology. Not at all. I am saying that toxic theology is often a key part of people's depression, anxiety, and various struggles in life. Genetics, medical conditions, childhood conditioning, life challenges, lack of resources and support—all these things play a part in our struggles with our happiness and well-being. Yet, theology can either help us or hurt us if we're hurting or heading that way.

Here's an example of what my former church taught (and what many "conservative" churches today still teach):

- To complain about or oppose a spiritual leader is to oppose God.

- Women have to have sex with their husbands even if they don't want to because that's what scripture teaches.

- Sin isn't always the reason you're depressed or having marriage problems but that's usually the case and the first place you should look.

But wait (unfortunately) there's more! Church members were told that their faithfulness to God could be measured by their church attendance, tithing, and evangelistic outreach. Control, shame, guilt, and fear were used to ensure the behaviors the church leaders wanted.

Any spiritual environment like this leaves people on the side of the road, beaten up, and left to fend for themselves. All the while, the church leaders and members step right over them as they go about "obeying God."

It's not like what I describe above was taught overtly every Sunday. It didn't have to be because it was woven throughout the culture. It was often communicated in subtle ways. I learned the hard way that something is tragically wrong when we're told that our obedience is more important to God than our happiness and well-being. I learned how tragic it is when we're told that if we trust and obey God, our happiness and well-being will follow.

Of course, all this is being taught by "spiritual leaders." These are the people who we were told to listen to. We were told to be humble. We were told to trust. The problem was I didn't see leaders being humble. I didn't see leaders listening to anyone but themselves. The higher up they were, the more isolated and insulated they were. That meant they were listening to almost no one but themselves.

I began to question how spiritual leaders who admit to being fallible could claim anything they taught was anything more than their *opinion* of what the Bible says. I began to think, "How can they say, 'This is what the Bible clearly teaches" as if they couldn't possibly be mistaken? How can anyone say, "God is saying this, not me" while admitting they are just human and fallible?

I began to see that the perfect way to try to control others (even if it's not intentional) was to claim to know the truth of God and to say they are speaking the truth of God. It didn't take me long in my private practice to realize that so much of what I had been taught about God wasn't helping people. It was hurting people.

I began to see that teaching about a God who threatens and punishes people to gain compliance results in frustration, resentment, anger, and even hate in the very people who are trying so hard to love God and to love each other.

A God who wants to control us and threatens us when we don't love him back is a God who fosters anxiety, depression, anger, and rebellion. And that kind of a God would deserve people resisting and rebelling.

My office was full of people who desperately wanted to be happy, have healthy relationships, who wanted to enjoy their careers, and who wanted to love being in a community of God's people! Yet, the theology they were taught created and nurtured fear, not faith.

A fear-based, guilt-based, and shame-based theology is not compatible with happiness, healthy relationships, success in life, and feeling at home in a community of God's people. It's only compatible with creating environments, within the community and within each person, that sets us up for being unhappy, depressed, angry, and wanting to fight back and stand up for ourselves.

The kind of theology I'm talking about takes away one of the greatest gifts of God: our autonomy. Even the most "humble" person is unable to be healthy and happy if someone else is demanding compliance "or else"! It's impossible to love someone who demands we love them back.

We get that when it comes to our marriages and friendships. We even get that when it comes to the workplace. The old "Command and Control" leadership style is not so easily accepted any longer—even though it is still prominent. Control makes us less human. It turns us into an object without dignity or rights. It makes us want to fight the one controlling us, not love them.

I'll admit that I didn't see all this until I became a therapist and saw people hurting so much. It took that for me to see how bad theology creates enormous human pain. My clients were people who loved God. Yet, they never felt they measured up to God's instructions, demands, and expectations. They just didn't feel "good enough" when it came to God and in many other areas of their life as well.

Ultimately, they all just wanted to be happy. Yet, many (not all) even felt that wanting to be happy or successful in life went against "seeking God or his Kingdom first." All because of toxic theology!

It took me working with people one on one, in all their pain, to realize that much of what I had been taught growing up and as a young adult (about God and the Bible) not only didn't help people, it hurt them. It hurt them spiritually, emotionally, and psychologically. It kept them in their depression and in their anxiety. It kept them in toxic relationships. It kept them in fear, guilt, and shame. It kept them from being whole and from being healthy.

I eventually concluded that a God who controlled people or threatened people didn't know how to love and couldn't be God. I came to believe that God can either love us or try to control us—but he can't do both. And what's interesting is that if God *is* trying to control us, he's failing miserably.

Alan Allard is a former therapist now coaching clients on how to thrive in life. He is an expert in treating trauma, including spiritual abuse and religious trauma. Alan has been quoted in The New York Times, U.S. News and World Report, California Executive, and other media outlets. He is married to his high school sweetheart and together they have five grandchildren who all live within a mile of each other. Find more at Alan's website: www.alanallard.com.

44

SEEING GOD DIFFERENTLY WILL CHANGE YOU

M. KATHRYN ARMISTEAD

Once you see God differently, you will be profoundly transformed.

*F*red was a healthy twenty-five-year-old married to his high-school sweetheart, Emily. One day he began having terrible headaches. When Fred went for a check-up, the doctor could find nothing wrong. But the pain persisted and Fred started requesting more medication. Because the doctor couldn't find anything out of the ordinary, he decided that Fred was faking just to get drugs. Knowing that he wasn't an addict and angry at being written off, Fred left the doctor's office feeling dejected. (All names and personal information have been altered to protect confidentiality.)

Despite the pain, Fred and Emily decided to visit family in a nearby city. As the evening wore on, Fred felt worse and worse. Finally, Fred's dad drove him to the emergency room at the university trauma center and demanded that Fred see a specialist. The doctor ran tests and discovered that Fred's trigeminal ganglion—a nerve located near the temple at the side of the head, in front of the ear—was dangerously enlarged. The doctor had no doubt that Fred was in constant pain. She admitted Fred for additional tests.

Alone in his hospital room, Fred tossed and turned. Just as he was falling asleep, Fred sat up with a jolt. Initially blinded by a bright light, he squinted. There at the foot of his bed was a man dressed in white—someone Fred thought he recognized. It was Jesus! Then Jesus said softly, "Your sins are forgiven. You are healed." Jesus vanished. Fred put his hand to his head. He was pain-free. Fred grabbed his phone and called Emily. "I'm healed! I'm healed! Jesus healed me!"

As the doctor made her rounds the next morning, Fred told her that he was fine—no pain. He did not, however, inform her that Jesus had healed him. He didn't want her to think he was crazy. The doctor examined him and found that the nerve was indeed its normal size. She scratched her head and said, "It's a miracle. But let's go ahead to do more tests anyway." Fred replied, "No, I'm healed. I'm going home."

Everyone was elated to see Fred back to normal—his old self. Everything was fine…for three months. Then the pain returned. "Jesus took it back," Fred told his pastor. "Jesus took my healing back. Why?" Fred was crushed. When he returned to the hospital for follow-up, the doctor tried different treatments, but nothing worked. Finally, the doctor said, "I'm sorry. There's nothing else we can do."

Fred tried to cope with the pain, but he had to quit his job. He filed for disability but was denied—twice. Now his marriage was on shaky ground too. His friends drifted, and Fred lost hope altogether. When Fred came to counseling, he was a shell of the person he had been. He also felt angry and abandoned by God. He asked his therapist: "Why did Jesus heal me just to take it away? Why is God punishing me?" During the therapy that followed, Fred spent hours unpacking what happened. He especially reflected on Jesus's words: "Your sins are forgiven." What did that mean?

Religious experiences—vividly real personal encounters with the divine, while not commonplace, are surprisingly common. This is because, in our culture, everyone has idiosyncratic images of God based on their developmental history—people, North and South, in urban and rural settings, senior citizens, adults, youth, children over five, believers and non-believers—everyone. And these various images and understandings compete, engage, and sometimes interfere with the God of the Christian faith as portrayed in the Bible and church tradition. Also, religious caregivers do not have the luxury of saying that a vision with religious ideation is simply a psychotic episode or a psychological response to crisis. But we do need to be discerning and guided by our approach and our own informed understandings of God. While it is significant that Fred experienced his vision during a time of acute distress, it is not satisfactory to say that is all that it was and dismiss Fred's healing as only "in his head." This would shortchange and dismiss all that is at stake for Fred and others like him.

Fred was convinced that God was present with him in a powerful way in that hospital room; because it was, as he said, "the most real thing that had ever happened" to him. Yet, Fred was afraid to ask the question that most concerned him: Why did God fail me? Until he could wrestle with that, Fred lived with a punishing sense of guilt, which underscored Jesus's statement about Fred's sin. It was also easier for Fred to feel that he deserved God's punishment than to risk exploring the possibility that God failed him. To him, those were the options.

It is a long-standing observation in the fields of psychiatry and pastoral counseling that a change in the client's God signifies a change in the client. That is, when there is a change in a person's image of God—the way a person sees God—there is also change in the person's sense of self. This was certainly true for Fred. During therapy Fred came to realize that he believed in God despite God's fickle behavior. He also discovered that he did not like this God—one who could give healing and then yank it away. Who could trust a God like that? Yet Fred kept seeking.

Through therapy, Fred gained insight into what he was asking for when he called on God. Sure, he wanted pain relief, but it also dawned on him that he was asking for God to shore up his shattered and wounded self. He wanted his Heavenly Father to rescue him, like any father would do. But it wasn't until Fred was able to let go of who he thought God was and what God should do that he was able to experience a deeper understanding of who God could be for him. Slowly Fred began to see God differently. Of course, there is a lot more to the story, but over time and with counseling, God became more loving, accepting, and yes, forgiving—someone who could be trusted. Fred also began to have more self-confidence, because he trusted himself more too. In addition, his sense of humor resurfaced—an indication of growing wholeness and increasing psychological maturity.

As Fred was better able to manage his anxiety, he reported that he felt as though a burden had been lifted. He connected this with God's healing. Fred said: "God is a lot more, much bigger that I knew. Yes, God did heal me in that hospital room. God is still healing me. I may still have pain, but God stands by me, sustaining me. God never left me. I was wrong about that. Now, I use the pain to remind me to lean on God. I'm becoming more forgiving of myself and others too. My wife has certainly noticed."

In Fred's case, the more trustworthy God became, the more resilient Fred became; such that, armed with renewed hope, Fred went back for additional tests and later surgery. The surgery was successful for the most part, although Fred still experienced pain from time to time. But he had enough relief that he was able to return to work and get on with his life.

The presence of God is often experienced by persons as immanently real. It is sometimes understood as a sign of divine favor and received as a precious, although heavy gift. These experiences may be understood as signs of God's personal and abiding love. For some, it is only in this relationship that they sense acceptance and affirmation of their fragile sense of self. Because understandings of who God is and what God does are forged within a particular sense of self, they reflect the history of the self, both conscious and unconscious—a person's story as lived in a particular context. Although it must also be said that some religious experiences are not happy occasions but rather, horrifying indications of mental illness and instability. Yet, through the care of a religiously-informed therapist, persons can gain a clearer understanding of who the Divine is to them and how this particular understanding came to be part of their story. And as God's steadfast lovingkindness is experienced more fully, transformation in the direction of wholeness is not just possible but likely.

M. Kathryn Armistead is Managing Editor of Methodist Review, *an academic, peer-reviewed journal. She earned her PhD from Vanderbilt University and is a retired Diplomate in the American Association of Pastoral Counselors and a United Methodist clergyperson. Her latest book is* Live Faith. Shout Hope. Love One Another. *(Market Square Books, 2022). Find her at www.kathyarmistead.com.*

45

THE TRANSFORMATIVE POWER OF RELATIONAL GRACE

MAX E. BUTTERFIELD

Live your life to the fullest by loving God, and people,
to the fullest.

I have some training in clinical psychology, but I'm not a therapist. I'm a researcher. I study the way we think about each other, and I explore how those thoughts affect our lived experiences together. Sometimes it can surprise people to find out that psychology involves research and number crunching, but the human mind is complicated. Figuring it out is a team effort, and there's a lot we still don't know. As I prepared to write this essay, grace was on my mind because it's not something psychologists have studied much. We talk about grace far more often in theological contexts than psychological ones, but I think it's time for psychologists to play catch up.

Grace is an interesting concept for a variety of reasons. It has at least seven different definitions. As a result, each of us probably has a slightly different understanding of what the word grace means, and that's ok. We're different people. We lead different lives, and we find ourselves in different circumstances. Although the type of grace I'm interested in here is often referenced in the Bible, its meaning there isn't always completely clear either. What we see in the Bible can be difficult to interpret in modern contexts because the version we have today comes from a mix of languages, authors, and writing styles. The text has been derived from both oral and written materials. It's the richest tapestry of historical literature in existence, and it's not even close. It's filled with poems, parables, pericopes, and prophecies. There are also genealogies, allegories, letters, and more.

Let's talk a little more about those letters. Many of them were written by a man named Paul, and he spoke a lot about the transformative power of grace. At one time, Paul was a scholar and religious leader who was very hostile to Christianity. In the wake of the death, and subsequent disappearance, of Jesus Christ, Paul spent his days trying to snuff out the growing Christian movement. However, he had a life-changing encounter with the resurrected Christ. From that point forward, he traveled to different places, telling people about his own mistakes, and about the transformative power of God's grace in his life. He started churches in different places, gave them a simple message about Christ, and then went on his way.

Fast forward a few years. The social, political, and religious elites in the Greco-Roman world became concerned with this growing Christian movement. Paul was a big part of that. The grace-based message was a threat to the status quo. Paul was a threat to the status quo. He was thrown in prison in Rome. While there, he heard about some trouble brewing at several churches he had started in his travels. The locals had already forgotten even the basic message he'd left them with, and they'd started arguing. A lot. So, he wrote them letters: "Dear Friends. Please stop it. Also, Timothy says hi." Okay, he said a little more than that, but his general message was straightforward.

(a) We're all imperfect.

(b) God loves us and invites us into relationships anyway.

(c) Those relationships, with God, and with others, transform our lives and our souls.

Scholars read Paul's letters and see different things. Some think they weren't written by Paul at all. Instead, they think they were probably penned under his name as a pseudonym to give them governing authority. Others even think they might have been form letters sent to all churches across the world. They would have been circulated as something like, "Dear Insert Name Here." A lot is actually uncertain about these letters, but the uncertainties don't diminish the message. If anything, they amplify it. The message of grace is meant for everyone.

How do we apply this to relationship psychology in our modern context? Well, what we know is that God sees all our imperfections and loves us anyway. Even better, God loves us not just in spite of who we are, but because of who we are. God doesn't control us, tell us what to do, or force us to change. God waits. God loves. God gives grace. Can you imagine a world where we also did that for each other, a world where we did that for ourselves? We intuitively understand what it means to have a grace-based relationship with God, but what if we applied the same principles to our relationships with the people around us, or to our relationship with our own selves?

It's easy to see the imperfections of others. The jerk who cuts you off in traffic: Imperfect. The boss who doesn't listen to your brilliant ideas: Imperfect. The family member who seems to be disagreeable for no reason in particular: Imperfect. Similarly, it can also be tempting to over-focus on our own imperfections and mistakes, and that's not enriching either. Deep down we know we can be pretty lousy sometimes. We feel like frauds. Or imposters. We have doubts. We don't feel good enough. Choose your own personal shortcoming. We all have them. We know it. We feel it. We're imperfect. Wouldn't it be wonderful if we could respond to ourselves with the same grace God offers to us?

This offer of grace means that God invites us into transformative relationships, but what does that really mean? First, it means that God invites us to connect with God. That's easy. That's great. Who wouldn't want a grace-based relationship with the most loving being in the universe? However, there's more to the story. Part of the deal is that God is also inviting us to connect with each other, to have unity with one another. One of the biggest problems in the early church was that folks were constantly bickering, so when Paul wrote his letters, one of his main points was that they needed to cut it out. Unity, he said, is not negotiable. I can just picture it, "So help me, if you Christians don't start getting along back there, I will turn this chariot around right now!"

Remember the jerk who cut you off in traffic? The boss who wouldn't listen to your ideas? The disagreeable family member? They're imperfect, sure, but God invites us all into relationships anyway. Our relationships with God, and with each other, will transform our lives and our souls, if only we will let them. I want to emphasize, though, that showing grace to others doesn't mean that we always have to agree. It doesn't mean that we have to accept abuse or maltreatment. We can't control other people. We can only control our response to them, and that's the story of relational grace. We're called to let people make their own choices, and that means sometimes we have to make our own hard choices. By definition, showing relational grace isn't going to be easy. There are always going to be bumps in the road, and our relationships with others are never going to be perfect. People can be really awful sometimes!

Unfortunately, though, we're all people. In our own special ways, we're all awful. We all need grace in our lives. The good news, though, is that the transformation is up to God. That's the beauty of grace. Its power doesn't have anything to do with us. We're called to show grace, but it's God who transforms the jerks, the bosses, the family members, and us. It's God who transforms us all. We just have to trust that God is big enough, good enough, and patient enough to bring us together and finish the job. Despite our imperfections, despite our shortcomings, despite ourselves, we're designed to love each other, to live in community with each other, and to be in relationship with each other. If we offer ourselves to God and to each other, it will transform our lives, and God will transform our souls.

That transformative grace is the story of Paul's letters, and it's the story of Jesus Christ. It can be our story as well. Today, I encourage you to live your life to the fullest by loving God, and people, to the fullest. Show them grace, just as God shows it to us.

Max E. Butterfield is a psychology professor at Point Loma Nazarene University in San Diego, CA. He teaches a variety of courses, and his research explores how subtle details influence our thoughts, emotions, and behaviors. He also enjoys spending time with his family, training for endurance sports, rockhounding, eating, sleeping and making people laugh. Preferably all at once.

46

The Trinity Within

Allison Bailey Jorgensen

I want to propose a thought experiment, for the sake of illustrating how we might look at our 'Selves' in relation to God. But first, I need to outline a schema that Dr. Dick Schwartz proposes for us on how we define the 'self.' The chart below visualizes a way of conceiving the components that comprise the Self. This schema has been labeled "Internal Family Systems."

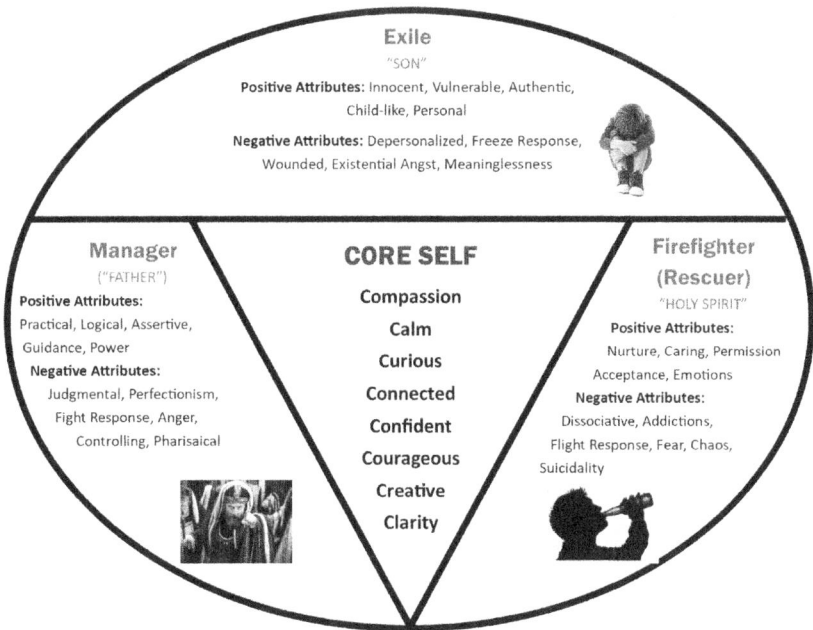

We all need (and struggle) to have each of these parts balanced to find our "Self." If you think about it, the ultimate in mental illness might be thought of as the parts of ourselves becoming estranged and disintegrated from each other (think 'multiple personalities'). Integrating our 'parts,' then, puts us on the path to wholeness and integration. As we allow for integration, balance and acceptance of all of our parts, we become whole…Just as God, the Three-in-One, is whole and integrated with the parts of Father, Son, and Holy Spirit (using the traditional words for the Trinity).

Let's apply the Internal Family System, this tri-part concept, to the Holy Trinity:

- Father or 'Parent': (commensurate with 'The Manager' part of our Self)

- Son or 'Child': (commensurate with 'The Exile' part of our Self)

- Holy Spirit: (commensurate with 'The Rescuer' part of our Self)

Luke 22:38-39, 41-44 says the following…

> Then he said to them, "My soul is overwhelmed with sorrow to the point of death. Stay here and keep watch with me." 39 Going a little farther, he fell with his face to the ground and prayed, "My Father, if it is possible, may this cup be taken from me. Yet not as I will, but as you will." and 41-44 41 He withdrew about a stone's throw beyond them, knelt down and prayed, 42 "Father, if you are willing, take this cup from me; yet not my will, but yours be done." 43 An angel from heaven appeared to him and strengthened him. 44 And being in anguish, he prayed more earnestly, and his sweat was like drops of blood falling to the ground.

This time, as you think about Jesus in the Garden, I'm going to have you imagine how this situation might have played out if God was *NOT* 'Love Incarnate.'

We might picture this: The 'Father part' of the Trinity would've looked down at Jesus (without Love), and said: "Dammit, you HAVE to do this! You MUST do this because I am your Father, and I am commanding you to go to the Cross! Get your shit together and just DO it or I will smack you upside the head! In fact, I think you need to punish yourself. Inflict some pain on yourself! Then you'll be acceptable…And, YOU, Spirit, you're always excusing him, making him question my authority! You need to stop your whining!"

Maybe some of you have heard that type of communication from your earthly father, or some other authority figures in your life, or even within yourself when you are frustrated by your own behavior.

And then, The 'Son part' of the Trinity, would've responded (without Love): "You can't take away my identity this way! How can you ask me to do this, give away my life, turn my life into nothingness and without any personal reality? It's madness! And meaninglessness! Obviously you don't love me! I'm outta here! And YOU, Spirit, you're no help!" There may be times in your life where you responded in this way to others, or even within yourself.

And then, the 'Spirit part,' (without Love) would've said to The Father: "You are so full of yourself! How dare you ask this of him? And, you, 'Son,' look at you! You're pathetic, such a wimp! What's wrong with you? Here, have some tequila, that will make you feel better. Or better yet, how about you make a plan to exit this life, the ultimate choice of escape? That will solve it all!" You may have had these words and accusations swirling around in confusion when you are in pain.

But when we bring the addition of Love into this scenario, the picture becomes very different.

God the Loving Parent listens to Jesus' cry, "Let this cup pass from me." He gives him time to process, to cry, to actually sweat blood in his agony. And Jesus communicates to his Loving Parent that because of love, he will accept the cross. ("Not my will, but thine be done," Luke 22:42). And immediately, the Rescuer (Holy Spirit) sent angels to minister and comfort Jesus in his time of need, recognizing and validating his suffering and giving him the strength he needed to face the task ahead. (Luke 22:43) All three 'parts' show up, communicate, have a conversation, allow love to come into suffering, and the outcome becomes resilience in the face of pain, reconciliation, redemption, and resurrection.

We spend our lives trying to get the 'Protector' parts (the 'Manager' and the 'Rescuer') to deny the needs and anguish of our wounded, depersonalized Exile parts of ourselves. As the Manager (the self-righteous Pharisaical, judgmental tyrant father part) and the Rescuer (the escapist, desire for comfort, give me drugs and alcohol part of ourselves) duel it out in their desire to create survival and salvation for us, we become brittle. Binary systems are easily broken, are shallow, and eventually disintegrate. To find our way out of the binary, dialectical push-pull of the Manager <> Rescuer parts of ourselves, we need to allow for and embrace the wounded Exile parts of ourselves, as Jesus did, by entering into our suffering as humans so that we might participate in the glory of being human, as Jesus did. 1Peter 4:13.

As we approach the existential angst of the Exiled parts of ourselves, and create a conversation between the Loving Parent, the Comforting Rescuer, and the Wounded Child within, we find the Third Way that Jesus says He is. We find the stability of a triangle, like a mountain, the Rock upon which we stand.

Love changes our pain into something meaningful, makes us real, and valid, and our dying with Him in the human experience becomes His way to create redemption. The only way out of this painful human condition is through the Third Way of Jesus. Love changes giving up, letting go, and the nihilism of the Cross, into something meaningful and full of redemption. God as Love changes everything.

Allison Bailey Jorgensen is a Licensed Clinical Social Worker. She supports those struggling with suicidality, anxiety and depression, mood disorders, grief, and addictive behaviors by utilizing IFS, Somatic, Inner-Child, and Mindfulness modalities.

47

THE WHOLE-MAKING GOD WITHIN

SHERI D. KLING

Although we are traumatized people living in a traumatizing world, we can come to know and experience the Whole-Making God Within.

We live in a traumatized and traumatizing world. In a world where loved ones get sick and die, pain is unavoidable. But sometimes suffering comes at the hands of those who are supposed to love and care for us or from strangers bent on destruction.

Trauma in early childhood or adulthood can have devastating effects on our health and well-being. This was clearly shown in a study conducted in the 1990s by the Centers for Disease Control and Kaiser Permanente of San Diego, California, in what is now known as the ACEs (Adverse Childhood Experiences) Study.

In that research, 17,000 adults were questioned about their early lives and given a score from 1-10 based on their exposure to ten categories of adverse experience, including abuse, neglect, violence in the home, and other traumatic events. There was a shocking correlation between those experiences and the later development of chronic, debilitating health conditions and risky behaviors. The ACEs study and works like *The Body Keeps the Score* by Bessel van der Kolk, M.D., reveal the depth of scarring to the human psyche left by such trauma.

To anyone paying attention, it's clear that we in the United States are fragmented at all levels: in our society, in our relationships, and even within ourselves. Our culture doesn't help, with its worldview that splits mind from body, humans from nature, and tells us that we are machines living in a meaningless universe who only matter when we consume, consume, consume.

No wonder we are suffering. No wonder so many of us are hopeless, feeling like our lives will never change.

And Yet

And yet, there is healing and transformation available to us in every moment. Because there is a whole-making God active in the world and present within each and every one of us.

When we read mathematician-philosopher Alfred North Whitehead and psychologist Carl Gustav Jung, we find an integrating story that can be a balm to our painful fragmentation. In their work, we find that at both the levels of the cosmos and of the human psyche, there is:

1. A Universal Flow of Creative Life

2. A Universal Presence of the Sacred Within, and

3. A Universal Lure toward Healing and Whole-Making

The very good news for us is that these aspects of God can be encountered *within us*, in our most intimate experience as individuals, and within our collective web of life. These universals are also present in our relationships, whether intimate, social, or therapeutic.

A Universal Flow of Creative Life

Drawing from Whitehead and Jung, we can understand that there is an ever-flowing stream of creative life at the base of experience. We might think of this as the *eros* or creative fire within everything.

For Whitehead, this fire ignites the spark of every moment of becoming, giving that moment its "living immediacy." This primordial mystery—that rushing river of being and becoming—is the reason why there is something rather than nothing at all. We may even think of this *eros* as God's *desire* for embodiment, for incarnation, for actuality.

In the human psyche, *eros* is a pull toward relationship, toward connection with others. Is this same urge present in God as the desire that leads to the formation of a world? If so, then we may think of everything as interconnected in a divine web of relatedness and gravitational Love that both calls everything into being and holds it together.

This rushing river of *eros*, this universal flow of creative life, never stops. It is the hidden sacred spring of living water moving unseen within our everyday world. Jung thought of it as the collective life or objective psyche that we encounter in our depths as an "Other" that confronts and changes us.

The Universal Flow of Creative Life holds great riches. It's our source of dynamism, vitality, and novelty and we come alive ourselves when we live in relation to it. Tapping into its riches is essential for a life lived well where we can integrate our varied experiences into a coherent whole.

We access this living mystery when we can quiet our thoughts and widen our attention to weave in the stirrings and images arising from our unconscious depths. Spiritual practices like meditation, centering prayer, dream work, and walking a labyrinth all open us to the riches available from the Universal Flow of Creative Life.

A Universal Presence of the Sacred Within

When we think of a dynamic cosmos where everything is always in the process of becoming, moments arise ignited by the spark of God's Eros. But that spark doesn't just externally push that moment off on its own journey. No, that spark is part of the actual makeup of the moment!

In other words, every real thing begins with the *incarnation of God's self*. Even more, in its arising, God gives each moment its very *reason for becoming*. That vision is then either embraced as that moment's vision for itself—or not—because there are always many possibilities.

In other words, the drops of experience that make up every real thing in the world begin with the grace-filled outpouring of God's very own life and vision for possibility. This is how Whitehead describes God's nearness to us. God kick-starts every moment into being by *entering* it, by incarnating God's self as the living spark within its arising.

We might say that we internalize God in every moment of our becoming. In this way, God's sacred presence permeates the universe.

Similarly, when we think of the human psyche, Jung believed there to be an image of God in every person that he called the *archetypal Self*. Not the conscious ego, the Self is the structuring center of the human psyche that integrates and holds all aspects of the personality together. It is personal and yet also transcends our individual, personal life.

The archetypal Self is the centering and circling fluid presence of God within us. We might think of it as an eddy of living water that forms as the Universal Flow of Creative Life moves through us. This Self is the swirling meeting point of the streams of human and divine life.

A Universal Lure toward Healing and Wholeness

Where those streams of human and divine life meet, there is a lure toward healing and wholeness within the living and dying of a dynamic cosmos. In our world, the ongoing dance between continuous creation and perpetual perishing, between loss and renewal, is the beautiful and yet painful reality within which we live. This is why I say we are traumatized people living in a traumatizing world.

We might then ask, if God is forming every moment through the incarnation of God's self, then why does the world look the way it does? Why is there even trauma at all?

In a truly relational cosmos, God doesn't force particular outcomes into being but acts as a persuasive lure toward Beauty. According to Whitehead, the reason we have trauma, suffering, and disarray in the world is because every real *thing* has real *freedom*. Individuals ultimately choose for themselves whether they will actualize the vision that God offers. The poignant truth is that real freedom can mean real conflict and pain.

And yet, God works from within our very being to lure us toward wholeness and transformed futures by offering us those possibilities that God envisions as best for us in every moment. This is true regardless of our place of birth, our current or past circumstances, and regardless of the doctrines we believe or discard. It is true no matter our gender, the color of our skin or the content of our bank accounts. It is true for every one of us because this is how the world itself is continuously created. God offers us God's self in every moment; God's possibilities for our wholeness are as near to us as our next breath.

Although Carl Jung rarely talked about the reality of God outside the psyche, he did famously say in an interview with the British Broadcasting Corporation (BBC) that he didn't "believe" in God, but *knew* that God exists. Ultimately, Jung believed our religious statements and ideas are always filtered through human consciousness while pointing to something indescribable and inaccessible to us directly.

Instead of speaking of a transcendent God, Jung describes the archetypal Self as the knowing and wise part of the human psyche that sees our wholeness and potential and draws us toward that vision.

The Self mediates the symbols that arise from the collective unconscious that draw us toward individuation—a process of growth to develop our unique gifts and genius in the world along with the ability to relate more authentically to others. This movement integrates the opposing energies within us—moving us toward wholeness—and brings to consciousness what has been unknown to us about ourselves. Often, these unknown aspects hold great energy and psychological riches when we can integrate them into our conscious personality.

Psychological shadow work to bring unconscious aspects of ourselves to the light of consciousness heals our emotional reactivity. It allows us to live in the present moment and respond from the flow of creative life. Spiritual practices like dream work and Ignatian discernment open our perception to the vision that God has for us in every moment and helps us live into transformed futures.

When we open our awareness to these three aspects of God (Universal Flow of Creative Life, Universal Presence of the Sacred Within, and Universal Lure toward Healing and Whole-Making) and adopt practices to encounter them, we can then experience for ourselves the kind of transformation and rebirth that help us actualize the value and Beauty that we can then joyfully offer the world.

Even if we come from traumatized beginnings, we find seeds of hope in the encounter with the healing, wholeness, creativity, and novelty at the heart of Reality. Contemplating new ideas about our Whole-Making God and adopting spiritual practices that make that God *real* for us can then restore our relationship with the Universal Flow of Creative Life, root us in the Universal Presence of the Sacred Within, and open us to the Universal Lure toward Healing and Wholeness.

Sheri D. Kling, Ph.D. is an author, speaker, singer, and spiritual mentor who draws from wisdom and mystical traditions, relational worldviews, depth psychology, and the intersection of spirituality and science to help people find meaning, belonging, and transformation. She regularly delivers dynamic "Music & Message" presentations to groups, and offers courses, concerts, and spiritual retreats. Dr. Kling is director of Process & Faith and the John Cobb Legacy Fund and a faculty member of the Haden Institute. She sees her mission as midwifing wholeness in individuals, organizations, communities, and culture. Her work can be found online at www.sherikling.com.

48

THE KIND OF GOD, THE KIND OF MAN

DON NEUFELD

Masculinity modeled after a distant, harsh, controlling "Father" God has a significant impact on men and those who live with and love them.

As we sat down for their first session of counselling as a couple, Jeremy (not his real name) was quick to confirm that I was a "devoted Christian" and indicated it was important to him that I know that "only one truth" exists on which to base our lives, and by implication, the counselling. His wife indicated she was "struggling with being a godly wife." Jeremy shared that his wife did not like the word "submission", but that "God is a God of order", which for him meant that "when stuff hits the fan there is only one leader".

In the early sessions it became clear that Jeremy had difficulty hearing his wife and tuning into her deep distress about the state of their relationship. As she indicated, "he fights me on my experiences". On top of his full-time work as a manager in the service industry that often demanded on-call responsibilities seven days a week, his enthusiastic commitment to his ministry work in their congregation and to the parishioners led his wife to express significant discouragement with not feeling valued in the scope of his priorities.

The graphicness of this actual case example highlights a number of significant themes that characterize some Christian couples that I have worked with in my career as a social worker. The assumed characteristics and role definitions of men, rooted in a specific reading of especially Paul's letters in the New Testament, ends up looking very much like the dominant, aloof and controlling God of classical Christian theology. Professor Stephen B. Boyd describes such modelling of masculinity after images of God in his book *The Men We Long to Be: Beyond Domination to a New Christian Understanding of Manhood*. He speaks of how these images legitimize unhealthy characteristics in men such as invulnerability, isolation, and domination.

Further, the order gleaned from scripture of God->Jesus->Man->Woman enshrines a hierarchy between men and women that then becomes the basis of power dynamics in relationships. This amounts to both a privileged position of power and a burden of responsibility that play havoc in men's lives. This havoc often then falls on those who live with and love men.

Therapeutic work with Christian men, in relationship counselling, in individual and in group work, does well to consider the echoes of these images of God in situations where power has been wielded in destructive ways and emotional distance is evident in relationships. The assumed authority and entitlement of men living under the presumptions about male superiority and privilege too often lead to extremes. This is especially so when normal human insecurities are threatened and powering up becomes the ready answer. This powering up finds implicit and sometimes explicit justification and permission within some streams of Christian teaching and preaching. Messages of compassion and restraint of these human impulses, when present, fall far short of the broader societal endorsements of male dominance and violence.

In relationships with spouses, in parenting, within the workplace or in community settings, misapplied power in the hands of finite men hurts others, and in turn leaves men's lives and relationships in shambles. Lacking more fully developed toolboxes for life, the hammer continues to be the only available tool for a life that would be much better served by fine instruments of empathy, care and tenderness. Societal messages about true manliness that decry any sign of weakness, trivialize emotionality and honor competitive performance, leave men with deep dilemmas within their lonely selves. They are confronted with the contradictions between how they presume they are supposed to be as men and the outcomes which foster distance, fear and disdain in the eyes of those by whom they long to be loved.

For boys and young men who are schooled in Christian families and communities with a calling to lead, to be the head of the home, to provide and protect, to live up to the image of "Godly men" they are intended to be, the actualities of life can be daunting and ultimately devastating. Striving to establish their legitimacy from the playground to the workplace, from dating to the wedding day, from the locker room to the bedroom, the demands to perform are incessant and often take a deep toll on boys' and men's lives.

The looming voices of primarily men in their lives instill the "fear of God" should they fail on this quest. Fathers driven by their own fear of being seen to be inadequate, model their behavior after the dominant images of an angry and cold "Father God" who haunted them in their developmental years, inflicting the same destruction into subsequent generations.

The competitive and performative nature of this type of masculinity can lead to risky, extreme and isolating behaviors. Shame is always knocking at the door as any shortfall is bound to bring external criticism and internal messages of failure that can be overwhelming. The image of a controlling, demanding and harsh God who has presumably instituted these high expectations for men in the Bible, is a dominating presence for many. The need to follow the traditional definitions of masculinity and to enforce their dominant roles in families and communities goes unquestioned, as it is the only picture of masculinity that so many ever witness as legitimate. And with God as the ultimate and unwavering judge, men in good faith simply want to be faithful.

Open and Relational Theism offers relief to the burdens of performance and shame, and opens an avenue to lower the guard of aggression and power. A God who is fully loving and relational invites men to live not in the fear of shame brought on by failure and the threatening presence of an angry "father", but in a voice that is remarkably gentle and calm offers the potential for peace. Mimicking God's highest attribute of love, we take our cues for life from Jesus' life, who modeled sacrificial love including love for enemies and strangers.

Intimate relationships, parenting, and interactions with those in our work-places and communities, are lived from a place of grounded character-based strength, not through intimidation and detachment. The characteristics and role expectations of men are not simply determined by social mores of First Century society, but an openness exists in which each individual man, and men in general, can participate as full and unique persons according to their gifting and inter-ests. God has joined with his creation as we vision and develop healthier ideas of masculinity. Men join with women to envision and work towards relationships of mutuality, trust and love.

A clinical approach to men who are seeking counsel, whether for troubling behaviors that have prompted pressure from others, for internal states of stress and hopelessness, or due to addictions and risk of self-harm that is so pervasive, requires that we also offer ourselves as agents of such a loving God to bring soothing and hope. Men need invitations to safety and love, even when their behaviors may have caused harm to others or to themselves. An Open and Relational image of God offers a powerful and intriguing alternative that is life-giving. Introducing such a picture of God brings men into a realm of possibility for change. A new paradigm for masculinity arises, and has significant potential to bring healing for men, individually and collectively. God's love draws men towards lives of peace.

Don Neufeld *is a social worker in private practice specializing in services for men. He is the co-editor of* Peaceful at Heart: Anabaptist Reflections on Healthy Masculinity *(2019) and the co-author of* Living that Matters: Honest Conversations for Men of Faith *(2023). He is a student in the Master of Theological Studies program at Conrad Grebel University in Waterloo, Ontario.*

– 49 –

AGENTS OF CHANGE

LARRY PAYNE

Our religious beliefs can make a difference in our power to act.

*H*ave you ever felt stuck in a situation you could not change? It's frustrating and even frightening to lose what psychologists call "agency." Good theology and mental health practices will aid in regaining the power to change.

Some of the most disturbing stories of evil in modern culture are stories of imprisonment. The world was shocked in 2018 when a Canadian woman, Edith Blaise, and an Italian man, Luca Tachetto, were captured by Islamic terrorists. They were driving across west Africa to visit a friend when their lives changed forever. The terrorists stopped them and imprisoned them in a remote desert camp. In her book, *The Weight of Sand*, Edith recounted the terrible desert conditions, the isolation, and the fear that gripped her. Cut off from her boyfriend and the civilization she knew, she had no power to change what was happening to her.

I can't imagine how helpless Edith felt. However, I've talked with clients who felt helplessly trapped in their emotional state. They had tried to change but couldn't. Psychologically, their power to change, called agency, was diminished to the point of giving up. Like Edith in the remote African desert, they were held as an emotional hostage by the past. Only by gaining real agency can clients move toward wellness.

When psychologists talk with clients about agency, the idea is simple. Agency is the client's belief that they can think or act otherwise, in a manner different than what has been done in the past. Consider a toddler for example, who may want to climb onto a couch but can't pull himself up that high. Acting with agentic capacity, however, he pulls a short stool near the couch and uses it as a step to triumphantly climb and sit on the couch. He had agency to think and act to bring change.

Edith and Luca, prisoners in the desert, had little capacity for agentic actions. Their captors held all the power for food and water, shelter in the desert, reward and punishment, socialization, and movement. At times, the loneliness and despair were overwhelming.

It doesn't take a terrorist camp in the desert of Africa to rob us of the capacity for change. A woman may feel helpless to escape an abusive marriage. Having few employment skills and trapped by patriarchal beliefs, she feels she must submit with no way out. Or a man fighting addiction may think there is no hope of real change, hating what is happening yet seemingly locked into a daily cycle of desperation. Agency is compromised and negative moods descend like dark clouds each day.

One of the most interesting stories in the Bible concerns a woman with a chronic illness. According to the narrator, she had suffered some ailment that brought chronic bleeding, persisting for 12 years. As Jesus walked through a village in Galilee, the woman heard about his healing power. Desperate, she pushed through the crowd and grabbed his robe. Jesus felt her tug. When confronted, she admitted her bold action in seeking healing and the incredible cessation of her chronic condition! Jesus said gently, "Daughter, your faith has healed you. Go in peace."

The story of miraculous healing may sound strange to 21st-century Westerners, who want to know the mechanics of this healing. Perhaps it was the placebo effect or a flow of energy beyond our current medical explanations. More important for our focus today is the agency with which this woman acted. She had sought healing many times and took action again as Jesus came to her village. Far from being helpless, she believed she could act and did with boldness. Jesus affirmed her agency.

Our religious beliefs can make a difference in our power to act. Some theologians have taught that God predetermines and controls all events of the universe. They reject the idea of people having the freedom and essential capacity to choose the actions of their lives. In essence, this doctrine eliminates agency. We are not able to ultimately change anything, though it may appear on the surface we are doing so. Thankfully, a better view of God and the universe can be found. Progressive theologians teach that all creatures have agency because the very nature of divine love is noncoercive, pervading and persuading all conscious entities to make choices within their capacities. Thomas Oord has written, "God necessarily gives the gifts of agency and self-organization to entities capable of them because doing so is part of divine love…. If God were to coerce others by withdrawing, overriding, or failing to provide freedom, agency, or self-organization, God would need to renounce the divine nature of self-giving, others-empowering love." With this insight, we can say that agency is at the center of God's relationship to us. Agency is a God-given capacity and the Divine desires it to be fully functional in our daily life.

If we feel trapped and unable to act, how can we move toward reclaiming agency for well-being? Psychologists Daniel William and Heide Levitt offer three essential steps.

We must address our emotions. How we feel about ourselves and our circumstances is only an opinion, not a fact. Feelings change all the time. Yes, they are powerful, but we can actually choose what we will do with the way we feel. The kidnap victims, Luca and Edith, felt terror and helplessness when the criminals surrounded their car, ordering them at gunpoint to get out. As the days went by, however, they gained perspective. They began to reason about the situation and focused their emotions on hope, giving them energy to act. We reclaim agency when we use our emotions without allowing them to control us.

We also gain agency when we choose to build skills and information. We make mental preparation for action, applying agency to the situation. The abused woman decides she can't risk her health being destroyed and discreetly calls a hotline to get help. The addict admits losing his job is a real threat and he chooses to attend the AA meeting this week. These small steps of self-determination are the demonstrations of agency that build momentum for change. Luca started learning Arabic, the language of his captors. They were willing to talk to him and he took advantage of that to develop a skill. He also learned about Islam because he saw the terrorists treated fellow Muslims in a different way than infidels. Edith found a new power when she obtained a pen and paper. She began to write poetry, hiding the works under her clothes. It freed her mind from the oppressive loneliness and fear of death.

A final element in agency is the determination to push through obstacles. Change is not easy for anyone. The situations may be very difficult, or our fears may hold us back. If we continue to push forward however, exploring, experimenting, and trying again, our agentic power will increase.

Jesus recognized this agency as a blossoming faith in the woman who touched him. He commended her for the boldness that reached out to him as a collaboration with God for her wellbeing. We find the same with Luca and Edith. They did not surrender to their captors. Instead, they outwitted them. They made faux conversions to the faith that allowed them to be together. Then, in the middle of the night and a ferocious sandstorm, they ran from the camp. Before dawn they had covered six miles of desert terrain and flagged down a truck driver on the highway. He took them to a city where the police gave shelter. Within a matter of hours, they were delivered. They had spent 450 days in the desert prison but escaped to live free again.

Agency is the capacity to think and act differently. It is a foundation of mental health and well-being. Agency is a part of God's uncontrolling love for our lives. On your journey, unleash that power for the best you can achieve.

Larry Payne has served during a 45-year career as a pastor, hospital chaplain, and professional counselor. He holds a D.Min. in pastoral theology and a Masters in professional counseling. He works as an LPC with Betterhelp.com. His podcast, Tracks for the Journey, *explores theology, counseling, and history (www. tracksforthejourney.com). Running, genealogy, and chores keep him busy at the Bright Star Farm in Texas.*

50

RELATIONAL THEOLOGY AND RELATIONAL PSYCHOTHERAPY

DONN PETERS

Are we aware of our own biases in the kind of God we create?

Molly's Story

Molly's God was not a relational God, but she desperately needed a relational therapist. Molly grew up in a conservative Christion home. She attended churches that presented to Gospel as a clear choice between right and wrong, with the catch that if you chose wrongly, you would spend eternity in hell. Primary to her experience was that she was "in it alone". No one was there to hear her questions and concerns. They were there to tell her what to think and what to choose. She found this somehow attractive and repelling all at once.

Molly had internalized a version of God that was primarily a lawgiver and judge. He gave the law, which is very clear, and judged her failings to keep the law and seemed not to care about her experience.

In working with her I chose to take a curious and collaborative stance with her. I was interested in how she became to be the person she was with me. I had to remind her that I was curious and was not seeking to judge her but wanted to get to know her. I also acknowledged my biases, particularly around religious issues. Often, I would ask her "Do you have any responses to how I'm interacting with you today?" Or "How is it for you to be in this relationship with me?"

Open and Relational Theology

Thomas Jay Oord has been writing on the topic of Open and Relational Theology for more than 20 years. Along the way, he found it necessary to redefine some historical theological concepts. Primary among these was the re-definition of love. Whereas classical theology had defined a loving God as a bit capricious, sometimes nurturing and caring while at other times cruel and uncaring, Tom's contribution is to see God's love as uncontrolling. A controlling love coerces an uncontrolling love influences. A controlling love operates by fear and threats of punishment. Uncontrolling love respects the autonomy of the individual. A God who uses controlling love stands apart, outside of our experience issuing commands and consequences for not following them. A God who uses uncontrolling love experiences our pains and joys and is "in it" with us.

Open Future – This issue addresses God's foreknowledge. Does God know the future? Open theologians say God can only know what is knowable, the future has not happened yet and is therefore unknowable.

Relational God – What are God's primary attributes? Classical theology defines God's nature as omnipotence, omniscience, and omnipresence which emphasize God's power and control. Relational theologians say God's primary attribute is love, all else is subordinate to love. As a loving God, God cannot control but only influence humans. As a loving God, God seeks a relationship with us humans. Rather than being seen primarily as the lawgiver and judge God is seen as the "fellow traveler" who is moved by our experiences.

Theodicy – The question that bedevils Christian theologians and philosophers of all sorts is the problem of evil. It is the central question in the book of Job. In the history of thought, the problem of evil is stated as the theodicy trilemma and is presented as early as Epicurus in *De Ira Dei*, 13, 20-2 and stated as 1. If God is unable to prevent evil, then he is not all-powerful. 2.1 If God is not willing to prevent evil, then he is not all-good. 3. If God is both willing and able to prevent evil, then why does evil exist? David Hume restated it as "Is God willing to prevent evil, but not able? Then He is impotent. Is He able but not willing? Then He is malevolent. Is He both able and willing? Whence then is evil?"

Relational Psychology

Relational psychology employs relational rather than mechanistic metaphors. During Sigmund Freud's (1856-1939) time the major technological achievement was the invention was the steam engine. Water heated to steam could be harnessed to do useful work. Freud's theory changed over the years as he thought more

240

deeply about the nature of the human psyche. By 1923 he published "The Ego and the Id" which became known as his structural theory. In keeping with the mechanistic metaphor of the steam engine, he saw the id as a seething cauldron of incestuous and murderous desires. This energy, which he called libido was harnessed by the ego to perform useful work of the psyche. Later he added the idea of a superego that functioned much like a whistle on the steam engine, tooting its warning when the pressure became too high.

Freud was following the tradition of Descartes and Newton in describing human functioning using machine metaphors. There was a significant amount of pushback, especially from the religious thinkers of the time, but eventually, the ideas took hold. For example, Neuroscientists believe they are explaining human behavior when they can reduce it to a complex machine-like set of efficient causes.

Freud died in 1939 after emigrating to London from his beloved Vienna in 1938. Prior to his death, he exerted strong control over the psychoanalytic movement. Early followers became heretics and were disbanded because of ideas or practices deemed non-compliant with the model he developed. After his death, a few brave souls in the British Psychoanalytic Society began to publish new ideas. While the new ideas produced many controversies those putting forth the ideas were not summarily dismissed.

There arose a great controversy between Anna Freud, Sigmund's never-married daughter, protector of the tradition, and Melanie Klein. The differences are hard to understand by the outsider, and therefore won't be mentioned here except to say they brought about the "controversial discussions" of 1942 and 43. Two important names came to the forefront Ronald Fairbairn and Donald Winnicott. Fairbairn changed the nature of libido. Freud's libido in blind mechanistic fashion sought only discharge, Fairbairn's libido was "object seeking" or better understood as relationship seeking. They solved the differences in the name of peace but at the cost of metatheoretical and theoretical integrity.

In the years after the war, many of Freud's followers emigrated to America. One such person was Heinz Kohut who left Vienna shortly after Freud. He developed Psychoanalytic Self Psychology which borrowed ideas from the British group. Harry Stack Sullivan a non-analyst but reader of Freud developed ideas that were to become Psychoanalytic Interpersonal Psychology. Contemporary analysts such as Robert Stolorow, Stephen Mitchell, and Estelle Shane furthered the development of what has become known as Relational Psychoanalysis.

The relational therapist fosters a spirit of curiosity and collaboration. The effect of these changes was to replace mechanistic metaphors with relational metaphors. Donald Winnicott changed the basic metaphor from a steam engine to a mother with baby which focuses on the development of the self through relational interactions between the mother and baby. This led to a plethora of research focusing on early mother-infant interactions.

Other changes in the therapeutic process were the establishment of a spirit of curiosity and collaboration rather than a spirit of the "knowing analyst" leading the self-deceiving patient to the truth. One other change of note was that the contemporary analyst saw themselves as active rather than passive in the co-creation of the therapeutic relationship.

The relational analyst is aware of his/her own biases. This includes a deep awareness of the analysts own inner world. His/her personal contributions and organizing principles to the treatment setting. It involves a minute-by-minute awareness of the transference-countertransference fluctuations in the interactions with the clients or clients. This awareness forms the basis of the analyst's understanding of the client's inner world and how it came to be. At points in the therapy, the analyst will state some of his/her understanding and check with the client to see if this makes sense. At other times the analyst will ask the client something like this "How do you feel about our interaction today?" Imagine God asking us humans how we feel about our interaction with him/her. Imagine God asking, "How do you experience me?" or "How do you experience my revelations to you?" Imagine a God who actually wants to be in a relationship with us and desires to share our experiences and hear from us.

What is it about us humans that we create a God who is primarily about power and control? A God who is primarily a lawgiver and judge, certain to punish our failings. A God who is distant and removed? Why do we prefer an omniscient and omnipotent God who knows all of our past, present, and futures but so often chooses not to act? Why do we prefer a God who allows evil and then claims it was in the service of good? And we call that a loving God.

Are we aware of our own biases in the kind of God we create?

Donn Peters received a Doctor of Psychology from BIOLA University in 1991. In June of 2020 he received a Doctor of Psychoanalysis from the Institute for Contemporary Psychoanalysis in Los Angeles. He is currently writing a dissertation on "The Relational turn in Psychoanalysis and Theology" for Tom Oord's Open and Relational Theology doctoral program.

51

ENABLING PRESENCE

RON WRIGHT

God's uncontrolling love is a presence that influences in a similar way as a psychotherapist who provides a caring, attuned, loving presence in therapy.

"I seem to always end up hurt and I don't know what to do. Why am I always the one hurt? What do you think I should do? Please just tell me and I will do it!"

$\mathcal{T}$he words above are sentiments that therapists commonly hear, and which represent a lot more complexity and nuance than one might expect out of such a seemingly simple plea. As a therapist, how might I hear these words? Do I take them at face value? Might there be a danger in telling a client what to do? Do these words reflect deeper assumptions that the person is making about themselves that are problematic? Might these words also reflect assumptions that are being made about God? What really is at work behind these words?

As I reflect upon these words as a therapist, I am also confronted with questions about what I think brings about help or healing through therapy. Is help or healing brought about through instruction and telling people what to do? Do I need to take control for therapy to be helpful or healing? What is the role of the client's freedom and agency in the therapeutic process? Is there a connection between the help or healing provided and *how* I am in the room as a therapist?

My hope in this essay is to connect the uncontrolling relational *presence* that I view as the necessary element for help or healing in the therapeutic process with my understanding of the importance of God's uncontrolling relational presence. To make this connection I intend to describe some of the psychological dynamics involved in control, how those dynamics might relate to our understanding of who God is, and how reframing power as potency, and not as domination or control, is central for healing and for an understanding of the uncontrolling relational presence of God.

The dynamics of control

Our earliest experiences with our caregivers begin to shape how we understand who we are, who others are, what it means to relate to another, and how we are to be in those relationships. Attachment theory posits that about fifty to sixty percent of people experience secure attachment with caregivers which allows them to develop an understanding of themselves as trustworthy and loveable, of other people as caring and concerned, and of relationships as places where attuned, sensitive, and loving mutual interdependence are found. Unfortunately, that means about another forty to fifty percent of people experience some kind of insecure attachment.

The first insecure attachment, avoidant, reflects an experience with caregivers where one develops an understanding of themselves as having to be independent, self-sufficient, and competent, of other people as neglectful and rejecting, and of relationships as places that are to be escaped because of the expectation of harm. The second insecure attachment, anxious, reflects an experience with caregivers where one develops an understanding of themselves as unlovable, worthless, and needy, of others as inconsistent in their sensitivity and care, yet also desperately needed, and of relationships as places that are craved and clung to no matter what happens.

In this brief summary of attachment styles we can begin to see that the ways we come to understand ourselves, others, and how to be in relationships impact how we might value or resist control. For example, the securely attached person seeks to be in a mutual and interdependent relationship, the avoidantly attached person seeks to resist control and to establish independence, while the anxiously attached person may seek out the control of others due to their feelings of low self-worth and need to merge with another. Adding to this picture of the relational dynamics that are at work in an understanding of control are psychological dynamics relating to the need for security and certainty.

When anxiety is experienced, we are all motivated to move towards those people, ideas, places, and things that we have associated with safety and assurance. In the face of anxiety, an avoidantly attached person will be even more motivated to establish their autonomy and to move away from relationships while the anxiously attached person will find added motivation to seek proximity and submission to another.

Controlling God

Research within attachment theory suggests that we often relate to God in a similar way as we have learned to relate to our caregivers. This makes sense given that God is not embodied, and we often refer to God in parental terms (e.g. Father). Taking what we have discussed about attachment dynamics and applying it to how we come to understand and relate to God yields some interesting insights.

For those who have experienced their caregivers as neglectful and rejecting, they may come to God with expectations that God, too, is ultimately disinterested in them. If they experience pain or suffering in their lives, they may view this as confirmation of the rejecting God they expected. Even if they don't experience God as rejecting them, they may still view God as attempting to control them, and thus, they may distance themselves from God. It is difficult for those with avoidant tendencies to allow themselves to feel close to God. Given their experiences in relationships, this kind of intimacy is one that stirs up anxiety and so they will emotionally distance themselves from God. Faith, for these folks, may look more intellectual and cerebral than emotional. Questions, doubt, and skepticism may play a more central role in the faith journey of those with avoidant tendencies as they use their intellect to maintain distance from God.

For those who have experienced their caregivers as inconsistent in providing care and concern and have therefore learned to submit and cling in relationships, they may relate to God through submission and attempting to stay emotionally close to God. Due to their assumption that they have nothing to offer, they look to others, including God, as places of security that they must hold on to. They expect to submit to God. This is due to the anxiety that comes with emotional distance and fear of abandonment. They also may desire for God to control them as a way of staying close to God. It is difficult for those with anxious tendencies to allow themselves to feel separate from God so they may cling to God. Faith, for these folks, may look more emotional than intellectual. A desire for certainty, security, and doing the "right thing" may play a more central role in the faith journey of those with anxious tendencies as their anxiety and fear of abandonment motivate them to move as close to God as possible.

Uncontrolling relational presence

So what do those who are avoidant or anxious in their attachment need in therapeutic settings? How might this also relate to an understanding of God? Often power is understood in terms of control and domination and is therefore something to distance from (if one is avoidant) or to submit to (if one is anxious). This is why therapists must be aware of how power might be understood within the therapeutic setting and why the simple plea at the beginning of this article is one that must be intentionally contemplated by the therapist. It is easy for therapists, too, to understand power as being strictly about control or domination. But what if there is a different way to understand power?

Erich Fromm, a psychoanalyst who focused on the dynamics of anxiety involved in our capacity for free will, reframes power as the capacity to be able to do something or to display mastery of some ability. Potency, as the alternative understanding of power for Fromm, is an expression of a self that feels alive. When one feels potent one does not need to dominate or control. Instead, giving is viewed as the highest expression of potency. It is through giving that one experiences their own aliveness, and this giving enhances the other's sense of aliveness. This perspective is what Fromm is getting at when he says, "Love is a power which produces love; impotence is the inability to produce love."

When therapists "give" their presence, care, and concern without attempting to control or dominate this dynamic is at work. For the avoidant client, the uncontrolling presence that the therapist gives is one focused on being an alternative caring expression to the harmful, neglecting relationships that the avoidant person has learned to expect. For the anxious client, the uncontrolling presence that the therapist gives is one focused on being the patient, consistent presence that counters the expectation that they have nothing to offer and will be abandoned. What is therapeutic in each of these instances is not how the therapist controls or forcefully changes anything, but rather how the potent and enabling relational presence that the therapist provides calls forth a new response in the client.

It is this dynamic of the uncontrolling relational giving of presence that provides, for me, a powerful metaphor for God as well. The God who IS love continues to express that love to us through being present with us, not through controlling all that happens to us. Loving presence wooing us towards love.

Ron Wright *is a professor of psychology at Southern Nazarene University and is also a licensed psychologist. He earned a Ph.D. in Clinical Psychology and an M.A. in Theology from Fuller Theological Seminary. Wright has been a Fulbright Scholar in Romania and was a Scholarship and Christianity in Oxford (SCIO) Visiting Scholar in Science and Religion. He consults with pastors, church leaders, and congregations about the impact of psychological dynamics on faith and life together for communities of faith. Ron can be easily reached at rwright@snu.edu.*

52

SORRY, THAT WON'T WORK FOR ME

ANGELA

Rather than rescuing, we are told, "God is with you in suffering."

I walked out of church in the middle of the message. I honestly could not listen to another sermon which idolized a God of love, contradicted by his own actions.

Don't we all enjoy a good superhero movie? We cheer as Christopher Reeves swoops down and sets the universe back in order. We expectantly anticipate the fairy tale ending as our hero conquers oppression, darkness and injustice. And, of course, what is a good movie unless everyone lives happily ever after. I wonder if our draw to these fantasies is the imagination deep within our souls, to know that there is a supernatural being who can control the universe, who is innately good and loving. A superhero who sees "me" and fights for my honor. A force for good who gets the last word. I want to imagine that there is. I wish my imagination had never met reality.

Understanding the neuroscientific and physiological implications of mental and emotional anguish had been only theory and hypothesis until recent developments in medical technology. It is now possible to view the brain, measure and benchmark physiological changes associated with trauma, PTSD, depression, and anxiety. These discoveries have given psychologists and physicians insight into treating those whose lives have been devastated. But at the end of the day, we still wish our superhero had protected us. We fiercely struggle to make sense of what forms our faith and what we experience?

I believe efforts in mental health care have mismanaged a powerful component in the healing and helping processes. This integrant is spiritual trauma. Confusion, anger and hopelessness caused from a disconnect in what we understand about God, his role in humanity and what we experience. A trauma, that regardless of educating, resourcing, and therapy approaches, still leaves an enormous hole in the souls of the suffering. A trauma that asks, "If God loves me, if God is all powerful, then why was I not protected, why was my loved one not healed, why did my parent leave me, why are innocent children being abused, why are people starving, why the holocaust..."

The question, "why," crosses cultures, societies and religions. The majority of civilizations believe in some supernatural presence or powerful persona. Many ascribe this presence to God. This God is typically believed to be eternal, all powerful, all knowing, and by most measures, just. In the Christian faith, we believe this God embodies sacrificial love. This God loves unconditionally with a relational "fatherly" love. Yet, the definition of love seems counter, at times, with the actions or lack of action of an all-powerful, loving, God.

If the battle had only been relative to traumatic events, maybe I could have forged through a little less mangled. Frankly, I could do the hard work of healing. Therapy helped me process pain and equipped me with coping skills. I had accepted that my abuser had a mental illness. I processed the shame, the anger, and navigated the PTSD. And still, there was this hole. I resonated with the Dark Night of the Soul, as described by George Sand. "We do not die of anguish, we live on. We continue to suffer. We drink the cup, drop by drop." My spirit was still broken and void. What did I do with that space in me that longed for connection with a holy higher, with a purpose. The place that yearns to believe in a loving God, but doesn't trust this God's love.

How God is framed and his role in suffering can cause further trauma, confusion and hopelessness. Those who have suffered loss or trauma oftentimes are provided with damaging scripture references about the sovereignty and omnipotence of a good God who cares more about our souls than our comfort. These references are used in attempts to console and comfort the hurting by touting the mystery and sovereignty of a higher power.

My references to God were understood through the lens of a sacred, inerrant or literal interpretation of the Bible. God is Omniscience, Omnipotent, Omnipresent and Immanent. God controls all things, causing or *allowing* both good and suffering in some quest for his own glory or creations' ultimate good. If it doesn't make sense or seems to contradict, then you are thinking too much, don't have enough faith or are undermining a holy almighty God. Sorry, that doesn't work for me.

God is, many times, likened to a loving parent who does good to his children, provides for and protects them. However (like any good father??), he doesn't rescue *all* of them, alter outcomes or intervene for *all* because, "some have lessons to learn." This God doesn't overstep his ***own*** boundaries and choices to infringe upon free will. So rather than rescue, we are told he is there with us in the suffering, he hurts with us, his grace is sufficient, we won't "understand" until we get to heaven. Viewing God from this perspective can be extremely disorienting. What parent having an ounce of love would not run to, risk their own life and rescue their child from being violated, kidnapped, killed or otherwise harmed. The theological gymnastics required to maintain this belief system is exhausting.

It was once explained to me by a kindly saint, that God cannot act against his own instituted boundaries in granting free will. I ask, then, "who makes the bloody rules?" Does this approach not undermine the claim of being all-powerful and all-controlling? Is this holy mystery what we offer because it makes us uncomfortable to poke at the indiscretions in the historical Christian interpretation of scripture for fear that we may actually see holes in our faith? I walked out of church that day.

Hours of psychotherapy, mindfulness, neuroscience research and at times medication and I still hit a wall. The questions and confusion of faith fueled anxiety and despair. I had no energy left. I longed to believe there was a good God. I longed to believe in love. At the core of my agony was the intrinsic gravitational expression of good and love which called to me. I needed to believe there was a God who loved, and saw, who cherished a little girl.

But, what if God doesn't control all things. What if he doesn't "allow" suffering. What if he isn't sitting on the sidelines anticipating that glorious "return" when our dimly lit glass will be removed, it all makes sense, and we break out in a chorus of "O Happy Day."

Enter center stage—Thomas Jay Oord and *The Uncontrolling Love of God*. As if…a LOVING God, directed a loving friend to share this absolute insane, object-able, questionable, disruptive narrative of how we understand God and Love! It was an immediate and transformative moment. I sat staring at the pages. Tears streamed down my face. In a moment I found freedom from darkness and lost hope. Years of confusion, anguish, and emptiness gave way to this newfound truth. God had not ordained my abuse. God was not lurking beneath mystery while standing silently on the sideline. He need not manifest his glory in some mysterious redemptive agenda at the expense of a little girl.

What if God is the fullness of love like we desperately want to believe. What if we frame his power through his creation and the call of those who carry the name of Christ? Jesus summarized scripture in a simple command, to love. What if God's power is limited to love, calling and influencing his creation to partner in love and good? This God I can trust!

I am working on a research project exploring spiritual trauma resulting from trauma and loss. In a survey, I asked what explanations or counsel was offered regarding God's role in suffering. Does one's beliefs relative to God help or impede the healing process? Participants in the survey were familiar with Tom Oord's work *God Can't* or were provided with a summary of Open and Relational Theology. The final question asked whether understanding God from an uncontrolling or ORT viewpoint would have been beneficial and/or helped expedite healing. An overwhelming 94 percent so far have indicated understanding God from this view would have made a difference. This God. That works for me!

Angela is a healthcare administrative professional. She is currently working on a research and survey project exploring spiritual trauma in relation to trauma and loss. Her interests in neuroscience, psychology and open and relational theology are spurred by stories of others as well as her own journey. (Angela does not want her last name published.)

53

FAITH, FREEDOM, AND FROMM

NATHAN D. CROY

If someone wants to embrace freedom, they should prepare for anxiety too.

*A*s Rati sat in my office, she wasn't weeping or angry, she was frozen. "I don't know if I want to get married to him or not. This wedding has been arranged since I was 12 and I had kind of accepted it. It happened to my other siblings, so I wasn't ever surprised. Now that it's here, I mean, he's not a bad person! I just…I don't know. People have asked me if I want to get married, if I hate the idea of an arranged marriage, all of that, but no one has asked me if I wanted to marry *him*. And now, I just don't know."

Rati (not her real name) moved from India to America for college. She came from a very wealthy and powerful family. They were conservative and maintained many cultural traditions, including arranged marriages. As her wedding day approached, her anxiety was growing. This man she was supposed to marry, she had only met him once, briefly, about 5 years ago. They had spoken online and by phone many times, but he remained a relative stranger to her.

Her time in America had introduced her to new concepts, customs, and cultures. None of her friends or roommates were expected to marry someone that had been chosen for them by their families. She was aware there were countries where arranged marriages were not the norm, but it was different when she experienced it first-hand. There seemed to be a very different set of expectations and outcomes in marriages, dating, and generally living life. Experiencing the reality of what she knew about vaguely had struck a chord with her. For Rati, the choice she was preparing to make extended far beyond the pending marriage. She was choosing between cultures, risking rejection from the family she was financially dependent on while finishing graduate school, and possibly being abandoned by some of the most important people she has ever known.

With the wedding date steadily marching towards her, Rati knew she would have to make a choice. It was clear that either choice would involve the risk of significant loss. That is why I asked her a different question,

"Rati, you've told me what other people have expected from you; your friends in college, a few men you've met, and your family. But there's one thing I haven't heard yet. What do you want?"

Many patients freeze at the question, "What do you want?" They frequently say they don't know, they're not sure, or they hope someone else will tell them. The bad news is that, of all the things therapy, religion, community, or relationships can give you, the one thing they cannot give someone is a want. It would be like asking someone to help me change my preference from raw broccoli to cooked broccoli! Others cannot alter my preferences. They can influence outcomes by controlling access to potential choices, they can encourage me to engage in certain activities, they can even threaten abandonment, rejection, or death for failure to comply. Ultimately, even if a person chooses to conform to the expectations of others, they may still be powerless to change their *want*. When this happens, when there's incongruence between our values and our drive (or our *want*), we experience anxiety.

For Kierkegaard, anxiety served a similar purpose to the emotion of healthy guilt. In the same way that guilt motivates people to engage in relationship repair after they have done something to damage the relationship (either with themselves, others, or God), anxiety pushes people to seek out congruence between their *want* and their behaviors. This anxiety only exists if there is freedom to choose how a *want* is expressed. In The Concept of Anxiety, Kierkegaard defined anxiety as "the dizziness of freedom" because, without this freedom to choose, we won't have to worry about acting congruently or not. We wouldn't even have to mourn the loss of being able to express our sense of self, our *want*, in the world. Freedom and anxiety are inextricably intertwined. Humanity, because we have the burden of awareness of our existence, cannot have freedom without anxiety. In the same way guilt can serve a healthy purpose (relationship repair), anxiety can be just as healthy (repair of authenticity).

Reflecting on the expansion of authoritarianism in the late 1930's, Fromm wrote *Escape from Freedom* (1941). He wanted to understand how Hitler could come to power with minimal resistance from the general population Having red Kierkegaard, Fromm built on those principles of anxiety and freedom. Fromm saw that when anxiety seemed to be overwhelming, to the extent we cannot process it, people seek ways to avoid their anxiety. Since freedom is necessary for anxiety to exist, the fastest way to resolve anxiety is by escaping our freedom. Fromm wrote there are three primary ways we give up freedom:

1. Through seeking an authority to take over and make decisions for us (Authoritarianism),

2. avoiding possibilities where we must make decisions, especially if those decisions could result in failure or rejection (Destructiveness),

3. or when an individual gives up their identity by mimicking the world around them to "fit in" so they will feel accepted (Automaton Conformity).

Each of these escape mechanisms is effective at avoiding anxiety, but there is a high price. By choosing to escape our freedom, we sacrifice our sense of self. With authoritarianism, we sacrifice our independence for relationship. The irony is that those who choose this means of relief are mutually submissive to each other. Fromm points out how the person "in charge" is dependent on others to submit to their will. He likens it to intimate partner violence.

This pattern would later be reflected in the "abuse cycle" developed in 1979 by Lenore E. Walker. For Fromm (and Walker), the evidence of this dependent submission is realized when the meek person in the relationship stands up to their bully. Suddenly, the bully becomes contrite, apologizes, and tells the formerly meek person how they're needed, and wanted, and the bully can't live without them! For a brief moment, the interdependence of these two people is revealed. Often, the timid person will relent, accept the bully back into their lives, and the cycle begins again.

The second form of avoidance is destructiveness. When the world feels too large, when there are too many demands, when there are too many opportunities to be hurt or taken advantage of, the easiest way is to avoid the opportunities. This can work for a while, but as we mature, the world offers more and more chances to grow. These possibilities for growth contain threats of failure, of ridicule, and (the seemingly) inevitable rejection. Instead of accepting the risks that come with growth, they "destroy" the possibilities. Keeping their world small is the only way to maintain control. The more people someone interacts with, the greater the chances of disappointing someone. Suicide, according to Fromm, is the last, desperate, attempt of destructiveness to save a small part of the self from the rest of the world.

Automaton conformity is the final, and most common, form of escape from freedom. Blending in with everyone else is an insidious loss of self. At the end of life, a person who has done everything "right," but with no soul invested in their actions, may think to themselves, "Well what was the point of all that?!" It would be akin to spending all your money on what someone else wants for themselves. Then, when looking at all the acquired goods, there's a sudden realization: "I didn't want any of this! Why did I buy it?" In the same way, if someone were to get a receipt for everything we spent our time on, they may wonder, "Why did I spend my time on this? I don't even like it!"

Unfortunately, this realization often comes too late. That is why automaton conformity is destructive. The world often rewards this form of escape. The rewards can be monetary, verbal, or material. When everything is quiet, sometimes the awareness of this emptiness creeps in and we begin to feel anxious. This sense of anxiety can be quelled with a nice dopamine hit from buying something newer, bigger, or better. Doesn't so much matter what it is, as long as it feels good; as long as it keeps the anxiety at bay.

Without intentionality, the church can be turned into an implement of escape using any of these means. When the church is made an authority, it can be used to absolve us of freedom, if only they'll tell us what to do (legalism). Destruction is possible through the creation of an us/them duality. Who's in, who's out? Are you a member or a visitor? This keeps our world small, but the relationships are clear and there is minimal risk of rejection as long as we "stay in our lane."

Automaton conformity is, in my opinion, one of the greatest risks, because it can create what some have called "functional pharisees." Christian schools accept many people from various walks of life. If one of these people acts outside of strict bounds *and is caught*, they are expelled and/or shamed until they leave. Those who have already learned how to hide their unsanctioned actions experience no punishments. These schools end up graduating people who comply with the rules and people who break the rules, yet they look identical.

The good news is that scripture, and Fromm, offer an alternative: Freedom. Defined as "spontaneous relationship to [humanity] and nature, a relationship that connects the individual with the world without eliminating his individuality" (Fromm, 1941, p. 29), freedom is the answer to the unhealthy avoidance of authentic living. Embracing freedom is not an easy task because of the accompanying anxiety. As it has been shown, living without true freedom leads to a half-life, a life without authenticity, a life of fear, avoidance, and half measures.

Freedom creates anxiety. When anxiety encourages people to create congruence in their life, it's healthy. There's also unhealthy anxiety. Unhealthy anxiety occurs when fear (the experience of a threat) is projected into the future. Fear triggers a reaction in the mind and body as if the threat had an object, a source, something we could run away from or kill. This is known as the fight, flight, freeze, faun response. If the threat exists in the future, if it's anticipatory, then all those same survival responses are triggered, but there's no object for us to address. All this motivating energy just sits inside of us with nowhere to go. As a friend from Texas said, "When you're looking for a place to hang your hat, any nail will do." In other words, if someone has all this energy inside of them, it's going to go somewhere. Turning it inwards is self-destructive and if we take it out on someone else (who isn't the threat), it's a meaningless displacement. The alternative to fear and unhealthy anxiety is a simple, but not easy, thing: Faith.

Faith is placing complete trust in someone or something. Trust doesn't work like a light switch. It's more like a dimmer and there are dozens of them. It makes sense to trust your mechanic to work on your car, but not trust them to repair your roof. Sure, some skills may be transferable, but that's not what a mechanic specializes in. There can be a high amount of trust in some places, a low amount of trust in others, and it would be healthy. When all the dimmer switches are turned to 100%, that's faith.

Fear and faith are opposites. Christians are encouraged to put their trust in God when they are afraid (Psalm 56:3, Isaiah 41:10, I John 4:18, John 14:1, Luke 8:50, Hebrews 13:6). Christians can also, to a lesser degree, trust their world to be somewhat predictable. Therapists view safety as the *freedom* from threat caused by the environment. When someone feels as if they do not have the freedom to create a safe environment, or the freedom from an unsafe environment, it would make sense their trust, and faith, would be low.

Experientially, this makes sense. If I'm surrounded by lions (that I don't trust), I'm going to feel threatened (fearful). If I trust myself to get out of the situation, or trust God to shut the mouths of the lions, I will be less fearful because I am less threatened. Learning to trust ourselves, to create and maintain trusting relationships, and learning to trust that God is with us in our lives, our experiences, our pain, and our joy.

Nathan D. Croy *is a clinically licensed marriage and family therapist and a licensed clinical addictions counselor in Overland Park, KS. In 2017, he founded Existential Family Therapy and created a group practice. He lives in Kansas City with his wife, Catie, and two daughters, Evaline and Amelia.*

54

WE NEED TO LET THE SOUL MOURN!

ULRICK DAM

We need to learn how to let the soul mourn and to recognize
that God never causes evil.

There are many wonderful things about being a Dane. Great pastries, Søren Kierkegaard, and especially our supersecret vowels, that only we—approximately six million Danes—use. Of course, our Æ, Ø, and Å. In this essay, I need to teach you a word with one of these vowels. The word is 'Sjælesorg,' which might not be the easiest to pronounce if you are not a native Scandinavian. The 'æ' in sjælesorg sort of sounds like the 'a' in 'any' and the ending -rg has a soft sound, more like a 'w.' I hope your tongues will survive trying to pronounce 'sjælesorg.'

In any case, Sjælesorg is the Danish word for pastoral caring, which is the part of the pastoral job, where we offer social, emotional, or spiritual support for members of our congregation. The Danish word 'Sjælesorg' is a combination of two words: 'Sjæle-,' meaning the 'souls,' and '-sorg,' meaning 'mourning' or it can also mean something like 'caring deeply.' It would literally translate into 'the mourning of the soul' or something like 'caring for the soul in a time of grief.' Danish can be a tricky language sometimes. Sjælesorg points towards the notion that pastoral care is about creating a space for the soul to mourn, grieve, and come to terms with loss and pain. In my experience, this is a very helpful framework for pastoral care.

The question then stands: How can we create a space for the soul to mourn? Firstly, I will introduce some of the ideas I've learned from Open and Relational theology about the uncontrolling love of God. Secondly, I will give you some pointers on how to practically open up a space for the soul to mourn.

So when we consult people in pain or grief, one question often comes up: *"Why? Why did this have to happen to me?"*

Why does evil happen? It might be one of the largest theological conundrums. Some people come to quite simple answers. For example, the answer could simply be that this evil is just God's plan. God needs to send you through pain for the greater glory. In essence, the evil stems from or is allowed by God. Easy, right? But that does not really fit our view of God, does it?

Before I encountered Open and Relational theology and the ideas of God's uncontrolling love, I always dreaded this sort of conversation. I had nothing really to contribute to the mourning person. I could do little more than listen and be a shoulder to cry on. When asked: *"Why?"* my brain just went blank.

Diving into the uncontrolling love of God, I learned something particularly important. I learned how to respond, as a pastor, to the question of why evil exists. I encountered a theological framework which can truly state, "evil never comes from God!"

When we experience true evils and believe that evil never comes from or is allowed by God, that implies God must be limited in some ways. God could not singlehandedly prevent this evil from happening. God's way of acting in the world has been limited, by God's own choice, to voluntarily self-limit. This is why we are saying God's love must be uncontrolling.

This is a limitation that God chose voluntarily upon creating our universe, the free agency of humans and other creaturely entities. Instead of being controlling, God keeps acting in our life today, through uncontrolling love, by being completely self-giving and others-empowering. Some critique this view and say it makes God impotent, but I do not see it that way. God is extremely potent, powerful, and mighty. God keeps inspiring, luring, and calling Creation into God's loving path and plans. And God works and acts in all sorts of ways, that could only be done by an almighty God.

Sometimes God heals by inspiring doctors and scientists to find the best treatments. Sometimes we see miraculous healing, where the cells themselves cooperate with God and a person is healed. But God is not just singlehandedly removing the cancer. God works in cooperation with creation, without being controlling. God never causes evil. God never allows evil, but God cannot singlehandedly remove evil. Evil stems from the free choice, all entities of creation have, to either cooperate with God or not. Thomas Jay Oord beautifully describes this:

"a relational God of uncontrolling love can't singlehandedly prevent evil done by free creatures, smaller organisms, or inanimate sources. A loving God without the ability to control can't be rightly blamed for causing or allowing evil. God can't prevent evil singlehandedly" (*Open and Relational Theology*, 85). God needs partners to function as God's hands and feet in this physical world to prevent evil and act out love and grace.

After I dove into the ideas of God's uncontrolling love, I started getting a grip on how to answer these questions. I got something to hold on to. I was able to perform sjælesorg; to create a space for the mourning soul. Looking back, I can see three major things I've learned.

Firstly, we need to show up and be authentic in a loving relationship with the person we are sitting with—and with God. We need to listen to the other person and listen to God's inspiration. What does Love lure me to do? To say? I place myself as an open and willing channel for God to act and speak into the mourning soul, who often doubts whether God cares at all and who often is closed off to experiencing God for itself. I am in a position of being God's partner. I can help to connect the mourning soul to the very being of God once again.

Secondly, we must have faith that evil never originates from God. God never causes or commits evil. Evil is the complete antithesis of God's very being. Evil most often originates from Creatures not cooperating with the divine. Sometimes this is done deliberately, sometimes accidentally. In sjælesorg, we must learn to sit with sorrow and not try to answer why this evil has occurred. It is not God's plan in any way, shape, or form. Evil can never be in God's being.

Thirdly, though we cannot explain why evil strikes, we can point towards an open future. God works through uncontrolling love to squeeze all the possible good out of evil. This does not mean that God allows evil for God's greater purpose. But once evil has struck, God works to squeeze all the possible good out of that evil. In sjælesorg our first step is to grieve and mourn; to let the soul bleed. Bleeding is not a bad thing; it cleans the wound and makes it ready for healing. When the wound is ready for healing, we can point towards the open future of God, and all the ways God draws us into a new tomorrow. In Revelation 21 God says: *"I am making everything new!"* (Rev. 21:5 NIV) Healing means that the broken soul will be made new and whole again.

These three ideas have been very important to me in sjælesorg. They have helped me to be a better counsellor, a better pastor, and a better friend and father. Pastoral care is not a discipline merely for pastors—another reason to call it sjælesorg. Caring is something we all do, all the time. When my son falls outside and scrapes his knee, my wife will embrace him and care for him. When you are called up by a heartbroken friend, you listen and you care. We all care all the time, these three points will help us be better caretakers in all aspects of our lives.

One last addition, which will not go on the list, is equally important. God does not have a physical and localized body. God does not have arms and hands to embrace the mourning. God can't even give a simple pat on the back. But you have hands and feet, and God can inspire you to embrace someone, give a pat on the back, or call up someone. When you do that, you act out God's love, you become God's hands and feet. Loving responses are how God is calling you to act. I love the way Robert Mesle says that "your experience of love can move your hands and arms to touch with gentleness, to hug with protectiveness, to reach out to others in ways that enact the causal power of your love in the world." (*Process-Relational Philosophy*, 2008, p. 64)

In other words: The ultimate love is given to us through God so that we are fully shaped by love. Love is not only a warm fuzzy feeling on the inside but an active power of good in the world that works to promote overall well-being. This love can move my hands and feet to reach out and enact the causal power of love, as Mesle puts it. Love is God's primary way of inspiring and moving humans. Love creates empathy, understanding, and connectedness. It creates a will to change unfair structures, and to stand up for the defenseless. Love inspires us to, physically and mentally, embrace people around us. Therefore, all constructive and robust sjælesorg must start from the point of love!

Ulrick Dam is a Danish Theologian with a Master's degree in Church leadership and development. Ulrick is pastoring a church and does leadership consulting. Ulrick has published some books and papers in Danish and is currently working on his first international book publication. Befriend him on Facebook to follow his work.

55

THE KEY TO ENEMY LOVE

SCOTT J. GREGG

The Uncontrolling Love of God helped me overlook deficits and focus on human goodness and enemy love.

I have been on a ten-year journey to find better ways of understanding myself, God, and the world. "Deconstruction" is a buzz word currently. Many people are rethinking inherited ideas that may be harmful or don't make a lot of sense. In 2012, I started to question the answers that familiar systems had handed me. I was fortunate to find open and relational theology and the work of Tom Oord early on in my journey. I encountered beautiful ideas that helped me address critical questions and look at life in fresh ways.

In this essay, I will discuss a meaningful shift in my thinking during these years, namely my move from a deficit-oriented perspective towards a non-pathologizing perspective. I will also consider how the Uncontrolling Love of God helped prime me for a non-pathologizing approach to therapy and life. Lastly, I will explain why it is my belief that a non-pathologizing perspective is the key to enemy love.

Deficit-oriented Perspective

I will start by briefly sharing what I mean by a deficit-oriented perspective. A deficit-oriented perspective tends to focus on weaknesses, deficits, and failures. From this perspective, the primary questions are "what's wrong?" "what's bad?," or "what's lacking?" People who view life from this perspective make negative judgements about the world. The deficit-oriented perspective leads to a shame and blame cycle where the self is condemned and the other is villainized. This view of the world is fatalistic and positive change is often dismissed as an impossible dream. One who holds this view is in danger of succumbing to hopelessness and despair.

Deficit-oriented Systems

In youth and young adulthood, my thinking was oriented towards deficits. I carried some shame, and I sensed that others were a threat to me. These extreme beliefs led to periods of moderate depression and social anxiety. Two familiar systems that I hoped would be helpful actually served to reinforce my deficit-oriented beliefs. Namely, my religious community and the mental health field.

I was part of a religious community that emphasized sin. I was told that I have a sin nature which made me tempted to engage in sin. I was also told that if I did sin, I would be separated from the love of God. The implication was that I should stop sinning so God would not punish me or leave me. I picked up that Jesus could be a friend to me, but that God was looking at me with a critical eye. In hindsight, it's easy to see how sick this is but when I was young, I carried the weight of this narrative.

Perhaps surprisingly to some, my early studies in psychology also served to reinforce a deficit-oriented perspective. The mental health field has traditionally been informed by the Medical Model. Practitioners who employ the medical model tend to look for pathology in the individual client and determine if the symptomology meets criteria for a "psychological disorder." Severe disorders are considered chronic, and any significant recovery can feel like a baseless hope. The Medical Model frames a person's emotional pain as symptoms, diseases, or disorders. Within this framework, the client often carries the stigma of one who is "damaged" or "broken." Whether it was intended or not, I started off my career asking, "what's wrong with my client?"

Non-Pathologizing Perspective

Two systems of thought helped me emerge from a deficit-oriented perspective, Open and Relational Theology and Internal Family Systems Therapy. I will briefly discuss these in the coming paragraphs, but first I hope to describe what I mean by a non-pathologizing perspective. While the deficit-oriented perspective is characterized by individual weaknesses, deficits, and failures, a non-pathologizing perspective looks for strengths, resources, and resiliencies. The non-pathologizing perspective views people as having the good instinct to work towards survival within their environment. The focus is not on problems with the individual but on how they adapted in a relational context. Several therapies utilize a non-pathologizing approach including Internal Family Systems Therapy, Emotionally Focused Therapy, Acceptance and Commitment Therapy, and Sensorimotor Psychotherapy, among others.

The non-pathologizing approach to therapy starts with the radical belief that every person, no matter how destructive their behavior, has goodness within them and is capable of healing. The non-pathologizing approach recognizes and appreciates that people value themselves enough to protect themselves. Extreme beliefs, emotions, and behaviors emerge from extreme contexts and originate with the good intention to survive. Destructive actions are not minimized nor is accountability dismissed, but there is a belief that a person can make better sense of their life and reach some level of self-acceptance and self-efficacy.

An Open and Relational Contribution

Thomas Jay Oord's ideas about the Uncontrolling Love of God laid a foundation for my embrace of non-pathologizing approaches to therapy. In the following paragraphs, I consider how the Uncontrolling Love of God is compatible with non-pathologizing therapies.

Freedom

Like the God of Uncontrolling Love, the non-pathologizing therapist emphasizes freedom. The person is empowered by the therapist to make decisions about the direction of the therapeutic process. The therapist does not come with a rigid agenda and often encourages the person to lead. Concerning God Tom states, "Our divine parent is always involved but never controlling. God gives space, listens deeply, and works with creation to bring about good. Our source gives freedom of choice without micromanaging or manipulating."

Synergy

Like the God of Uncontrolling Love, the non-pathologizing therapist knows that healing happens in a collaborative relationship. Whereas a more traditional approach to therapy may have the therapist prescribing a treatment or cure, the non-pathologizing approach is one in which the therapist works together with the client on equal footing. Tom writes that "God needs our cooperation" and he calls this cooperative partnership "indispensable love synergy."

Safety

Like the God of Uncontrolling Love, the non-pathologizing therapist prioritizes safety. Internal Family Systems has a saying that "all parts are welcome." This means the client can bring every part of themselves to therapy and they will not be judged, condemned, or abandoned. The non-pathologizing therapist knows that a healing relationship includes the whole person, wounds and all. Tom states, "God is present to every part of us, even those parts we don't consciously feel." And he adds we don't have to "worry that God might punish, damn, or ignore us."

Hope

Like the God of Uncontrolling Love, the non-pathologizing therapist always hopes. Founder of Internal Family Systems, Dr Richard Schwartz, frequently calls himself a "hope merchant." He sees himself as selling hope to hopeless parts of us. He can do this because he actually has hope that significant and lasting positive change can take place. He even goes as far as to guarantee he can help. Tom states, "God responds to all that is negative, frustrating, and painful with resilient hope." God never gives up on us.

Compassion

Like the God of Uncontrolling Love, the non-pathologizing therapist extends compassion. The non-pathologizing therapist is fully present with others in their pain. The therapist's compassion also includes listening for how the pain came to be and creates an atmosphere where the pain can be discussed openly. Concerning God Tom states, "The Perfect Lover is everlastingly sensitive and universally compassionate."

Non-Pathologizing and Enemy Love

The non-pathologizing perspective appeals to me because I believe it to be the foundation for enemy love. Therapists tend to learn quickly that perpetrators were once victims at a different point in the lifespan. I admire IFS founder, Dr Richard Schwartz, because he has worked with the most severe populations and remained steadfast in his assertion that people are good. I believe he can maintain this perspective because he works to see people in their contexts, considers the multi-dimensional complexity of their inner world, and looks for humanity deep within.

It is my firm conviction that pathologizing people, no matter how wounded or destructive, leaves us in a blame and shame cycle. This doesn't mean accepting a non-pathologizing approach is easy. It is extremely hard. We can all think of things so heinous that it feels like we've been punched repeatedly in the gut. In my career I have counseled perpetrators of sexual abuse, domestic violence, and murder. One woman I sat for therapy with killed her child. What's astonishing when you get close is that they are still human. And the safer they feel the more you see it. Our tendency to label people as bad without knowing their story or getting close enough to see them is a major problem for our species. I suggest that the non-pathologizing perspective holds the key to learning to love more like God.

In conclusion, the non-pathologizing perspective as developed in therapeutic approaches like Internal Family Systems has the potential to change the world. Dr Schwartz has a deep intuition that his model has applications far beyond the therapy room. Frankly, I could not be more convinced that he is right. I also believe that Tom Oord's view of an open and relational God fits like a glove with these non-pathologizing therapies. I hope to see more collaboration between open and relational theology and non-pathologizing therapies in the future. The ideas here can help us build relational bridges in a world that desperately needs it.

Scott J Gregg is a Licensed Marriage and Family Therapist in the states of California and Idaho. Scott is a contracted therapist with the United States Air Force. Scott also owns a private therapy practice with his wife Andreina who is also an LMFT. Scott has a newborn son Elias, and he enjoys sports and hiking.

56

SO WHAT HAPPENS WHEN WE ASSUME?

DANIEL HELD

Why we cannot heal without first challenging our prior assumptions.

I have a few old classic movie scenes and lines that are impossible for me to forget, even if I wanted to do so. One that stands out in my memory involves *Cool Hand Luke*. My favorite line from that movie? "What we have here is a failure to communicate."

My memory of this infamous line is triggered in my mind whenever I feel misunderstood after repeated attempts to communicate with another person. What I find about myself is that understanding and being understood carries extreme value in relationships with those I love. I rarely experience love and misunderstanding at the same time.

In tracing my own failure to effectively and accurately understand others, who may in turn then question my love for them, the fault most often begins with my having made a hasty assumption. Assuming the wrong thing about someone gets me into a world of hurt, especially in an otherwise loving relationship.

In my personal as well as professional experience over 76 years now, I've found the #1 ingredient in a loving and helpful relationship to be accurate understanding as produced by successful communication. And the #1 cause of a failure to communicate is an unquestioned assumption. Assuming an untruth about another, be it a spouse, a child, or anyone else is anything but loving and helpful.

This pertains to self-love as well as other-love. We all make assumptions about ourselves that are also untrue. We believe lies about ourselves. We misunderstand ourselves in ways that threaten our ability to love ourselves. Yet, if we learn to question our assumptions and change our inner self-talk to better know and understand ourselves (the object of a great deal of our psychotherapy experiences), we then grow to love and appreciate ourselves far better than before.

Now let me test this out by asking you a question about another type of assumption. Is it possible to assume something about God that is untrue? To actually believe a lie about God. To misunderstand God enough to actually threaten our love relationship, at least on our end?

Let's say, for instance, that we assume that a loving God would stop bad things from happening to good people. Have you ever made that assumption? If so, what happens to your love for God when bad things do happen to good people? People you've even prayed for and counted on God to protect or bless or perhaps heal? If we make such an assumption about what a loving God would or should do, then what happens when God doesn't comply with our assumptions? What then happens to our faith? Our loving relationship? Our communication? Our prayer life?

Looking back over my many years as both a licensed therapist and ordained pastor, the best healing work I've ever achieved has been in areas where old assumptions were questioned and replaced on the part of my clients and parishioners. Over time, I have gathered what amounts to a top ten list of wrong assumptions harmful to relationships, communication, and mental health.

Assuming that our human brains are completely rational. In reality, much of our brain function is not rational. The part that is, our frontal lobe, doesn't begin developing until we reach our adolescent years. In fact, the first part of our brain to develop is the limbic system that surrounds our amygdala, which lacks the capacity for reason but is our brain's first responder to every event of our lives in between womb and tomb.

Assuming that our first response to life's events is typically correct. In fact, our first response is overly cautious especially where any change of circumstance is concerned. Our brain's first reaction to any change is to more often perceive danger and initiate stress hormones such as adrenaline and cortisol pumping to our muscle groups, preparing us for survival by means of fight or flight.

Assuming that all change is dangerous and threatening. In fact, some change is and so it is wise to exercise caution. But most change is merely difficult, not dangerous, and is far more likely to contain opportunities than threats. Progressive change is more often a friend than it is an enemy.

Assuming that changing our mind is a sign of weakness. In fact, it is a sign of strength. What is a sign of weakness is our inability to change and adapt to changes going on around us. This is why in scripture even God is noted to have a change of mind on the occasion of our changing human circumstances.

Assuming that another person's behavior means anything at all about us. In fact, it means a lot about that person but next to nothing about ourselves. For the most part, it's simply not about us.

Assuming that anyone else can cause our feelings to change. In fact, we cannot cause another person's feelings or vice versa. Feelings are caused by our own thoughts or actions. They come and go based on what we are thinking or doing at that moment. It might be nice if we could make each other happy or unhappy, but reality just doesn't work that way.

Assuming our parents and others in authority knew or should have known best. In fact, what we humans know or believe is often ignorance or distortion of truth passed on from one generation to the next. It's probably safe to say we do the best we can at the time based on what we then think we know. What we think is right at any given time may be known to be wrong years later.

Assuming that being unloved means being unlovable. In fact, everyone is lovable, but many people have not been loved and, as children without rational brain functioning yet developed, do assume they are then unlovable. That is what interrupts their ability to love either themselves or others, even their own lovable children.

Assuming that love is a feeling. In fact, "like" is a feeling, and pleasing others is something we and others do "like," but it has nothing to do with love. Love is a decision to help others or ourselves get whatever is needed for personal empowerment. Getting whatever is wanted, even if opposite that which is needed, may feel like "love" but is actually just "like" pretending to be "love." Helping others and pleasing others can be quite the opposite, as every parent has easily discovered.

271

Assuming that love is controlling others. Love empowers others by means of influence. It informs others' decisions with truth as a better alternative than a lie. It will never decide for others who, by God's creation, are already capable of deciding for themselves. Love's power is in its ability to multiply itself by empowering others to better control themselves.

I could go on and on here with any number of different assumptions many of us carry around unquestioned in our minds. My point is simply this: failure to challenge and correct wrongful assumptions is the root cause of hurtful emotions and relationships. They are the root cause of failed communication. A failure to communicate with ourselves, others, and even with God is hurtful and in need of healing. A failure to accurately understand ourselves, others, or God is a failure to be fully loved and loving.

As a Christian therapist who seeks to follow Jesus into the healing work of restoring a right understanding of God, neighbor and self, I challenge assumptions. I challenge my own assumptions first through my own prayer for right understanding, successful communication, and loving influence. Then I challenge my client's assumptions for the sake of their own healing in order to save them from their own failure to love, and to communicate their own accurate understanding in relation to themselves, others, and God.

Why do I do this? Because if I understand Jesus accurately through Christian scripture, he came challenging our assumptions from womb to tomb. And by faith I believe he did so for the sake of our own healing. Healing that saves us from our own failure to love in relationship with ourselves, others, and God. And because, without Jesus, what we may have here is a failure to communicate.

Daniel K. Held, M.Div., M.S.W., LISW *is a licensed therapist in Ohio and the author of* Love's Resurrection: its power to roll away fear's heaviest stone *(Higher Ground Books & Media, 2018) and* Redeeming Gethsemane: when our age of loneliness meets the woke church *(HGBM, 2021). Find his blog at* More Love Less Fear, *www.danielkheld.com.*

57

IN GOD'S IMAGE

GREG HOOVER

*God can't control others; if we want more positive
relationships, neither should we.*

*I*n the words of Thomas Jay Oord, "Essential kenosis considers the self-giving, others-empowering love of God revealed in Jesus Christ to be logically
primary in God's eternal essence." Oord also writes, "Essential kenosis says God
cannot override, withdraw, or fail to provide the power of freedom, agency, or
existence to creation. Consequently, God cannot control creatures or creation." In
this essay, we'll unpack Essential Kenosis a little, and in the process, we'll explore
its relationship to mental and emotional health.

Simply put, God is a universal Spirit without a localized body whose essential nature is uncontrolling love. We see this theme running throughout the
Scriptures. The two parts of this insight invite us to think about a few of its implications for psychological and emotional healing.

First, it suggests that God can't stop suffering *singlehandedly*—whether physical, emotional, or psychological. But why not? It's important to note that God is
not constrained by any outside force or principle. Rather, God's very nature is
uncontrolling love; and in the words of the New Testament, "God cannot deny
himself" (2 Tim 2:13). This suggests that God needs our help to bring about what
God wants, including the healing of our own emotional struggles and damaged
relationships. This implies that we need to be actively involved in the pursuit of
our own mental health, rather than passively waiting for God or others to "fix" us
or a significant relationship.

Next, since God is Spirit and does not have a localized body (John 4:24), we realize that God does not have hands to reach out and stop someone from being abused, a physical shoulder to cry on during hard times, or arms to give a hug to a hurting child. As people of faith, we strive to become God's metaphorical "hands." This inspires us to partner with God for the healing of our bodies, our souls, and our world. Moreover, this active partnering with God is not only good for those we help, but it also provides meaning to our lives and increases our social interest in those around us. This practice in itself is psychologically healing and can assist in managing the "common colds" of mental health, including depression and anxiety. We see this idea elucidated in the work of psychiatrists Victor Frankl and Alfred Adler, respectively.

Finally, since we are made in God's image (Gen 1:27), we also are called to imitate God's uncontrolling love in our own lives and relationships. Practicing this principle is not only spiritually sound but is essential for our own psychological and emotional wellbeing. It is also an effective strategy to help maintain and nourish healthy relationships with the significant people in our lives, which contributes to our own mental health. This third point will be the major focus of this essay.

Before my ordination to the priesthood, I worked professionally in mental health for many years, and I continued that work through pastoral counseling and spiritual direction. Throughout this process, I've come to believe that many common mental health issues and emotional difficulties spring from our habit of trying to control the uncontrollable. This includes other people, especially those closest to us.

As we will soon see, this insight suggests that trying to control others is perhaps the single most damaging thing we can do to our relationships, as well as to our own psychological and emotional well-being. But if we follow God's example of treating others with uncontrolling love, we will not only preserve and improve our significant relationships, but our own mental, emotional, and spiritual health.

The psychologist William Glasser founded a therapeutic system known as *Choice Theory* (the philosophy behind his system) and *Reality Therapy* (the practical application of Choice Theory). This essay will integrate elements of *Choice Theory*, the psychological idea that the only person's behavior we can control is our own, with *Essential Kenosis*, the theological insight that God's essential nature is uncontrolling love. Furthermore, it will give a spiritual foundation to the practical therapeutic principles of *Reality Therapy*, and a psychological application to the theological principles of Essential Kenosis.

Choice Theory is based on the basic idea that each one of us only has the power to control ourselves. Furthermore, it teaches us that trying to control others, especially the significant others in our lives, damages those relationships as well as our own emotional health.

According to *Choice Theory*, the source of much emotional struggle is failed or failing relationships with people important to us. These relationships may include spouses, children, parents, friends, and coworkers. Furthermore, Glasser encourages therapists to recognize that most emotional problems that bring someone to therapy stem from a current relationship that is not working. Although Glasser limits these relationships to human interactions, I believe that if our relationship with God is not "working," we may experience similar emotional struggles.

Choice Theory provides ten axioms, of which the first five are most apropos to this essay. They are:

(1) The only person whose behavior we can control is our own.

(2) All we can give another person is information.

(3) All long-lasting psychological problems are relationship problems.

(4) The problem relationship is always part of our present life.

(5) What happened in the past has everything to do with what we are today, but we can only satisfy our basic needs right now and plan to continue satisfying them in the future.

Understanding these axioms of Choice Theory helps us to realize the distinction between *external control psychology* and *internal control psychology*. External control psychology is very common, and we might say it is the default way we tend to understand life and our relationships with others. It is the belief that our thoughts, behaviors, feelings, and experiences are determined by forces outside ourselves. This may include such forces and factors as other people, society, family history, a spouse, or other various external influences.

In contrast to this is internal control psychology, which according to Choice Theory is the more mentally healthy perspective. Internal control psychology is much less common, but can be learned and applied to our personal lives. Simply put, it is the insight that we are responsible for our own choices and the consequences that come from them. In the words of Albert Ellis, the founder of *Rational Emotive Behavior Therapy*, "The best years of your life are the ones in which you decide your problems are your own. You do not blame them on your mother, the ecology, or the president [and I would add God to this list]. You realize that you control your own destiny."

In theological language, we might say it is psychologically and emotionally healthy to follow God's example of treating others with uncontrolling love. As Thomas Jay Oord has suggested, God's essential nature is uncontrolling love, God loves everyone and everything thing, and so God can't control anyone or anything. To this I would add: *And neither should we.*

Following the example of the God in whose image we are made, we can learn to love others, inspire others, support others, encourage others, and not try to control others. But how do we begin to do this, and reach our full potential in Christ? Perhaps Choice Theory may offer us a clue.

Glasser suggests that external control psychology tends to operate by seven destructive, unhealthy habits. They are the seven deadly habits: Criticizing, Blaming, Complaining, Nagging, Threatening, Punishing, Bribing or Rewarding to Control.

Fortunately, there is a way to break these unhealthy habits. That can be done by replacing them with their more constructive counterparts. They are the seven caring habits: Supporting, Encouraging, Listening, Accepting, Trusting, Respecting, Negotiating Differences.

By prayerfully and mindfully becoming aware of the Seven Deadly Habits and replacing them with the Seven Caring Habits, we can begin to live out our calling to treat others with the same uncontrolling love that God models so well for us. Doing so will not only improve our relationships—which are essential for our wellbeing—but also improve our own mental and emotional health.

To summarize: We learn in Genesis that humans are created in the image of God, and we learn in 1 John that God is love. By integrating Essential Kenosis with Choice Theory, we can discover a practical process of spiritual, mental, and emotional healing that is biblically grounded, psychologically cogent, and can preserve and restore the relationships we need for a full and meaningful life. From this, we learn a simple but powerful lesson: Because God's essential nature is uncontrolling love, God can't control others singlehandedly; and if we want to have less emotional struggles and more positive relationships, neither should we.

---

*The **Rev. Greg T. Hoover**, an award-winning writer, is a professional actor, behavior therapist, and Episcopal priest. Greg loves his children, the outdoors, hiking, traveling, horseback riding, and playing guitar. He is the author of* The Pain Killer *(Black Rose Writing, 2022), which explores a famous series of unsolved murders from the perspective of Open and Relational Theology.*

58

Communion as the Therapeutic Center of Uncontrolling Love

Heather G. Hunnicutt

*Through the lens of uncontrolling love, the communion
table is the exemplar for, and undergirding of,
the therapeutic alliance.*

What does it mean to become-in-relationship as part of post-traumatic spirituality? This is the question I wrestle with in my work. I am a trauma therapist by trade, as well as ordained clergy and trained theologian, and what I hear most frequently from survivors is not the question of *where* God was in their trauma, but *why* God did not stop it. Yet one of the premises of open theism is the way in which it affirms individual freedom to witness and participate in the world and, by so doing, become-in-relationship. Nowhere in Christian practice is the witnessing-participative nature of the faith so evident as at the communion table.

The story of the table is one critical to faith. The Christian community's identity is founded upon a trauma, but it should be noted that the communion ritual predates that trauma, for Jesus' supper with his friends comes before the Garden of Gethsemane, arrest, trial, assault, and killing the next day. The communion table remains a symbol of a love that holds fast and perseveres. It is an open offering of remembrance and grace. Augustine describes the communal act thusly:

> For what you see is simply bread and a cup—this is the information
> your eyes report. But your faith demands far subtler insight: the bread

is Christ's body; the cup is Christ's blood. So now, if you want to understand the body of Christ, listen to the Apostle Paul speaking to the faithful: "You are the body of Christ, member for member." [1 Cor. 12.27] If you, therefore, are Christ's body and members, it is your own mystery that is placed on the Lord's table!

It is the communion table that serves to remind us of Christ's presence as grace itself, which we may choose to participate in bodily. As we participate, we touch, taste, and feel the reality of God—and the freedom God offers—into greater being, and are thereby transformed.

The communion table is the foundation of worship for my own tradition, the Christian Church (Disciples of Christ), at which we gather weekly. Usually placed at the end of the service, the act of communing is the apex of our fellowship, reminding the body of and proclaiming our mutual interdependence before we take our leave one from another. It is a centering experience, this communing, and here the center holds. It is where we choose to join in the suffering and joy of the other. The presence of God, in Christ, through the Spirit, comes to the table, and we are healed as we participate in the communal act.

When we "show up" to experience and participate in the act of remembering, it is, as Augustine writes, "our own mystery placed on the Lord's table." We place on the table our hope for becoming, trusting in the Holy Mystery to show up, recognizing the wounds each of us carries in the approach. God asks us, in the ritual remembrance, to enter into the grief of those around us, too. If we are honestly to do so, we must remember the pain of this death every time we come to the altar. We must feel in our body (and in our bodies) what it means to grieve along with God the sins of empire and patriarchy, systems that harm and oppress. We must stand against repressing our grief in favor of comfort, for the raw dread of death has no redemptive gloss in this place. There is, in a love that does not force its own way, an inherent danger as real as the cross. There is, in a love that does not force its own way, a hope as real as the resurrection.

In many traditions, mine included, we often close our communion with the line, "For as often as you eat this bread and drink the cup, you proclaim the Lord's death until he comes" (1 Cor 11:26) Communion, Paul says, is mute testimony, a proclamation that life is not always what it seems. There are ways to remember life persists beyond the grave; one move toward resurrection life is enacted each week at the table. In this space, we recognize our being resurrected though remembering. Having been met by God and the Other, we have begun to live more fully.

We may carry the gift of that meeting, too, outside the church's walls and into the world-at-large. We may notice our opportunities for meeting more fully having been nourished in our own becoming. This healing is available not only within the walls of our churches, but also in therapeutic communion.

Just as Jesus in the garden evaluated the ways of life and death before him, so, too, must traumatized clients choose what they are willing to countenance. As I am wont to say to clients, "It's a real risk, and a real choice." In the therapeutic relationship the survivor is not left to do this alone. Survivor and therapist look at the life the client is living over against the life "before" and the hoped-for "after." In the meeting of holy communion, which is to say, truly encountering both God and another human being such that their life touches yours, all are changed. This is the liminal space in which healing is enacted. In that space, living and meeting become our communion. In that space, our communion can mark the beginnings of salvation.

In a very real sense, therapist and client take turns offering the bread of their bodies and the wine of their blood to one another. The client says, "This is my body" each time she is present to her trauma, present to that which has cost her what she knew of life. The therapist offers, "This is my blood, my passion for you and life and becoming offered in response to your trauma." On the altar of pain, a holy consubstantiation occurs, an offering of self to community and God enacted in this microcosm.

If we are to honestly enter into the grief of others as clinicians, we must remember the pain of this loss every week when we come to the altar (in this case, the therapy room). We must remember the work of Jesus in choosing the cup that did not pass from him. We must also remember that we cannot (and should not) force change or growth, but rather love with the hope of it.

The therapeutic communion is situated within a relationship that acknowledges the realities of life and death, the death could have won the day and the life that somehow prevailed. The therapy hour can be transformed into the real presence of God between therapist and client every time they come together. There is no visible change in the pair, no mystical transfiguration of either person. Yet the hour is consubstantiated in the sense that both persons are becoming more substantial *with* one another, *through* one another, and *in* one another and God.

This is the mystery of healing: That two broken persons choose to enter a mutually vulnerable relationship, taking turns being brave and witnessing the other's courage. For though the therapist rarely shares their own life's experiences with trauma clients, they must choose to hear the unspeakable, to join the client in pain so sharp, agony so deep, it threatens their own well-being. We offer our bodies and blood trusting that the God who is in all things chooses to be present in that place, too. We offer our bodies and blood expecting they will be not only who we are, but also more than we are, a hope for *becoming* realized in this present presence. We offer our bodies and blood uncertain of how precisely the mystery of healing works, trusting the God who suffers with us, too, to become more sub-stantive, more embodied, in the process.

Like communion, therapy is a ritual that can help survivors move through their trauma in the context of a safe-enough relationship. Like any other ritual, it can take time to establish comfort and safety. For example, most of us did not memorize the words to the Apostles' Creed upon our first recitation thereof. We had to practice within our community, to feel the words in our mouths, to make connections between its lines, phrases, and postures. In like manner, we must prac-tice therapy, the vulnerabilities, expressions, and unique language inherent thereto. When we have practiced these things with a safe-enough other, and when we have been challenged to allow others to meet our needs, we may begin to remember the community and our place within it. This is exactly what can happen in good therapy-as-ritual. The communion of therapy can infuse much-needed hope on the way to courageous living.

Heather G. Hunnicutt holds a bachelor's degree in psychology, a master's in pro-fessional counseling, a master's in theological studies, and a doctorate in theology. She is a licensed professional counselor where she specializes in trauma recovery. Heather is also pastor of Salem United Church of Christ. She spends her days with her five children, seeking after joy and transformation.

59

Do You Want to be Self-Actualized?

TRACY LOCKE

Self-actualization is a scary prospect. Would you actually want that?

*I*f I were to try and control my clients, it would mean I have an agenda, an idea of the way I wanted them to go. I'll let you into a secret. I do want them all to get better, to feel happy and to get the most out of life but that's the only agenda I have. The way my clients achieve that is up to them and I'm fully aware that many won't achieve it and indeed, don't want to.

Some clients I've noticed over the years find comfort in their known misery and anxiety. It is familiar, so feels safe. To get well, feels dangerous, as if to turn against that known misery, would be disloyal to it. It's as if in some ways, people feel protected by it.

With sadness too, particularly when that sadness is caused by bereavement, it can feel disloyal to the memory of the lost person to be free of the pain. The pain illustrates how much that person loved the lost person.

So to try and free someone from those particular emotional cells, can feel like doing some people a disservice. So as counsellors we have to accept where people are in their healing journey. To be aware of our desire to fix but also aware that in fixing a person in the way we might want to, could strip that person of something very important to them.

And it's when I'm thinking about that, that I think about Jesus asking the paraplegic at the pool at Bethesda if he wanted to be well, whether this is what Jesus was aware of. (John 2: 5–9) Maybe the man's identity was tied up in being there to catch the blessing offered by the waters, maybe there was a community feeling to being there that meant he felt belonging to a disabled family, which he may lose if he were healed.

I think about this story, because not only am I a counsellor /Psychotherapist, but I am a paraplegic. My paralysis was caused by spina bifida and therefore it is a condition I have had from birth. If Jesus appeared now, would I want to be healed? The answer is more complex than a simple yes or no.

I've had stage 4 bladder cancer too, which has added to my physical diffi-culties, but would I swap it for a life completely healed? Physically yes I would. Life is more difficult and now in my 51st year of life, it's more painful. Who likes pain?…OK I know some of you do, let's not go there. I don't and I'd get rid of it in a heartbeat if I could.

However, my disability and my cancer have made me who I am. They have given me emotional strength; they have given me a particular type of lens on the world and they have given me empathy and compassion for others. And for me, that's the bit I wouldn't swap out for healing, because to me, that is healing.

In recent years the counselling world has realized that empathy is not as use-ful as compassion in therapy. Empathy is walking in the shoes of another, maybe even getting down in the hole with someone, but sometimes if you do that, you can't get yourself or the other person out. Compassion gives you a spacious view of a person's predicament which enables you to hold that person emotionally and help them find their own way out. It is empowering.

And if you can encourage self-compassion in a client, then a client can have a more healing and healthy mindset. You wouldn't trust a person who was judg-mental with your pain and if you were judgmental of yourself, you wouldn't trust yourself. That's what leads to addiction, anxiety and depression. It's disconnection with the self.

So people like Gabor Mate who have developed approaches like Compas-sionate Inquiry are now very popular. People are beginning to see that helping a person befriend themselves is the beginning of healing.

To believe that the God of the Universe loves you, well that's a few stages on from that may be. We are good at loving others, but not "as we love ourselves" because more often than not we don't love ourselves. We carry younger versions of ourselves around, who we judge for getting into trouble or being in the wrong place at the wrong time.

Friends do not control. They hope for the best for their friend. They support a friend to a better way of life that is chosen by their friend, not them.

The Good Samaritan (Luke 12: 25-37) supported the injured person, put him up in an Inn and paid for his care. He was quite hands-off really and certainly didn't determine the nature or the outcome of the healing. If he'd said how the chap should heal, what he should believe and what he'd done wrong in getting beaten up, the man would perhaps have switched off and checked out of life and given up.

Being uncontrolling in your love and in your life in general, frees people to be the people they were born to be. Happy, healthy and loving. I guess you might say "self-actualizing."

So much is said in churches about the importance of telling people where they went wrong. That we are responsible for a person if they've made mistakes and we don't tell them how they've gone wrong, to "correct" them. However, I'd say the important thing is to be uncontrolling, which is linked to being non-judgmental. We are told in the Bible many times, not to judge, yet churches are notorious for it.

I was an Adventist and left when my children came out as LGBT. I was told I was being controlled by the devil because I didn't kick my son out. (My son was 14 when he came out). Would my son have learned love sleeping rough in the UK at 14 or has he learned love from a mother who has loved him and his sibling enough to leave the church behind, because to me uncontrolling love is the answer to just about every question?

Jesus wept. With us, not as judgement. Yes he flipped tables but that was against a system, not an individual. Its right to be angry, when systems are not compassionate. It's right to metaphorically flip tables. Nothing would change to make the world better if we didn't, but individuals are better off loved without judgement or control.

It's the way counsellors all over the globe change lives every day and it's how God reaches souls every day too. The question is, are we open to that healing/self-actualizing?

Tracy Locke *was born with spina bifida in 1970. She qualified as a teacher with an honors degree in Education in 1993 and as a Psychotherapist in 2000. She taught from her wheelchair for 7 years, taught Counselling to adults and now works in the Staff Psychological Wellbeing Service for Hywel Dda Health Board as a Psychotherapist. She lives with her husband and two children who are both neuro divergent and their two dogs in West Wales, UK.*

– 60 –

THERAPEUTIC CONTROL

JAVIN MATHER

Knowing what we do and don't have control over can be scary.
Let's quell some of that fear.

*E*ven the word "control" can muster up various negative connotations, especially in the world of counseling and psychology, perhaps bringing to mind stories of abuse, manipulative partners, or toxic parental/family relationships. Such responses are more than valid for many of us, especially taking any trauma background into account. Nonetheless, I feel "control" is also something capable of redemption, and such a concept interweaves rather appropriately with how it conceptually applies to both therapy and the character of God.

To say there are only two extremes of control in regard to love, being either controlling or uncontrolling, does not do the nuance and beauty of humanity justice, as the stories I encounter in my years of counseling clients speak to breadth and depth of both human strength as well as self-destruction. Control is a key player in the heart of this spectrum. As a concept, control is not wrong or evil, though we sadly live in a world where it is more often than not utilized in the name of more nefarious pursuits than those that are loving and constructive. I would contend having a healthy understanding of control, as guided by love for others and self and in context of God's character, inform much of the therapeutic relationship as well as human interactions/behaviors more generally.

Whether due to biological survival mechanisms, environmental stressors, relational tensions, or an amalgamation of the three, our minds tend to default towards focusing on disruptions, abnormalities, or anything really that threatens our well-being in some capacity. Such forces are oftentimes situations beyond our control or in which we have limited control. In fact, we might define trauma as "any situation or event that occurs abruptly in which we do not have control or control is taken from us and with which we do not have the ability to cope immediately." As such, discussing control is important. The presence of even multitudes of factors and situations over which we have no control does not, in fact, negate or erase the things we do have control over, even if their quantity feels minimal by comparison.

Viktor Frankl, counseling philosopher and Holocaust survivor, would contend we have empowering control in what attitudinal values we choose in the face of uncontrollable circumstances, in turn connected to how lives are hopefully driven by personal meaning we've achieved. Alfred Adler might contend that control is exercised primarily in the context of building social relationships and our positions and influence within them, both for the sake of meaningful connection as well as a sense of survival and place in the world. Albert Ellis, creator of reality therapy, might even say control is at the heart of facing our direct realities and our role and responsibilities therein to ourselves. Control, when guided and governed by love among many other positive traits and stances, can be truly instrumental in one's well-being and even healing, and I cannot help but wonder if this is a manner similar to how God approaches the concept of control.

Control, guided by love, allows my clients permission to finally see themselves as valuable, important beings in the scope of their own lives and experiences, not merely recipients of trauma, strife, and dysfunction, tidal wave after tidal wave. They can see their own thoughts and opinions finally having weight and can see themselves as being just as relationally desirable by their friends as they view them to be. Control can influence healthy decision making and coping, again allowing a client to recognize what things they have immediate or gradual governance over in their own lives to respond to toxic situations and patterns in finally new and unique ways. Control can aid them in improving their self-concept and self-esteem, perhaps finally giving them courage to draw upon support and resources needed to leave behind negative situations and relationships.

When spirituality is sometimes addressed in counseling, this idea of control operating out of love and other strengths bear a positive impact on discussion of God and God's place in the lives of clients who identify with Christian faith. Instead of God bearing toxic control as the arbiter of horrible things, we reinforce those things as having occurred as the result of choices and evil of others; what control God may have to some extent is nonetheless loving in seeking to use the situation for our growth towards God.

Uncontrolling love might perhaps be viewed as control being relinquished in situations that it could easily exist, whether we're talking about God's presence in a given situation or situations in our own lives in which we release ourselves of feeling an obligation to control that is doing our well-being more harm than good. Personal agency and autonomy as people is intimately connected to our sense of love and relationship, both controlling and uncontrolling; control is not so much the problem as is the motivations and intent behind it, though lack of control in some situations might be deemed the most loving course of action.

I see love in control in that our planet is perfectly distanced from the sun such that we do not burn or freeze to death and can uphold life across millennia. I see love in control in the design, organization, and structure of oh so many biological, ecological, and environmental systems on this earth both in nature and living creatures. I see love in control in the boundaries and healthy cautions loving parents give their young children to keep them safe. Control does not infer an utter lack of love, but rather, its execution and intent are governing factors in whether or not a given kind of control is loving or unloving in its outcomes.

By contrast, there is an inherent kind of uncontrolling love in the counseling relationship, as I do not seek to engage in decision making and advice giving for my clients; if they only arrive at healthier choices and perspectives due to blatantly direct intervention and instruction on my part, how can they fully personalize and own those things for themselves in such a way to garner effective consistency? Control is nonetheless present in our conversations, but it serves more as a topical guiding force, open-ended enough in nature to validate their own reflections and free will as opposed to my spelling everything out for them in some concrete, maybe cold-hearted manner. Control as executed by God is perhaps done in a similarly guiding manner, not forcefully or coercively, but prominently enough to allow things to happen in such a way that our agency and free will as humans is not utterly negated in the process.

Upholding love for self, love for others, and the idea of God ultimately being loving (though not devoid of others traits nor devoid of power) is integral to the , counseling process. Even the smallest shred of love for self, however hidden deep down, must be present for the simple fact that someone enters my office in hopes of achieving change in their lives, sometimes even including feeling in control of them again in the face of all they've come through. Love for others is central to any healthy, meaningful relationship and is also integral to relational repair in the face of conflict patterns, infidelities, and toxic communication.

God as guided by love is central, in my mind, to the concept of holding space, that even in situations where God's presence feels far off, God is nonetheless sitting right next to us, experiencing the full breadth of our pain with us, and existing solely for us in a peaceable, judgment-free manner in those very moments.

I've seen the beauty and power of what truly redeemed control can look like as a therapist. While I cannot speak to the depth and detail of how God exercises control in some situations and does not in others like a trained minister or professional theologian might be able to, I can say that any control God does engage with in creation and in our lives is ultimately guided by love and augmented by myriad other traits, to the benefit of creation and to the upholding of us as God's beloved.

Javin Mather is a licensed clinical professional counselor in Idaho, having practiced for 11 years now across agency settings, hospital/triage care positions, college/university settings, in state/federal capacities, and via his private practice, Storyboard Counseling. He earned his Bachelor of Science degree in psychology from Boise State University in 2008, and Master's studies in counseling were completed at Northwest Nazarene University in 2011.

61

JADE/D

SHANNON DAVY MIMBS

The therapeutic context provides sacramental space for persons to redefine, experience, and embrace God's uncontrolling love.

*D*ear Jade,

I hope this letter finds you and your family doing well. As mentioned in our last session, I often send out follow-up letters 2-3 months after services. There are various reasons I believe this to be important; but to sum it up, it celebrates the tremendous growth that I've seen in you. Let me start by saying that I'm so very proud of you! Some people who come to therapy think it's a sign of weakness or just someone needing help with problems. But you quickly understood the heart of what it is—entering conversation with someone who helps sort through past experiences, gameplan about present situations and work towards a better future. And you didn't simply come to a class or lecture.

You grabbed the truth that it's a process, one in which you'll get out of it what you put into it. Rather, we will get out of it what we put into it. And we know that's because your story, perspective, and voice matter greatly. You, Jade, matter.

So, my celebration is not only that you rocked showing up to sessions (though that was awesome, no doubt). You genuinely gave "100" in owning your story, talking through some painful parts of your past, and deciding whether you wanted to put in that four-letter, wordy-dird—"w-o-r-k." And that you did. Deep down you weren't looking for an Abracadabra or quick fix. You were searching for ways to find meaningful, substantial, significant relationships. And, yes, I remember your comment in the beginning—"I don't need no one." Yet, you were hungry to understand your place in this warzone of a world.

I think that in many ways you discovered even more that you have a place, moment-by-moment, in every connection around you. Like you said in one session before, "Maybe I just need what I didn't experience when I was growing up: genuine acceptance and loving relationships."

This sacramental space for presence and healing is what therapy is all about. We discovered the truth that love is healing, life-giving and has the best interest of you and everyone else in mind ("Facts!"). It energizes reality itself, having a center with no borders. You were open-minded, considerate, and honest during this process. That, no doubt, is worth celebrating.

So, let's review some of the feedback that you shared in your survey. And, yep, I'm going to use your words throughout the letter. I'm pretty sure you remember why.

1. "Yeah, I trashed the idea—'It is what it is'… I've learned that sometimes, 'It is what it shouldn't be'."

Wow! You went from understanding the world as being a movie script in which you simply zombie along, to seeing the vibrancy of life all around us. You began to wonder what it might mean if the future is being written day-by-day, moment-by-moment, by numerous factors ("Pick up the pen"). And I still remember the million-dollar question you raised—"If God, like my grandma says, makes everything happen, why should I even care what I do?" Slowly but surely, I watched you unplug from the notion that God is the ultimate gamer—pressing buttons, calling all the shots, while kicking back controlling every character ("He's sippin' a Red Bull and has me on single-player campaign mode"). I think it's (using your words) "badass" that you began to consider the possibility (and logic) that if God is ultimately love, and love is uncontrolling, then the world isn't a game at all. You said it's more like improv in high school. That's a good way to put it.

Choice by choice, you began to break down some unhealthy habits (e.g. isolating yourself from your family and friends). You wrestled with whether certain attractions or distractions gave you traction towards building the person you want to become ("Get a grip!"). You discovered the power you possess in lining up choices and habits with the goal of growing up. And you dug in. Day by day, you began to slow down and consider the future-changing impact of your words, attitude, and actions. Like after that math test on fractions, you realized that "integers are where it's at!" Wholeness or integrity is the goal. Why settle for being a fraction of the person you have the potential to become?

2. "This is, for real (for real), bigger than me."

Of the many things I celebrate, Jade, is how you came to realize the connection between everything. You pushed past the idea that "everything happens for a reason." And there was the "aha" moment when you helped break down the nerdy statement, "Transformation is personal but not privatized." Seriously, you've helped in my own process of becoming, as we're all under construction in so many ways. And considering our connection with everything around us, you explored why things have affected you as they did. We're hardwired for love; and giving and receiving love (whether "healthy" or "sick" love, as you referenced) shapes our character and that of the world. In the big picture, it transforms reality as we know it—all the way around.

There's a powerful freedom in realizing that the world (and everything existing) is in a constant vibrancy of becoming. It reminds me of our first session of looking at therapy as "journeying from fragmentation towards wholeness." I'm so thankful you helped me understand how to explain this differently. My mantra was a tad bit outdated and somewhat confusing. But your take on the preposition was spot on. If I used the word "to," it seems to imply a "jump," while "towards" sounds like a journey. And this journey is a dancelike experience of developing healthier relationships. If we're to become more and more our best self, it's in the context of who we are with others and the world around us ("I am because you are").

In so many ways, Jade, I think this is at the heart of you "growing up" in which love becomes your guiding compass every day. It's that ever-so-gentle nudge for you to choose the most loving choice possible, moment-by-moment. It surely has a ripple effect in the world. You've taken the pen in hand and realized the story is yet unfinished. Put in a different way, like when you brought the guitar to session, you're playing a new song. It's one that's beautiful, creative, and needs to be heard by your family and friends.

3. "I've learned that I can change after all, and the future can be better."

Here's the kicker. You're no longer "stuck" in the past as if it defines you. Cycles of behaviors can be broken and healthier ways of navigating the world are at your fingertips in living a life of love. You've made so much progress in this area. Jade, this is a gamechanger—knowing that there's not one set of tracks for each of us, as if we're limited to one direction with a predetermined stop ahead.

When we first met, you viewed the future as being rather hopeless. Happiness seemed more like a mirage and healing from past pains more like wishful thinking. However, I've witnessed you blossom in your faith, hope and love. There's been an incredible shift in your openness to a future that can look better than what you've been through.

Now, this doesn't mean that there won't be challenges, hardships, or loss. Those "dark nights of the soul" are common to us all at times. Yet, you're no longer driven by your impulses or reactionary. The power to choose love in each situation you may face opens new chapters of creativity, shares goodness with the world and radiates to others the beautiful person you're becoming. As I've told you in every session, I believe in you…and Love does too.

Sincerely,

Shannon

Shannon Davy Mimbs serves as a therapist at a counseling agency. He earned his MDiv and MACMHC from Pentecostal Theological Seminary. He is pursuing doctoral work in Open and Relational Theology at Northwind Theological Seminary. He and his wife, Allison, live in Georgia and prize their three children as their greatest treasure.

62

THE STORIES THAT SHAPE US

JASON C. WHITEHEAD

We tell stories to tell the world who we are. Sometimes stories heal, sometimes they cause harm.

There are no whole truths; all truths are half-truths. It is trying to treat them as whole truths that plays the devil.

Alfred North Whitehead

Therapists are trafficking in human possibilities rather than settled certainties.

Jerome Bruner

We create, imagine, and organize ourselves out of stories. When we first get to know someone, we are often prone to sharing facts and historical details. When we're ready for them to know us, we tell them a story.

Stories shape our sense of self and how we make sense of experiences. They are how we organize our worlds and communicate who we are to others. But there's a difference between sitting down and writing a story, and the self-created narratives that shape us. Human stories are often messier than the carefully crafted books we read. Whereas those often have a beginning, middle, and end, ours generally devolve and divert in chaotic ways.

Some of our stories have beginnings that branch off from the middle of a previous story. Some beginnings give birth to second beginnings before a middle arises. Some endings aren't endings at all. Instead, they loop back to the middle of an old story, providing unsatisfying conclusions, and leaving us stuck.

Although we share some similarities, human stories aren't as clean as their fictional counterparts. We are messy, chaotic, embedded storytellers. What we don't fully remember, we're prone to make up.

Memory research tells us that we often imagine parts of a story so that it's cohesive. Our brains aren't computers or databases. When we remember, we're rebuilding or reconstructing an experience. Every time we tell a story it's rebuilt from the ground up.

The stories that shape us aren't old documentaries. At best, they're historical fiction, part fact and part imagination. The trouble comes when we mistake our memories for complete truths. This tends to make the stories that shape us rigid and unyielding.

Those inflexible stories that we all carry are the reason therapists exist. While there are many schools of thought, I see our role as sacred listeners. Our presence to these reified stories, these half-truths masquerading as whole truths, is an act of creative-responsive love.

Every time we ask a question, we're generating a possible version of a life.
David Epston

As we become aware of ourselves as storytellers we realize we can use our stories to heal and make ourselves whole.
Susan Wittig Albert

Our stories shape us, and we shape our stories. Since every story we tell includes a healthy dose of imagination, we are constantly making connections and choices about our stories and identities.

Therapy, as an act of creative-responsive love, attends to these choices in the context of a relationship. It's the reason why two simple words, "say more," permeate the culture of our profession. "Say more" is an intervention of the highest order. It is an invitation to a storyteller, an acknowledgement that the story is important, and that there is always more to tell.

For therapy to embody creative-responsive love it must be able to present an open world. It's a world of choices and accountability. A world rife with possibility and responsibility. There is no need for therapy and therapists if choice and change aren't possibilities.

Our greatest work is in co-creating the kind of sandbox that allows people to share the stories that have shaped them and question those stories as well. As therapists, our capacity to tolerate ambiguity is vital. We are called into relationships where people are certain the stories they tell are the whole truth. And, we have to both believe them and coax them into expanding a story.

This takes creativity and responsiveness. It is a (sometimes) gentle process of prodding at the cracks in a story. Love is believing a story and believing it's not the last word. Every story has fissures in it. These are the overlooked details, the tiny moments of glossed over resistance, or the overshadowed moments of resilience and flexibility.

As sacred listeners we're hearing a story twice. At the first level, we hear what we're told. We're letting the story breathe and have life. At the same time, we're peering into those cracks and fissures. We're drawing attention to them and asking for more. Creative-responsive love means we don't settle for a simple story. It means we believe in someone's capacity to reshape their stories.

For stories to heal, they must become complex, breaking the bonds of rigidity and simplicity. Our questions and "say mores" aren't the end. They're the beginning of teaching and embodying ways to question how we tell our stories. The goal of creative-responsive love in therapy is that it becomes an uncontrolled force in someone's life. Our goal as therapists is to help you embody creativity in your lives so that you are empowered with choice. You can choose how to tell your stories rather than the story dictating how it will be told.

The capacity to choose how we will tell a story is transformative.

In countering the effects of a problem-saturated story, it is important to develop as rich, detailed, and meaningful a counter-story as possible.
Jill Freedman & Gene Combs

Every new beginning comes from some other beginning's end.
Seneca

Our stories shape us, we shape our stories, and our choices matter. Every new beginning comes from some other beginning's end, which may be attributed to Seneca, but I know it from the song *Closing Time* by Semisonic. This presents us with an opportunity to explore how stories have multiple meanings and possibilities, and how our choices in telling them matter.

The first story about this quote deals with its origins in Stoic philosophy and ethics. Seneca was a Stoic philosopher (among other things) who wrote around the same time Jesus walked the earth. Early Christianity was heavily influenced by Stoicism. Augustine incorporated Stoic principles, ethics, and logic into his theological writing. Someone also created a series of fake correspondence between Paul and Seneca. I don't think we can underestimate the impact of Stoic philosophy on early Christianity.

My imperfect story about Stoic philosophy is that it has to do with being intentional in how we approach and engage in life. It is about a responsibility to being present to the world as it unfolds around us and taking in everything we can of life. Hence, this quote from Seneca could be about being present to the beginnings and endings we all experience, as well as the grief and excitement they can produce.

Now, the song by Semisonic complicates our Stoic story a bit by making it contextual. On the surface, *Closing Time* seems to refer to the last call at a bar. Its imagery, tone, and tempo seem to point us in the direction of life outside the bar when the doors close. In this interpretation it is a story about finding your people and heading out into the world together. It creates some cracks in the Stoic story by giving it some additional context and possibility.

However, the final fissure to the story of the song comes when you look into the history of its writing. Dan Wilson, the songwriter, explained that the song is about the birth of his son. And, when you go back and read the lyrics, the meaning of the song changes and the context for the quote comes alive in different ways.

A nine-word story that takes us from first-century Stoicism to the closing of a bar to the birth of a child. All true depending on the storyteller, but much richer and more complex when taken together. You see, we now have a story (whatever it was we believed about this quote when first reading it), and we have a counter-story (whatever it is we believe having read these different experiences of the quote). Because of this diversity, we have choices to make.

Therapy, as creative-responsive love, is about developing possible choices and stories. It is an act of love to tell someone, "yes, I believe you…and there's more to it." We listen to the stories and help explore the counter-stories. We love both who they are, and who they are becoming in all its fits and starts.

I wanted a perfect ending. Now I've learned, the hard way, that some poems don't rhyme, and some stories don't have a clear beginning, middle, and end. Life is about not knowing, having to change, taking the moment and making the best of it, without knowing what's going to happen next. Delicious Ambiguity.

Gilda Radner

Delicious ambiguity. If I had to settle on a phrase that encompasses what it means to embody creative-responsive love in therapy, this would climb to the top of the list. Co-creating and savoring the new beginnings that come from the end of an old beginning is our work together. And it is good, delicious work.

Jason Whitehead *is a Licensed Clinical Social Worker and Associate Certified Coach. He earned his Ph.D. in Religion and Psychology from Iliff School of Theology and the University of Denver. He is the author of* Redeeming Fear *(Fortress Press, 2013) and Lead Curator of ReFrame, an app-based discipleship community. Jason loves woodworking, pickleball, and good beer.*

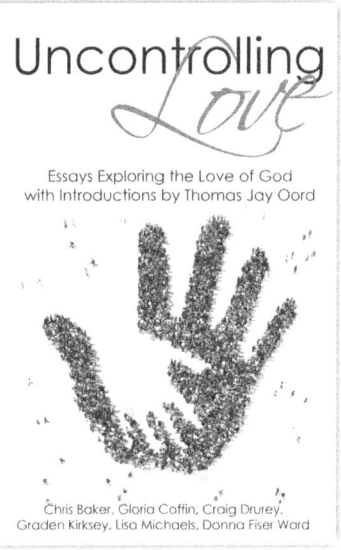

Made in the USA
Coppell, TX
01 March 2023

13570956R00174